The Bible:

Book of Prosperity

King Jesus Publications – Publishing the Word of the Kingdom

The Bible:

Book of Prosperity

Dr. Michael W. Grant Sr.

KJP

King Jesus Publications
P. O. Box 64
Winnsboro, La. 71295
318.435.9010

The Bible: Book of Prosperity

If you would like information about the ministry, interested in becoming a partner, please write:

King Jesus Worship Center
P. O. Box 64
Winnsboro, La. 71295

Unless otherwise indicated, all Scripture quotations are from the KING JAMES VERSION

Published by King Jesus Publications KJP
P. O. Box 64
Winnsboro, La. 71295

Dedication

I dedicate this book to my God

To my Loving Wife and Family

To the Benjamin, Grant, and Johnson Family

To my Church Family - King Jesus Worship Center

To the Body of Christ for whom it is written

To King Jesus Worship Center (Winnsboro)

To King Jesus Worship Center (Monroe)

To King Jesus Worship Center (Rayville)

To King Jesus Worship Center (Lancaster, TX.)

To King Jesus /New Vision Worship (Dallas, TX.)

To Drs. George and Clarice Fluitt

To Leroy Thompsom Ministerial Association

Wisdom Keys – Study to show yourself approved unto God

Contents

Wisdom Keys – Words are Seeds Containing Your Future

Introduction

Saints all of the world are in disagreement on whether God want prosperity for his children. The answer to this dispute can be found in the Word of God. God people are destroyed because of a lack of knowledge. Many people are against prosperity because they have seen so many false teachers using the word to manipulate for their own ungodly purposes. However, this does not change the Bible concerning what God desire is for his people.

Jesus first public sermon gives man the answer to the question of prosperity:

Luke 4: 16 – 19
16 And he came to Nazareth, where he had been brought up: and, as his custom was, he went into the synagogue on the Sabbath day, and stood up for to read. 17 And there was delivered unto him the book of the prophet Esaias. And when he had opened the book, he found the place where it was written, 18 The Spirit of the Lord is upon me, because he hath anointed me to preach the gospel to the poor; he hath sent me to heal the brokenhearted, to preach deliverance to the captives, and recovering of sight to the blind, to set at liberty them that are bruised, 19 To preach the acceptable year of the Lord.

Jesus gives an outline to the purpose for him coming to the earth. He came to preach the good news to the poor. Then he brings out the condition of the poor. He explains they are brokenhearted, captives, blind, and bruised. The exact opposite to the word poor is prosperity. When a person is poor, they are in bad shape. When a person has prosperity, they are in good shape. God sent Jesus to the earth to become poor that through his poverty men can become rich. Is God for prosperity for humankind? Yes, this was his purpose for Christ coming to earth. Before you Judge wrong, consider that rich men without Jesus is poorer than material poor men.

Rev. 3:17, 18

17 Because thou sayest, I am rich, and increased with goods, and have need of nothing; and knowest not that thou art wretched, and miserable, and poor, and blind, and naked:18 I counsel thee to buy of me gold tried in the fire, that thou mayest be rich; and white raiment, that thou mayest be clothed, and that the shame of thy nakedness do not appear; and anoint thine eyes with eyesalve, that thou mayest see.

He tells the rich in the Laodiciceans Church that they are poor, wretched, miserable, naked and blind. Yes, there are two classes of the poor. The rich poor and the material poor. Jesus came to save both from hell and to feed them his Word. Because true prosperity is first, rich toward God, then rich with wealth, health, peace and long life on earth. Many that are rich in Christ are being rejected even now. Jesus told that church, He was going to vomit them out of his mouth. Why? Because they were poor with God, and not helping the poor as they are commissioned. Just keep in mind Lazarus and the rich man.

In this book is every scripture for your study on the word prosperity. It will contain every chapter from the Bible where the word prosperity is written. Other chapter will be on the words prosper, prospered, prospereth, prosperous and prosperously.

In addition, scripture where the word prosperity is written, you have every scripture that contain that Hebrew word. These scripture are listed for your study, meditation, prayer and confessions. This book is a great tool for ministering on prosperity. It has detailed word such in Hebrew on the word prosperity.

History of the King James Version

The King James Version (KJV), commonly known as the Authorized Version (AV) or King James Bible (KJB), is an English translation of the Christian Bible for the Church of England begun in 1604 and completed in 1611.[2] First printed by the King's Printer Robert Barker,[3][4] this was the third translation into English to be approved by the English Church authorities. The first was the Great Bible commissioned in the reign of King Henry VIII (1535),[5] and the second was the Bishops' Bible of 1568.[6] In January 1604, King James VI and I convened the Hampton Court Conference where a new English version was conceived in response to the perceived problems of the earlier translations as detected by the Puritans,[7] a faction within the Church of England.[8]

James gave the translators instructions intended to guarantee that the new version would conform to the ecclesiology and reflect the episcopal structure of the Church of England and its belief in an ordained clergy.[9] The translation was done by 47 scholars, all of whom were members of the Church of England.[10] In common with most other translations of the period, the New Testament was translated from Greek, the Old Testament was translated from Hebrew text, while the Apocrypha were translated from the Greek and Latin. In the Book of Common Prayer (1662), the text of the Authorized Version replaced the text of the Great Bible – for Epistle and Gospel readings – and as such was authorized by Act of Parliament.[11] By the first half of the 18th century, the Authorized Version had become effectively unchallenged as the English translation used in Anglican and Protestant churches. Over the course of the 18th century, the Authorized Version supplanted the Latin Vulgate as the standard version of scripture for English speaking scholars. With the development of stereotype printing at the beginning of the 19th century, this version of the Bible became the most widely printed book in history, almost all such printings presenting the standard text of 1769 extensively re-edited by Benjamin Blayney at Oxford; and nearly always omitting the books of the Apocrypha.

The King James Version is word to word translation. This make it easy to go back and study the original Hebrew (Old Testament) and Greek (New Testament) words in the Bible. Most Bible student know that a word like **prosperity** can have several different Hebrew words in its original written language. It is this understanding as a Bible student we have to take advantage of as we study to show ourselves approved unto God. Almost every word in the King James Version can be traced back to the original Hebrew or Greek word.

The Translation

James VI of Scotland took over the English throne from the Tudors in A.D. 1603. He was promptly crowned King James I of England. At that time, the number of English translations of the Bible caused disunity in the kingdom.

In January of 1604, James I called a conference of theologians and churchmen at Hampton Court in order to hear and then resolve things that were amiss in the church. He sought to deal with ecclesiastical grievances of all sorts. A number of those present pressed the new king for a new translation—one that would take the place of both the Geneva Bible and the Bishops' Bible (so named because a group of Anglican bishops revised it), as well as thwart the Catholic challenge symbolized by the Douai-Rheims Bible. The actual proposal for a new translation came from a Puritan, Dr. John Reynolds, president of Corpus Christi College, Oxford. King James I was agreeable to the proposal.

Not everyone was initially open to the new translation, however. There were some from more conservative expressions of the Christian faith who initially resisted publication of the KJV. These were unwilling to accept *anything* rooted in the official Church of England, or produced under the auspices of the king (1).

The KJV is a word-for-word translation—though, many would say, not unbendingly so. In producing this translation, there were six panels of translators appointed by King James I, two meeting at Oxford, two at Cambridge, and two at Westminster. A total of 54 translators were involved in the project, and began their work in 1604. Of these six panels, two oversaw the translation of the New Testament, three oversaw the translation of the Old Testament, and one oversaw the translation of the Apocrypha. The six groups worked separately, and once their work was complete, it was sent to the other panels for comment and revision. The chief members of the six panels then met to make final decisions on all suggested revisions (2).

The translation procedure was based upon fifteen rules that were given to the team of 54 translators. For instance, the first rule states: "The ordinary Bible read in the Church, commonly called the Bishops' Bible, [was] to be followed, and as little altered as the truth of the original will permit." The sixth rule stipulates that no marginal notes be affixed "but only for the explanation of the Hebrew or Greek words, which cannot without some circumlocution, so briefly and fitly be express'd in the text." All 54 translators adhered to all fifteen rules.

The original Preface of the KJV tells us that the goal of the translation team was not to make "a new translation, nor yet to make of a bad one a good one... but to make a good one better, or out of many good ones one principal good one." So, dependence on the work of previous translators is acknowledged. The original title page of the KJV even states that it was made "with the former translations diligently compared and revised." (3)

13

Even though various preexisting translations contributed to the King James Version, it is primarily William Tyndale's work that is most pervasive. A 1998 scholarly analysis concluded that Tyndale's words account for 84 percent of the New Testament and 75 percent of the Old Testament books he translated. As one scholar put it, "His genius as a translator shines through in page after page and phrase after phrase (4)." Scholars agree that the KJV is at its very best when it keeps its wording close to that of Tyndale. It is at its worst when it does not. One linguistic critic lamented that in the KJV, "portions of those parts of the Old Testament that Tyndale did not translate, particularly in the prophetic books, are close to unintelligible (5)." (Job and parts of Isaiah are poorly translated.)

The King James translators avoided including interpretive marginal notes, but did include marginal notes with alternative translations of Greek words that have a range of possible meanings. Some today find this significant, especially in regard to the debate with KJV-only proponents (some people believe the King James Version is the only legitimate Bible), some of whom believe the precise wording of the King James Version was directed by the very hand of God. The fact that the KJV translators acknowledged possible alternative translations would seem to undermine this position.

The KJV generally renders God's Old Testament name, YHWH (or Yahweh), as LORD, using small capital letters. Interestingly, however, the KJV uses the term "Jehovah" for YHWH four times: **Exodus 6:3**, **Psalm 83:18**, **Isaiah 12:2**, and **Isaiah 26:4**. When the term Adonai Yahweh occurs in the Old Testament, it is rendered as LORD God.

The KJV translators began each verse on a new line. The beginning of each paragraph was marked with a pilcrow—¶ in the 1611 publication. Interestingly, however, these pilcrow marks disappeared after **Acts 20:36**. (One wonders of the printer just ran out of pilcrows.)

14

Since its initial publication, the King James Version has undergone three revisions, incorporating more than 100,000 changes. The most careful and comprehensive revision was published in 1769. The KJV is well known for its archaic language, using such terms as Thee, Thou, and ye, and verbs often ending in "-eth" and "-est" (loveth and doest). This is one reason some love the KJV. The language seems so elegant.

Unsurpassed in Beauty

A notable benefit of the King James Version is that it is virtually unsurpassed in poetic beauty. In fact, no other version comes near the literary beauty and elegance of the KJV. Yet, despite such modern sentiments, the truth is that the KJV was written in the *everyday language of 1611* and was engineered to be understood by the common people. Of course, back in those days, the majority of people could not read or write, and hence most people came to love the KJV through its public readings.

Important Keys to Bible Study

1. Remember the KJV was translated to English
2. Always research the definition of the original word
3. Allow the Holy Ghost to help you in your study
4. Don't be closed minded because of traditions
5. Seek the truth for yourself
6. Become an A student on words definitions
7. Study in detail the original Hebrew or Greek words
8. Study the Word for youself

Wisdom Keys – Give God access to all you have

Chapter 1

Prosperity is for the Body of Christ

Knowledge is the Key

Praise God for all the pastors and teachers that taught me over the years. From birth until now, God have always connected me with great men and women of God to teach me the Word of God. Having a person in your life to keep you educated in the Word is the most important thing in your life. The Holy Ghost is my Teacher. He always led us to Anointed Teacher of the Word.

Bible study is like school. We start out in the first grade and graduate from elementary and later high school. From there many go to college and get higher degrees. A degree is a term used to tell your degree of teaching on a certain subject. Good students of the Bible never stop seeking higher degrees in the Word of God. Many pastors in the community where I came up were not that educated when it came to things such as Bible history or word study. Some did not even have a high school degree. However, God ordained them for their assignment of that season.

Whenever there is a new season, there are changes necessary for that season. When winter season start, you have to get the coat out of the closet. The short sleeve shirt have to be exchanged for a coat. Many in the churches are still giving elementary teaching to students that are qualified for high school. Both the teachers and the students have refused to go to the next level. This is the time that you as an individual have to allow the Spirit of the Lord to lead you to a higher degree of teaching.

In my case, I followed the Holy Ghost to my next level. In 1987, after returning to Louisiana, God lead us to the Eagle Nest Church in West Monroe, Louisiana. The Pastors there were Drs. George and Clarice Fluitt. That church was an Eagle Nest as the name stated. We were in the nest and they prepared us to fly. It was here that I learned that I was a King and a Priest. Thank God for those Holy Ghost teachers of the Bible.

God ordained this church for those hungry for the next level in the Word. The pastors gave us detailed information on Bible history. I was taught in detail about the original language of the Bible. This teaching was a blessing to all present. This teaching is the foundation of this book. The name King Jesus Worship Center came from this teaching. Thank God for the leadership of the Holy Spirit. Praise God for the open mind to receive from a white pastor. Thank God for Holy Ghost Apostles.

This is what seasons of change is all about. When we submit to God, He will keep you on the right path. Dr. Leroy Thompson is my pastor. He is an Apostle for this generation in the area of prosperity. What better place to be to hear the subject of prosperity other than Darrow, Louisiana. We have to learn not to be closed-minded when it comes to prosperity. Apostle Thompson is ordained to teach on this subject.

The Choice is yours when it comes to whether you want prosperity in your life. There is always a choice between prosperity and poverty. Prosperity is the blessing; therefore, it will make you strong in every area of your life. Poverty is a weapon used by the devil through wicked men to keep humanity in bondage.

Poverty verses Prosperity

It is almost impossible to understand prosperity if you do not understand how evil poverty is. Poverty is a spirit used by the devil to keep men in a weak status on earth. Poverty is the destruction of the poor. Many have taught, that you cannot teach prosperity unless you have experience the benefits. They believe those who have the most are best qualified to teach prosperity. This thinking leaves out true Bible prosperity. True Bible prosperity start with how rich a man is toward God. So many multimillionaires are poor when it comes to God. However, the experience of poverty does help a person to teach on prosperity. Some men have never experienced poverty a day in their life. This is the reason so many in the church fight against prosperity for all people.

Many Christian lawmakers take the same stand that the rich man took with Lazarus. They say pull your own self up by your boot strap. They do not understand that some people do not have a boot or the strap. It is very easy to say that everybody can make it in America if they just try. True, but how far can a Lazarus in America make it without help. Did God expect the rich man to help Lazarus?

Luke 16: 19 – 24

19 There was a certain rich man, which was clothed in purple and fine linen, and fared sumptuously every day:20 And there was a certain beggar named Lazarus, which was laid at his gate, full of sores, 21 And desiring to be fed with the crumbs which fell from the rich man's table: moreover the dogs came and licked his sores. 22 And it came to pass, that the beggar died, and was carried by the angels into Abraham's bosom:the rich man also died, and was buried; 23 And in hell he lift up his eyes, being in torments, and seeth Abraham afar off, and Lazarus in his bosom. 24 And he cried and said, Father Abraham,

have mercy on me, and send Lazarus, that he may dip the tip of his finger in water, and cool my tongue; for I am tormented in this flame.

Apparently, God sent this rich man to hell because he refused to help the poor man. Standing behind a man-made word of capitalism will not overrule the Bible. Capitalism is the best system when governed properly. Many pastors in churches in this country have never experienced poverty. This is the reason they are against anybody that is trying to help the poor. Because of blindness, they think it is good for men to make a billion per year and have their employees making less than the poverty line. Lazarus could have been a hardworking man. He could have been working for a rich man that was just paying him minimum wage. This could have been the reason why

he man was begging. Maybe he did not have enough money to buy health insurance. Selah. The result, the wicked rich man ended up in hell. God will judge the wicked rich and the wicked in the church.

The Spirit of Poverty

Poverty (Hebrew reysh) – To be destitute, lack, needy (make self) poor (man).

Poverty

1 The state of having little or no money, goods, or means of support, destitution, indigence, pauperism, penury.

2. Deficiency of necessary or desirable ingredients, and qualities.

Poverty is a spirit from Satan planted in the mind of men that bring oppression to the human race. These ungodly thoughts cause men to seek wealth for wrong purposes. It causes men to serve earthly wealth rather than God. It is ideas implanted in laws to keep oppression on those who lack, have little resources, or other means of support. The same spirit oppressed Israel in Egypt.

This sprit is a bully that takes advantage of the poor to feed the wicked rich with more wealth. This was in the mind of slave traders that brought slaves from Africa to America. Men died in the civil war trying to up root evil enslavement of blacks in America. Jim Crow laws are still in place today that keep the poor chained in poverty. Poverty is not a race but a spirit that works through men to oppress men made in the image of God.

All over the world, men are dying every day fighting against this oppression on the less fortunate. As it is today, so was it in the time of Jesus. Christ lived in poverty-stricken areas in his lifetime on earth. This was so strong in his time, that Jesus said in Luke 4: 18, 19 " 18 *The Spirit of the Lord is upon me, because he hath anointed me to preach the gospel to the poor; he hath sent me to heal the brokenhearted, to preach deliverance to the captives, and recovering of sight to the blind, to set at liberty them that are bruised, 19 To preach the acceptable year of the Lord."*

The heart of Jesus ministry was to destroy poverty and bring prosperity back to the human race. First, he bring out that they need the good news of the Kingdom of God. He brings out next, that poverty breaks the hearts of men and put them in captivity. Jesus indicate that poverty blind the mind of men. In addition, it bruises men in ways only God can restore them.

The lost rich are poorer than the saved poor of this world. Because, the lost rich are hell bound. Whereas, the saved poor are heaven bound. One will have a mansion in heaven while the lost will have a house of torment. God desires both to be rich toward Him, and have material wealth. He blesses men so they can be a blessing. Jesus was made poor on the cross, that man through his poverty could become rich.

He died for the poor rich man to have true riches. The true riches are God and his Kingdom way of doing things. He desires rich men to be full of love and use his wealth to help the poor in this world. Then Jesus vows to give them a return that will make them richer now in this lifetime.

For the poor of this world, He died so that their eyes could be open to how to overcome the spirit of poverty. This will come through the spirit of wisdom, knowledge and understanding of Kingdom principals. In most cases the poor rich man still ends up in hell. Most poor men walk on in darkness on earth, and stay poor.

Jesus is the answer for the spirit of poverty. He has sent us his word, and anointed preachers and teacher to deliver humanity from the destruction of poverty. This book is a tool that God is using to bring men out of poverty. The wicked rich, lost rich and the poor have to receive the word and obey the voice of God.

Proverbs 10: 15 - *15 The rich man's wealth is his strong city: the destruction of the poor is their poverty.*

Proverbs notes two things: one, wealth gives man a strong dwelling place on earth. Two, the destruction of the poor is their poverty. Poverty destroys both the lost rich and the poor. It is not the white, black or brown man that destroy men. Our fight is thus against the spirit of poverty and not against flesh and blood. The poor in material goods have to allow God to lead them into Prosperity.

I teach the good news of prosperity all the time. Just as it was with Moses, so is it today with most poor folks concerning earthly prosperity. Moses told Israel God have houses that you do not have to build. A land already prepared with your name on it. Wealth other men have worked for, that he will give to you. They harden their heart toward Moses even as they do today. As with Moses, the people that believed went into the promise land.

Proverbs 22: 6 – 9
6 Train up a child in the way he should go :and when he is old, he will not depart from it.7 The rich ruleth over the poor, and the borrower is servant to the lender. 8 He that soweth iniquity shall reap vanity: and the rod of his anger shall fail. 9 He that hath a bountiful eye shall be blessed; for he giveth of his bread to the poor.

God inspire us to train up a child in the way he should go. Poverty is not the way to go. God teaches us that the rich rules over the poor. God desire all of his children to be the head and not the tail. He wants us to be lenders and not borrowers. Notice the borrower is servant to the lender. The writer explains that a person with a bountiful eye is blessed. That word bountiful is the Hebrew word (towb), the same word translated prosperity in the King James Version of the Bible.

God desire is for his children to have an eye for prosperity. Then will we see right and be blessed. This is a perfect example why we should study original Hebrew and Greek words from the Bible.

Poverty Revealed

Unlike in pass ages God through his word has opened the eyes of many through technology. What men use to hide concerning poverty is available by way of the internet, television and other ways of communication. This along is causing men both saved and lost to rise up and fight for the rights where prosperity is concerned.

One of the greatest weapons Satan uses against men is poverty. This year in 2014, Forbs reported the 85 richest people in the world have as much wealth as 3.5 billion people on earth. This is half of the population on earth.

Report states:

- Almost half of the world's wealth is owned by just one percent of the population.

- The wealth of the one percent richest people in the world amounts to $110 trillion. That is 65 times the total wealth of the bottom half of the world's population.

- The bottom half of the world's population owns the same as the richest 85 people in the world.

- Seven out of ten people live in countries where economic inequality has increased in the last 30 years.

- The richest one percent increased their share of income in 24 out of 26 countries for which we have data between 1980 and 2012.

- In the US, the wealthiest one percent captured 95 percent of post-financial crisis growth since 2009, while the bottom 90 percent became poorer.

Poverty is the destroyer of the poor. God said, "My people perish because of a lack of knowledge." This book is a blessed study guide to be used to increase our knowledge of Bible prosperity. The wicked rich Satan inspired men have always done all they can do to keep men from going forward.

So many missed informed preachers preach against prosperity. However, God said, "I wish above all things that you prosper and be in health even as your soul prospers. There are so many people in the church in poverty because of false teaching.

On one hand, some conservative's pastors that have wealth, accuse preachers that peach prosperity of preaching a liberation message.

Some call it a black liberation message. Then others assume because a person is preaching prosperity, they are robbing the poor of their needed wealth. God system of prosperity is the fastest and best way to get out of poverty. Jesus was a liberation preacher. Those that have not experience poverty look down on the poor and accurse them of being lazy. Others use not being married as the root cause of poverty in the poor community. The root cause of poverty is the love of money that is in the hand of the wicked rich. They don't understand why in poor areas men sell drugs, steal, fight, kill, prostute, and commit all kinds of crimes. The root cause is because they don't have jobs that pay enough to support their families. Then they are locked up and given a criminal record. Release from jail, and because of the record are hindered even more from finding good paying jobs. If you have not been around that it is hard to relate to what I am saying. If you have not been black in America there are so many things you cannot comprehend. If a person is not white he cant see what a white person see. The love of money is the root of all evil.

This Bible book of prosperity will help you as a person to study the word for yourself. This way you can be the judge of God word. It will list every scripture in the bible on the word prosperity. In addition, it will give the definition, original translation, and other words that have the same meaning of prosperity. These words were translated in different English words.

The word prosperity was not the original Hebrew, Greek and Aramaic word. This word was translated when converted to English using the King James Version. Satan has almost made it a curse word through the darkness he has planted in the minds of men.

The best definition for this word is as follow:

Prosperity – To have everything you need in life to be a blessing. It means to have the whole pie, verses having a piece of the pie. It means to be rich toward God and rich with earthly wealth. Prosperity cause one to go forward in life. It causes one to have peace and not war. Prosperity is not just material wealth as Satan has planted in the mind of men.

You can have all the money in the world and lose your soul. Therefore, that is not true prosperity. A man can be worth billions and have a killing disease, that is not going forward. When a person is rich with God, rich with wealth, rich with health, and rich with peace in every area of his life, then that is total prosperity. God desire you to have total Prosperity in your life.

In your study of the word prosperity, you will find translated words such as:

Good, better, well, goodness, best, merry, precious, fine, beautiful, glad, peace, whole, and favor to name a few.

Ask yourself these questions:

Does God want men to do well? Does the Holy Ghost want men to have the best? Is it God will for men to have peace? Did Jesus die for men to be merry? If your answer is yes, then prosperity is a blessed thing and not a curse thing.

The Laws of Prosperity

As we begin to study the laws of prosperity, it is very important to remember we are studying from God word and not man options. Let us read some basic scripture on which this book is rooted. When we read the Word, we have to believe it just as it is. When we see it in the Word, receive it, believe it and act on the Word, faith is release in our heart. Faith comes by hearing and hearing from the word of God (Rom. 10: 17).

The Apostle John said, " *2 Beloved, I wish above all things that thou mayest prosper and be in health, even as thy soul prospereth. 3 For I rejoiced greatly, when the brethren came and testified of the truth that is in thee, even as thou walkest in the truth. 4 I have no greater joy than to hear that my children walk in truth (3 John 2 – 4).* "

We should remember that John was not a young man when he wrote this epistle. He was a man that had walked with Jesus during his earthly ministry. He was inspired by the Holy Ghost to write this letter. If there were something wrong with prosperity, why would God desire this above all things for the believer? John brings out to us that prosperity is not just material wealth. John mentioned prosperity for the soul and the health of our body.

There are three forms of prosperity: Spiritual Prosperity, Soul Prosperity and Physical Prosperity. Spiritual prosperity has everything to do with a person being rich toward God and His Kingdom. Soul prosperity includes a God renewed mind. Physical prosperity includes health to your body, and producing the material wealth on earth that you need to go forward.

Spiritual and Physical Law

We must, as believers understand that laws govern everything in both the earth realm and the heavenly. Nothing takes place by accident. We must work the laws right to have prosperity in our life. There are laws that govern the spirit realm and the natural realm. Whether we are dealing with the law of gravity or any other physical law, we must understand the law and operate with wisdom to be successful in this life. God wisdom can be used to cause physical laws to operate in your favor.

Whether it is using the law of lift to fly airplanes or use the tax code to work in your favor. We have to have soul prosperity to go forward in this life. Wicked men use fabricated laws to lead men unto deeper poverty. Banks take advantage of government laws to charge high interest rate. They used freedom of laws to charge the poor high dollars for bounced checks. Companies owned by men, use laws to charge very high rates for products such as gas, oil, and other products. This caused more poverty on the poor. Free marked is good with regulations. This is the reason there are laws in place now to stop companies from buying other companies at their pleasure. Because wicked men only care about their own wealth. We as saints on the earth must stand up and fight for justice. Whatever we allow on earth, God will allow from Heaven.

John Rockefeller at one time had a monopoly on oil. Standard oil was in a league all by itself. This freedom without government made him the riches man on the planet. However, most of the people in the country were suffering. This man was a christian man that gave his tithes to the church. However, the government had to stop his company from controlling all of the oil. If not he could have raised the price so high, that poverty would have taken over most citizens in the country. Thank God, we had the right president in the country during that time. Many big companies were stopped in there track to stop the spirit of poverty during that season. We have to do the same in our season. Freedom is good, but freedom in the hand of the wicked is a killer. Wall Street and the wicked rich are working on the same evil until this day. Not all companies on Wall Street are wicked. It is wrong for one family to make billions a year, and workers of that company making less than fifteen thousand per year. That pay is poverty to any family.

The fasted way out of poverty is prosperity for the soul. When we have faith for prosperity, God will saturate our minds with wisdom to operate while in this world system. God has put wisdom in our spirit to be down loaded to the mind. When we allow him through the teaching of prosperity, he will give us, the fullness of his seven Spirits. These seven spirits have the ability to overcome or supersede evil laws created by men.

Isa. 11: 2 – 4

2 And the spirit of the Lord shall rest upon him, the spirit of wisdom and understanding, the spirit of counsel and might, the spirit of knowledge and of the fear of the Lord; 3 And shall make him of quick understanding in the fear of the Lord: and he shall not judge after the sight of his eyes, neither reprove after the hearing of his ears: 4 But with righteousness shall he judge the poor, and reprove with equity for the meek of the earth: and he shall smite the earth with the rod of his mouth, and with the breath of his lips shall he slay the wicked.

Isiah prophesied that God would rest upon on Jesus these seven anointing listed in the scripture. It was this reason that Jesus preached prosperity to the poor. God Spirit was upon him to preach the good news to the poor. This good news included Jesus becoming poor and through his poverty, we could become rich. Jesus was not poor during his lifetime. He became poor only after his arrest. Jesus received expensive gifts when he was born. A poor man has no need for a personal treasure. A poor man does not have money to give to the poor. Jesus had access to wealth all around him. He had money in the fish mouth. He had donkeys tied up waiting on him. The upper room was his whenever he needed it. Jesus Apostles and many of his supporters were rich.   Yes, Jesus preached a liberal message to the poor. He preached wisdom, knowledge and understanding of spiritual laws to come out of poverty.

The Prophets makes it clear that when these seven anointing are on a man he will be of a quick understanding in the fear of God. When a man fear or reverence God, he will believe God word over man word. The anointing cause men not to judge from what he hears on Fox, CNN or non-prosperity preachers. Through the anointing, God use men tongues to smite the earth realm by the Word. He uses them to write the Word.

With the seven Spirits of the Lord, we began to slay the wicked with the Word of God. Even now while you are reading this book, wicked imaginations are leaving your mind. For others this book is reinforcing the Holy Word already in your mind. The purpose of this book is to slay wicked imaginations planted by the wicked ones.

The Key to Spiritual Laws

Spiritual Laws include such laws as sowing and reaping. The Word says, "as long as the earth remains there will be seedtime and harvest. This is the key to having prosperity while we are on earth. Satan hates every preacher that has the boldness to preach this spiritual law to the poor. He knows the only way out for the poor is God laws of prosperity. See the mystery to all spiritual laws in the passage below:

Mark 4: 11- 20

11 And he said unto them, Unto you it is given to know the mystery of the kingdom of God:but unto them that are without, all these things are done in parables:12 That seeing they may see, and not perceive; and hearing they may hear, and not understand; lest at any time they should be converted, and their sins should be forgiven them. 13 And he said unto them, Know ye not this parable? and how then will ye know all parables?
14 The sower soweth the word. 15 And these are they by the way side, where the word is sown; but when they have heard, Satan cometh immediately, and taketh away the word that was sown in their hearts. 16 And these are they likewise which are sown on stony ground; who, when they have heard the word, immediately receive it with gladness; 17 And have no root in themselves, and so endure but for a time:afterward, when affliction or persecution ariseth for the word's sake, immediately they are offended. 18 And these are they which are sown among thorns; such as hear the word, 19 And the cares of this world, and the deceitfulness of riches, and the lusts of other things entering in, choke the word, and it becometh unfruitful. 20 And these are they which are sown on good ground; such as hear the word, and receive it, and bring forth fruit, some thirtyfold, some sixty, and some an hundred.

Jesus said the key to all spiritual laws in the Kingdom is this parable. Verse 14 is the key, "the sower sows the word." This key is seedtime and harvest. If there is no seed sown, there will not be a harvest. For prosperity, we have to apply this principal. This is why the wicked fight against prosperity being preached. Prosperity for the poor always comes through the principals of God. That is, the God kind of prosperity. You will be surprised, but sowing is not about just sowing money. Sowing money is necessary to reap money in return. Let us take a closer look at the parable.

Jesus indicated that the sower was sowing the word. The word was planted in the hearts of men. Some did not understand the word, these were seeds planted in shallow ground of the mind and heart. Because they did not understand, Satan stole the word. When you don't understand spiritual laws Satan will make sure he give you a false word against the sower, so you will give up what was sown. However, sowing and reaping is a principal that work.

Seeds were sown on stony ground; these hear how the laws of prosperity work. They began to give tithes, offering, gifts and other good deeds in the Kingdom. Then persecution and affliction come because of the word in their heart, and they stop applying the principal and poverty takes over once again.

The third type, hear the word and began to bring forth fruits to the Kingdom. Then they began to care more about the things of the world. This deception chokes the Word, and it becomes unfruitful. Then they do not bring forth fruits into the kingdom. They use the harvest that was coming on vacations, cars, houses, kids and other things. All of this is good, but the kingdom should come first.

Finally, the sower sowed the word into good soil. The good soil is a person that receives the seed of prosperity. He believes it in his heart and mind. He gives not only his tithes and offering, but he makes all that God has given him available to God. This man brings forth through spiritual laws the thirty, sixty, and hundredfold return.

Sowing Money was not the Key to the Parable

While sowing money, wealth and deeds are important this was not the main secret to the kingdom. The secret to the kingdom was sowing the Word of God. Death and life is in the power of the tongue. The tongue controls the destiny of a man, as a steering wheel determines the destiny of car.

Jesus indicates that the sower is to continue to sow the word even if it does not produce fruit right away. The sower in the parable sowed into shallow, stony, and thorny ground without anything to show. However, because he believed in the law of sowing and reaping, he kept on sowing. Finally, because of his faith, his seed made contact with good ground soil. We know that this good ground was a heart that received the word.

Remember the Lord governs all spiritual laws. The Lord is the one that make every good seed produce a crop. If a man has faith in Kingdom laws, God will make all grace abound toward him. The sower ended up with thirty, sixty and hundredfold return. This happen because the laws of the spirit override all natural laws.

If God cannot find a man heart to receive his word, he will turn a heart to believe just because you have faith in his principals. The farmer continues to sow his seed because he believes in the law of seedtime and harvest. We have to have the same faith in the seed of the Word of God.

Words are Seeds Containing Your Future

The Word of God rules in both the spirit and natural realm. In the natural realm, words rule over everything else. Words can determine whether you live or die. Whenever a man receives a promotion, someone gave the word for that to happen. If you can receive this powerful law it is the key that unlock all of the principals of God.

Romans 10: 8, 9 - 8 But what saith it? The word is nigh thee, even in thy mouth, and in thy heart:that is, the word of faith, which we preach; 9 That if thou shalt confess with thy mouth the Lord Jesus, and shalt believe in thine heart that God hath raised him from the dead, thou shalt be saved.

The writer says the word is near you even in your heart and your tongue. With the heart man believe, salvation come by confessing what you believe. This is the key to understanding the spirit realm. God sows his word in our heart. Once the word is in abundances in the heart, we speak it out of our mouth. Faith words spoken out of the mouth are loaded with the power of God.

When Jesus multiplied the bread and fish, both time it happen, because he used the laws of sowing the word. Yes brothers and sisters, the Lord travel in his word to manifest what we sow in faith. Jesus used these principal to stop the wind and the water in a bad storm. He cast out devils with his words. He raised the dead by just saying come forth. Jesus used the key to the kingdom, and left us a Bible to read about this spiritual law of sowing and reaping.

Hebrews 11: 3, Through faith we understand that the worlds were framed by the word of God, so that things which are seen were not made of things which do appear.

The Word of God framed the world. God is a speaking Spirit. When God created the heavens and the earth, it was by His spoken Word. God Spirit travels in the faith words that we speak. When we speak doubt or fear filled words demon spirit have access to bring these words to pass. Jesus ended this parable of sowing, by saying, " he that has understanding shall receive a bountiful harvest." If you do not have understanding, you will lose that which was sown into your heart.

This is the reason it so important to study the word of prosperity and speak God ordained words. If a man will not receive the seed of prosperity in his heart, he will never speak it out of his mouth. Then unbelief talk will bring a snare into their life. I encourage you to use this book for studing, meditation, and most important, to speak the word. When a man pray he is speaking the word. When you confess the word, you are sowing the word. What better way to get your harvest desires, than by speaking the Word of God. This book is loaded with the word of God. It is the combination of sowing seeds of money, wealth, deeds and speaking the Word that cause manifestation to push you forward. Let this Bible Book of Prosperity bring you the desires of your heart.

The root of poverty according to God Word

James 5:1 Go to now, ye rich men, weep and howl for your miseries that shall come upon you. 2 Your riches are corrupted, and your garments are motheaten. 3 Your gold and silver is cankered; and the rust of them shall be a witness against you, and shall eat your flesh as it were fire. Ye have heaped treasure together for the last days. 4 Behold, the hire of the labourers who have reaped down your fields, which is of you kept back by fraud, crieth:and the cries of them which have reaped are entered into the ears of the Lord of sabaoth. 5 Ye have lived in pleasure on the earth, and been wanton; ye have nourished your hearts, as in a day of slaughter. 6 Ye have condemned and killed the just; and he doth not resist you.
7 Be patient therefore, brethren, unto the coming of the Lord. Behold, the husbandman waiteth for the precious fruit of the earth, and hath long patience for it, until he receive the early and latter rain. 8 Be ye also patient; stablish your hearts:for the coming of the Lord draweth nigh.
9 Grudge not one against another, brethren, lest ye be condemned:behold, the judge standeth before the door. 10 Take, my brethren, the prophets, who have spoken in the name of the Lord, for an example of suffering affliction, and of patience.

The wicked rich have so much wealth laid up that it is in a rust stage. This wealth that was not given to whom it was due, will be a witness against the wicked multimillionaires and billionaires. The poor that worked for your companies is crying out to God even now. You have condemned, locked up and done evil against the poor. They didn't have enough wealth to fight against you. You told them to help their own self. You kept their pay very low by what God call fraud. But the Lord of war will fight for his people. He will take back all that belong to the poor. The wicked will be Judged by The LORD.

Chapter 2

Chapters on Prosperity

Definition

PROSPER'ITY, *n. L. prosperitas. Advance or gain in any thing good or desirable; successful progress in any business or enterprise; success; attainment of the object desired; as the prosperity of arts; agricultural or commercial prosperity; national prosperity. Our disposition to abuse the blessings of providence renders prosperity dangerous.*
The prosperity of fools shall destroy them. Prov.1.

PROS'PER, *v.t. L.prospero, from prosperus, from the Gr. to carry to or toward; to bear. To favor; to render successful. All things concur to prosper our design.*
PROS'PER, v.i. To be successful; to succeed.
The Lord made all that he did to prosper in his hand. Gen.39.
He that covereth his sins, shall not prosper. Prov.28.
1. To grow or increase; to thrive; to make gain; as, to prosper in business. Our agriculture, commerce and manufactures now prosper.

PROS'PERED, *pp. Having success; favored.*

PROS'PERING, *ppr. Rendering successful; advancing in growth, wealth or any good.*
prosperity

PROS'PEROUS, a. L.prosperus. Advancing in the pursuit of any thing desirable; making gain or increase; thriving; successful; as a prosperous trade; a prosperous voyage; a prosperous expedition or undertaking; a prosperous man, family or nation; a prosperous war. The seed shall be prosperous; the vine shall give her fruit. Zech.8. 1. Favorable; favoring success; as a prosperous wind.

PROS'PEROUSLY, adv. With gain or increase; successfully. Prosperousness

PROS'PEROUSNESS, n. The state of being successful; prosperity.

Prosperity

Deuteronomy 23:1-8

1 He that is wounded in the stones, or hath his privy member cut off, shall not enter into the congregation of the Lord. 2 A bastard shall not enter into the congregation of the Lord; even to his tenth generation shall he not enter into the congregation of the Lord. 3 An Ammonite or Moabite shall not enter into the congregation of the Lord; even to their tenth generation shall they not enter into the congregation of the Lord forever:4 Because they met you not with bread and with water in the way, when ye came forth out of Egypt; and because they hired against thee Balaam the son of Beor of Pethor of Mesopotamia, to curse thee. 5 Nevertheless the Lord thy God would not hearken unto Balaam; but the Lord thy God turned the curse into a blessing unto thee, because the Lord thy God loved thee. **6 Thou shalt not seek their peace nor their prosperity all thy days for ever.**
7 Thou shalt not abhor an Edomite; for he is thy brother:thou shalt not abhor an Egyptian; because thou wast a stranger in his land. 8 The children that are begotten of them shall enter into the congregation of the Lord in their third generation.

1 Samuel 25:1-20

1 And Samuel died; and all the Israelites were gathered together, and lamented him, and buried him in his house at Ramah. And David arose, and went down to the wilderness of Paran. 2 And there was a man in Maon, whose possessions were in Carmel; and the man was very great, and he had three thousand sheep, and a thousand goats:and he was shearing his sheep in Carmel. 3 Now the name of the man was Nabal; and the name of his wife Abigail:and she was a woman of good understanding, and of a beautiful countenance:but the man was churlish and evil in his doings; and he was of the house of Caleb.
4 And David heard in the wilderness that Nabal did shear his sheep. 5 And David sent out ten young men, and David said unto the young men, Get you up to Carmel, and go to Nabal, and greet him in my name:**6 And thus shall ye say to him that liveth in prosperity, Peace be both to thee, and peace be to thine house, and peace be unto all that thou hast.** 7 And now I have heard that thou hast shearers:now thy shepherds which were with us, we hurt them not, neither was there ought missing unto them, all the while they were in Carmel. 8 Ask thy young men, and they will shew thee. Wherefore let the young men find favour in thine eyes:for we come in a good day:give, I pray thee, whatsoever cometh to thine hand unto thy servants, and to thy son David. 9 And when David's young men came, they spake to Nabal according to all those words in the name of David, and ceased.
10 And Nabal answered David's servants, and said, Who is David? and who is the son of Jesse? there be many servants now a days that break away every man from his master. 11 Shall I then take my bread, and my water, and my flesh that I have killed for my shearers, and give it unto men, whom I know not whence they be? 12 So David's young men turned their way, and went again, and came and told him all those sayings. 13 And David said unto his men, Gird ye on every man his sword. And they girded on every man his sword; and David also girded on his sword:and there went up after David about four hundred men; and two hundred abode by the stuff

14 But one of the young men told Abigail, Nabal's wife, saying, Behold, David sent messengers out of the wilderness to salute our master; and he railed on them. 15 But the men were very good unto us, and we were not hurt, neither missed we any thing, as long as we were conversant with them, when we were in the fields:16 They were a wall unto us both by night and day, all the while we were with them keeping the sheep. 17 Now therefore know and consider what thou wilt do; for evil is determined against our master, and against all his household:for he is such a son of Belial, that a man cannot speak to him.

18 Then Abigail made haste, and took two hundred loaves, and two bottles of wine, and five sheep ready dressed, and five measures of parched corn, and an hundred clusters of raisins, and two hundred cakes of figs, and laid them on asses. 19 And she said unto her servants, Go on before me; behold, I come after you. But she told not her husband Nabal. 20 And it was so, as she rode on the ass, that she came down by the covert of the hill, and, behold, David and his men came down against her; and she met them.

1 Kings 10

1 And when the queen of Sheba heard of the fame of Solomon concerning the name of the Lord, she came to prove him with hard questions. 2 And she came to Jerusalem with a very great train, with camels that bare spices, and very much gold, and precious stones:and when she was come to Solomon, she communed with him of all that was in her heart. 3 And Solomon told her all her questions:there was not any thing hid from the king, which he told her not. 4 And when the queen of Sheba had seen all Solomon's wisdom, and the house that he had built, 5 And the meat of his table, and the sitting of his servants, and the attendance of his ministers, and their apparel, and his cupbearers, and his ascent by which he went up unto the house of the Lord; there was no more spirit in her. 6 And she said to the king, It was a true report that I heard in mine own land of thy acts and of thy wisdom. **7 Howbeit I believed not the words, until I came, and**

mine eyes had seen it:and, behold, the half was not told me:thy wisdom and prosperity exceedeth the fame which I heard. 8 Happy are thy men, happy are these thy servants, which stand continually before thee, and that hear thy wisdom. 9 Blessed be the Lord thy God, which delighted in thee, to set thee on the throne of Israel:because the Lord loved Israel for ever, therefore made he thee king, to do judgment and justice. 10 And she gave the king an hundred and twenty talents of gold, and of spices very great store, and precious stones:there came no more such abundance of spices as these which the queen of Sheba gave to king Solomon. 11 And the navy also of Hiram, that brought gold from Ophir, brought in from Ophir great plenty of almug trees, and precious stones. 12 And the king made of the almug trees pillars for the house of the Lord, and for the king's house, harps also and psalteries for singers:there came no such almug trees, nor were seen unto this day. 13 And king Solomon gave unto the queen of Sheba all her desire, whatsoever she asked, beside that which Solomon gave her of his royal bounty. So she turned and went to her own country, she and her servants.

14 Now the weight of gold that came to Solomon in one year was six hundred threescore and six talents of gold, 15 Beside that he had of the merchantmen, and of the traffick of the spice merchants, and of all the kings of Arabia, and of the governors of the country.

16 And king Solomon made two hundred targets of beaten gold:six hundred shekels of gold went to one target. 17 And he made three hundred shields of beaten gold; three pound of gold went to one shield:and the king put them in the house of the forest of Lebanon.

18 Moreover the king made a great throne of ivory, and overlaid it with the best gold. 19 The throne had six steps, and the top of the throne was round behind:and there were stays on either side on the place of the seat, and two lions stood beside the stays. 20 And twelve lions stood there on the one side and on the other upon the six steps:there was not the like made in any kingdom.

21 And all king Solomon's drinking vessels were of gold, and all the vessels of the house of the forest of Lebanon were of pure gold; none

were of silver:it was nothing accounted of in the days of Solomon. 22
For the king had at sea a navy of Tharshish with the navy of
Hiram:once in three years came the navy of Tharshish, bringing gold,
and silver, ivory, and apes, and peacocks. 23 So king Solomon
exceeded all the kings of the earth for riches and for wisdom.
24 And all the earth sought to Solomon, to hear his wisdom, which
God had put in his heart. 25 And they brought every man his present,
vessels of silver, and vessels of gold, and garments, and armour, and
spices, horses, and mules, a rate year by year.
26 And Solomon gathered together chariots and horsemen:and he had
a thousand and four hundred chariots, and twelve thousand horsemen,
whom he bestowed in the cities for chariots, and with the king at
Jerusalem. 27 And the king made silver to be in Jerusalem as stones,
and cedars made he to be as the sycomore trees that are in the vale,
for abundance.
28 And Solomon had horses brought out of Egypt, and linen yarn:the
king's merchants received the linen yarn at a price. 29 And a chariot
came up and went out of Egypt for six hundred shekels of silver, and
an horse for an hundred and fifty:and so for all the kings of the
Hittites, and for the kings of Syria, did they bring them out by their
means.

Job 15

1 Then answered Eliphaz the Temanite, and said,
2 Should a wise man utter vain knowledge,
and fill his belly with the east wind?
3 Should he reason with unprofitable talk?
or with speeches wherewith he can do no good?
4 Yea, thou castest off fear,
and restrainest prayer before God.
5 For thy mouth uttereth thine iniquity,
and thou choosest the tongue of the crafty.
6 Thine own mouth condemneth thee, and not I:

yea, thine own lips testify against thee.

7 Art thou the first man that was born?

or wast thou made before the hills?

8 Hast thou heard the secret of God?

and dost thou restrain wisdom to thyself?

9 What knowest thou, that we know not?

what understandest thou, which is not in us?

10 With us are both the grayheaded and very aged men,

much elder than thy father.

11 Are the consolations of God small with thee?

is there any secret thing with thee?

12 Why doth thine heart carry thee away?

and what do thy eyes wink at,

13 That thou turnest thy spirit against God,

and lettest such words go out of thy mouth?

14 What is man, that he should be clean?

and he which is born of a woman, that he should be righteous?

15 Behold, he putteth no trust in his saints;

yea, the heavens are not clean in his sight.

16 How much more abominable and filthy

is man, which drinketh iniquity like water?

17 I will shew thee, hear me;

and that which I have seen I will declare;

18 Which wise men have told

from their fathers, and have not hid it:

19 Unto whom alone the earth was given,

and no stranger passed among them.

20 The wicked man travaileth with pain all his days,

and the number of years is hidden to the oppressor.

21 A dreadful sound is in his ears:

in prosperity the destroyer shall come upon him.

22 He believeth not that he shall return out of darkness,

and he is waited for of the sword.

23 He wandereth abroad for bread, saying, Where is it?

he knoweth that the day of darkness is ready at his hand.
24 Trouble and anguish shall make him afraid;
they shall prevail against him, as a king ready to the battle.
25 For he stretcheth out his hand against God,
and strengtheneth himself against the Almighty.
26 He runneth upon him, even on his neck,
upon the thick bosses of his bucklers:
27 Because he covereth his face with his fatness,
and maketh collops of fat on his flanks.
28 And he dwelleth in desolate cities,
and in houses which no man inhabiteth,
which are ready to become heaps.
29 He shall not be rich, neither shall his substance continue,
neither shall he prolong the perfection thereof upon the earth.
30 He shall not depart out of darkness;
the flame shall dry up his branches,
and by the breath of his mouth shall he go away.
31 Let not him that is deceived trust in vanity:
for vanity shall be his recompence.
32 It shall be accomplished before his time,
and his branch shall not be green.
33 He shall shake off his unripe grape as the vine,
and shall cast off his flower as the olive.
34 For the congregation of hypocrites shall be desolate,
and fire shall consume the tabernacles of bribery.
35 They conceive mischief, and bring forth vanity,
and their belly prepareth deceit.

Job 36

1 Elihu also proceeded, and said,
2 Suffer me a little, and I will shew thee
that I have yet to speak on God's behalf.
3 I will fetch my knowledge from afar,
and will ascribe righteousness to my Maker.

4 For truly my words shall not be false:
he that is perfect in knowledge is with thee.
5 Behold, God is mighty, and despiseth not any:
he is mighty in strength and wisdom.
6 He preserveth not the life of the wicked:
but giveth right to the poor.
7 He withdraweth not his eyes from the righteous:
but with kings are they on the throne;
yea, he doth establish them for ever, and they are exalted.
8 And if they be bound in fetters,
and be holden in cords of affliction;
9 Then he sheweth them their work,
and their transgressions that they have exceeded.
10 He openeth also their ear to discipline,
and commandeth that they return from iniquity.
**11 If they obey and serve him, they shall spend their days in
prosperity, and their years in pleasures.**
**12 But if they obey not,
they shall perish by the sword, and they shall die without
knowledge.**
13 But the hypocrites in heart heap up wrath:
they cry not when he bindeth them.
14 They die in youth,
and their life is among the unclean.
15 He delivereth the poor in his affliction,
and openeth their ears in oppression.
16 Even so would he have removed thee out of the strait
into a broad place, where there is no straitness;
and that which should be set on thy table should be full of fatness.
17 But thou hast fulfilled the judgment of the wicked:
judgment and justice take hold on thee.
18 Because there is wrath, beware lest he take thee away with his
stroke:
then a great ransom cannot deliver thee.

19 Will he esteem thy riches? no, not gold,
nor all the forces of strength.
20 Desire not the night,
when people are cut off in their place.
21 Take heed, regard not iniquity:
for this hast thou chosen rather than affliction.
22 Behold, God exalteth by his power:
who teacheth like him?
23 Who hath enjoined him his way?
or who can say, Thou hast wrought iniquity?
24 Remember that thou magnify his work,
which men behold.
25 Every man may see it;
man may behold it afar off.
26 Behold, God is great, and we know him not,
neither can the number of his years be searched out.
27 For he maketh small the drops of water:
they pour down rain according to the vapour thereof:
28 Which the clouds do drop
and distil upon man abundantly.
29 Also can any understand the spreadings of the clouds,
or the noise of his tabernacle?
30 Behold, he spreadeth his light upon it, and covereth the bottom of
the sea.
31 For by them judgeth he the people;
he giveth meat in abundance.
32 With clouds he covereth the light;
and commandeth it not to shine by the cloud that cometh betwixt.
33 The noise thereof sheweth concerning it,
the cattle also concerning the vapour.

Psalms 30
A Psalm and Song at the dedication of the house of David.
1 I will extol thee, O Lord; for thou hast lifted me up,

and hast not made my foes to rejoice over me.

2 O Lord my God, I cried unto thee, and thou hast healed me.

3 O Lord, thou hast brought up my soul from the grave:

thou hast kept me alive, that I should not go down to the pit.

4 Sing unto the Lord, O ye saints of his,

and give thanks at the remembrance of his holiness.

5 For his anger endureth but a moment; in his favour is life:

weeping may endure for a night, but joy cometh in the morning.

6 And in my prosperity I said,

I shall never be moved.

7 Lord, by thy favour thou hast made my mountain to stand strong:

thou didst hide thy face, and I was troubled.

8 I cried to thee, O Lord;

and unto the Lord I made supplication.

9 What profit is there in my blood, when I go down to the pit?

Shall the dust praise thee? shall it declare thy truth?

10 Hear, O Lord, and have mercy upon me:

Lord, be thou my helper.

11 Thou hast turned for me my mourning into dancing:

thou hast put off my sackcloth, and girded me with gladness;

12 To the end that my glory may sing praise to thee, and not be silent.

O Lord my God, I will give thanks unto thee for ever.

Psalms 35

A Psalm of David.

1 Plead my cause, O Lord, with them that strive with me:

fight against them that fight against me.

2 Take hold of shield and buckler,

and stand up for mine help.

3 Draw out also the spear, and stop the way against them that

persecute me:

say unto my soul, I am thy salvation.

4 Let them be confounded and put to shame that seek after my soul:

let them be turned back and brought to confusion that devise my hurt.

5 Let them be as chaff before the wind:
and let the angel of the Lord chase them.
6 Let their way be dark and slippery:
and let the angel of the Lord persecute them.
7 For without cause have they hid for me their net in a pit,
which without cause they have digged for my soul.
8 Let destruction come upon him at unawares;
and let his net that he hath hid catch himself:
into that very destruction let him fall.
9 And my soul shall be joyful in the Lord:
it shall rejoice in his salvation.
10 All my bones shall say,
Lord, who is like unto thee,
which deliverest the poor from him that is too strong for him,
yea, the poor and the needy from him that spoileth him?
11 False witnesses did rise up;
they laid to my charge things that I knew not.
12 They rewarded me evil for good
to the spoiling of my soul.
13 But as for me, when they were sick, my clothing was sackcloth:
I humbled my soul with fasting;
and my prayer returned into mine own bosom.
14 I behaved myself as though he had been my friend or brother:
I bowed down heavily, as one that mourneth for his mother.
15 But in mine adversity they rejoiced, and gathered themselves
together:
yea, the abjects gathered themselves together against me, and I knew
it not;
they did tear me, and ceased not:
16 With hypocritical mockers in feasts,
they gnashed upon me with their teeth.
17 Lord, how long wilt thou look on?
rescue my soul from their destructions,
my darling from the lions.

18 I will give thee thanks in the great congregation:
I will praise thee among much people.
19 Let not them that are mine enemies wrongfully rejoice over me:
neither let them wink with the eye that hate me without a cause.
20 For they speak not peace:
but they devise deceitful matters against them that are quiet in the land.
21 Yea, they opened their mouth wide against me,
and said, Aha, aha, our eye hath seen it.
22 This thou hast seen, O Lord:keep not silence:
O Lord, be not far from me.
23 Stir up thyself, and awake to my judgment,
even unto my cause, my God and my Lord.
24 Judge me, O Lord my God, according to thy righteousness;
and let them not rejoice over me.
25 Let them not say in their hearts, Ah, so would we have it:
let them not say, We have swallowed him up.
26 Let them be ashamed and brought to confusion together that rejoice at mine hurt:
let them be clothed with shame and dishonour that magnify themselves against me.
27 Let them shout for joy, and be glad, that favour my righteous cause:
yea, let them say continually, Let the Lord be magnified, which hath pleasure in the prosperity of his servant.
28 And my tongue shall speak of thy righteousness
and of thy praise all the day long.

Psalms 73
A Psalm of Asaph.
1 Truly God is good to Israel,
even to such as are of a clean heart.
2 But as for me, my feet were almost gone;
my steps had well nigh slipped.

3 For I was envious at the foolish,
when I saw the prosperity of the wicked.
4 For there are no bands in their death:
but their strength is firm.
5 They are not in trouble as other men;
neither are they plagued like other men.
6 Therefore pride compasseth them about as a chain;
violence covereth them as a garment.
7 Their eyes stand out with fatness:
they have more than heart could wish.
8 They are corrupt, and speak wickedly concerning oppression:
they speak loftily.
9 They set their mouth against the heavens,
and their tongue walketh through the earth.
10 Therefore his people return hither:
and waters of a full cup are wrung out to them.
11 And they say, How doth God know?
and is there knowledge in the most High?
12 Behold, these are the ungodly,
who prosper in the world; they increase in riches.
13 Verily I have cleansed my heart in vain,
and washed my hands in innocency.
14 For all the day long have I been plagued,
and chastened every morning.
15 If I say, I will speak thus;
behold, I should offend against the generation of thy children.
16 When I thought to know this,
it was too painful for me;
17 Until I went into the sanctuary of God;
then understood I their end.
18 Surely thou didst set them in slippery places:
thou castedst them down into destruction.
19 How are they brought into desolation, as in a moment!
they are utterly consumed with terrors.

20 As a dream when one awaketh; so, O Lord, when thou awakest,
thou shalt despise their image.
21 Thus my heart was grieved,
and I was pricked in my reins.
22 So foolish was I, and ignorant:
I was as a beast before thee.
23 Nevertheless I am continually with thee:
thou hast holden me by my right hand.
24 Thou shalt guide me with thy counsel,
and afterward receive me to glory.
25 Whom have I in heaven but thee?
and there is none upon earth that I desire beside thee.
26 My flesh and my heart faileth:
but God is the strength of my heart, and my portion for ever.
27 For, lo, they that are far from thee shall perish:
thou hast destroyed all them that go a whoring from thee.
28 But it is good for me to draw near to God:
I have put my trust in the Lord God,
that I may declare all thy works.

Psalms 118
1 O give thanks unto the Lord; for he is good:
because his mercy endureth for ever.
2 Let Israel now say,
that his mercy endureth for ever.
3 Let the house of Aaron now say,
that his mercy endureth for ever.
4 Let them now that fear the Lord say,
that his mercy endureth for ever.
5 I called upon the Lord in distress:
the Lord answered me, and set me in a large place.
6 The Lord is on my side; I will not fear:
what can man do unto me?

7 The Lord taketh my part with them that help me:
therefore shall I see my desire upon them that hate me.
8 It is better to trust in the Lord
than to put confidence in man.
9 It is better to trust in the Lord
than to put confidence in princes.
10 All nations compassed me about:but in the name of the Lord will I
destroy them.
11 They compassed me about; yea, they compassed me about:
but in the name of the Lord I will destroy them.
12 They compassed me about like bees;
they are quenched as the fire of thorns:
for in the name of the Lord I will destroy them.
13 Thou hast thrust sore at me that I might fall:
but the Lord helped me.
14 The Lord is my strength and song,
and is become my salvation.
15 The voice of rejoicing and salvation is in the tabernacles of the
righteous:
the right hand of the Lord doeth valiantly.
16 The right hand of the Lord is exalted:
the right hand of the Lord doeth valiantly.
17 I shall not die, but live,
and declare the works of the Lord.
18 The Lord hath chastened me sore:
but he hath not given me over unto death.
19 Open to me the gates of righteousness:
I will go into them, and I will praise the Lord:
20 This gate of the Lord,
into which the righteous shall enter.
21 I will praise thee:for thou hast heard me,
and art become my salvation.
22 The stone which the builders refused
is become the head stone of the corner.

23 This is the Lord 's doing;

it is marvellous in our eyes.

24 This is the day which the Lord hath made;

we will rejoice and be glad in it.

25 Save now, I beseech thee, O Lord:

O Lord, I beseech thee, send now prosperity.

26 Blessed be he that cometh in the name of the Lord:

we have blessed you out of the house of the Lord.

27 God is the Lord, which hath shewed us light:

bind the sacrifice with cords,

even unto the horns of the altar.

28 Thou art my God, and I will praise thee:

thou art my God, I will exalt thee.

29 O give thanks unto the Lord; for he is good:

for his mercy endureth for ever.

Psalms 122

A Song of degrees of David.

1 I was glad when they said unto me,

Let us go into the house of the Lord.

2 Our feet shall stand

within thy gates, O Jerusalem.

3 Jerusalem is builded

as a city that is compact together:

4 Whither the tribes go up, the tribes of the Lord,

unto the testimony of Israel,

to give thanks unto the name of the Lord.

5 For there are set thrones of judgment,

the thrones of the house of David.

6 Pray for the peace of Jerusalem:

they shall prosper that love thee.

7 Peace be within thy walls,

and prosperity within thy palaces.

8 For my brethren and companions 'sakes,
I will now say, Peace be within thee.
9 Because of the house of the Lord our God
I will seek thy good.

Proverbs 1

1 The proverbs of Solomon the son of David, king of Israel.
2 To know wisdom and instruction;
to perceive the words of understanding;
3 To receive the instruction of wisdom,
justice, and judgment, and equity;
4 To give subtilty to the simple,
to the young man knowledge and discretion.
5 A wise man will hear, and will increase learning
; and a man of understanding shall attain unto wise counsels:
6 To understand a proverb, and the interpretation;
the words of the wise, and their dark sayings.
7 The fear of the Lord is the beginning of knowledge:
but fools despise wisdom and instruction.
8 My son, hear the instruction of thy father,
and forsake not the law of thy mother:
9 For they shall be an ornament of grace unto thy head,
and chains about thy neck.
10 My son, if sinners entice thee,
consent thou not.
11 If they say, Come with us, let us lay wait for blood,
let us lurk privily for the innocent without cause:
12 Let us swallow them up alive as the grave;
and whole, as those that go down into the pit:
13 We shall find all precious substance,
we shall fill our houses with spoil:
14 Cast in thy lot among us;
let us all have one purse:

15 My son, walk not thou in the way with them;
refrain thy foot from their path:
16 For their feet run to evil,
and make haste to shed blood.
17 Surely in vain the net is spread in the sight of any bird.
18 And they lay wait for their own blood;
they lurk privily for their own lives.
19 So are the ways of every one that is greedy of gain;
which taketh away the life of the owners thereof.
20 Wisdom crieth without;
she uttereth her voice in the streets:
21 She crieth in the chief place of concourse, in the openings of the
gates:
in the city she uttereth her words, saying,
22 How long, ye simple ones, will ye love simplicity?
and the scorners delight in their scorning,
and fools hate knowledge?
23 Turn you at my reproof:
behold, I will pour out my spirit unto you,
I will make known my words unto you.
24 Because I have called, and ye refused;
I have stretched out my hand, and no man regarded;
25 But ye have set at nought all my counsel,
and would none of my reproof:
26 I also will laugh at your calamity;
I will mock when your fear cometh;
27 When your fear cometh as desolation,
and your destruction cometh as a whirlwind;
when distress and anguish cometh upon you.
28 Then shall they call upon me, but I will not answer;
they shall seek me early, but they shall not find me:
29 For that they hated knowledge,
and did not choose the fear of the Lord:
30 They would none of my counsel:

they despised all my reproof.
31 Therefore shall they eat of the fruit of their own way,
and be filled with their own devices.
**32 For the turning away of the simple shall slay them,
and the prosperity of fools shall destroy them.**
33 But whoso hearkeneth unto me shall dwell safely,
and shall be quiet from fear of evil.

Ecclesiastes 7

1 A good name is better than precious ointment; and the day of death
than the day of one's birth. 2 It is better to go to the house of
mourning, than to go to the house of feasting:for that is the end of all
men; and the living will lay it to his heart. 3 Sorrow is better than
laughter:for by the sadness of the countenance the heart is made
better. 4 The heart of the wise is in the house of mourning; but the
heart of fools is in the house of mirth. 5 It is better to hear the rebuke
of the wise, than for a man to hear the song of fools. 6 For as the
crackling of thorns under a pot, so is the laughter of the fool:this also
is vanity.
7 Surely oppression maketh a wise man mad; and a gift destroyeth the
heart. 8 Better is the end of a thing than the beginning thereof:and the
patient in spirit is better than the proud in spirit. 9 Be not hasty in thy
spirit to be angry:for anger resteth in the bosom of fools. 10 Say not
thou, What is the cause that the former days were better than these?
for thou dost not enquire wisely concerning this.
11 Wisdom is good with an inheritance:and by it there is profit to
them that see the sun. 12 For wisdom is a defence, and money is a
defence:but the excellency of knowledge is, that wisdom giveth life to
them that have it. 13 Consider the work of God:for who can make that
straight, which he hath made crooked? **14 In the day of prosperity
be joyful, but in the day of adversity consider:God also hath set
the one over against the other, to the end that man should find
nothing after him.**

15 All things have I seen in the days of my vanity:there is a just man that perisheth in his righteousness, and there is a wicked man that prolongeth his life in his wickedness. 16 Be not righteous over much; neither make thyself over wise:why shouldest thou destroy thyself? 17 Be not over much wicked, neither be thou foolish:why shouldest thou die before thy time? 18 It is good that thou shouldest take hold of this; yea, also from this withdraw not thine hand:for he that feareth God shall come forth of them all. 19 Wisdom strengtheneth the wise more than ten mighty men which are in the city. 20 For there is not a just man upon earth, that doeth good, and sinneth not. 21 Also take no heed unto all words that are spoken; lest thou hear thy servant curse thee:22 For oftentimes also thine own heart knoweth that thou thyself likewise hast cursed others.

23 All this have I proved by wisdom:I said, I will be wise; but it was far from me. 24 That which is far off, and exceeding deep, who can find it out? 25 I applied mine heart to know, and to search, and to seek out wisdom, and the reason of things, and to know the wickedness of folly, even of foolishness and madness:26 And I find more bitter than death the woman, whose heart is snares and nets, and her hands as bands:whoso pleaseth God shall escape from her; but the sinner shall be taken by her. 27 Behold, this have I found, saith the preacher, counting one by one, to find out the account:28 Which yet my soul seeketh, but I find not:one man among a thousand have I found; but a woman among all those have I not found. 29 Lo, this only have I found, that God hath made man upright; but they have sought out many inventions.

Jeremiah 22

1 Thus saith the Lord; Go down to the house of the king of Judah, and speak there this word, 2 And say, Hear the word of the Lord, O king of Judah, that sittest upon the throne of David, thou, and thy servants, and thy people that enter in by these gates:3 Thus saith the Lord; Execute ye judgment and righteousness, and deliver the spoiled out of the hand of the oppressor:and do no wrong, do no violence to the

stranger, the fatherless, nor the widow, neither shed innocent blood in this place. 4 For if ye do this thing indeed, then shall there enter in by the gates of this house kings sitting upon the throne of David, riding in chariots and on horses, he, and his servants, and his people. 5 But if ye will not hear these words, I swear by myself, saith the Lord, that this house shall become a desolation. 6 For thus saith the Lord unto the king's house of Judah; Thou art Gilead unto me, and the head of Lebanon:yet surely I will make thee a wilderness, and cities which are not inhabited. 7 And I will prepare destroyers against thee, every one with his weapons:and they shall cut down thy choice cedars, and cast them into the fire. 8 And many nations shall pass by this city, and they shall say every man to his neighbour, Wherefore hath the Lord done thus unto this great city? 9 Then they shall answer, Because they have forsaken the covenant of the Lord their God, and worshipped other gods, and served them.

10 Weep ye not for the dead, neither bemoan him:
but weep sore for him that goeth away:
for he shall return no more,
nor see his native country.

11 For thus saith the Lord touching Shallum the son of Josiah king of Judah, which reigned instead of Josiah his father, which went forth out of this place; He shall not return thither any more:12 But he shall die in the place whither they have led him captive, and shall see this land no more.

13 Woe unto him that buildeth his house by unrighteousness,
and his chambers by wrong;
that useth his neighbour's service without wages,
and giveth him not for his work;

14 That saith, I will build me a wide house and large chambers,
and cutteth him out windows;
and it is cieled with cedar, and painted with vermilion.

15 Shalt thou reign, because thou closest thyself in cedar?
did not thy father eat and drink,
and do judgment and justice,

and then it was well with him?

16 He judged the cause of the poor and needy; then it was well with him:

was not this to know me? saith the Lord.

17 But thine eyes and thine heart are not but for thy covetousness, and for to shed innocent blood,

and for oppression, and for violence, to do it.

18 Therefore thus saith the Lord concerning Jehoiakim the son of Josiah king of Judah; They shall not lament for him, saying, Ah my brother! or, Ah sister! they shall not lament for him, saying, Ah lord! or, Ah his glory!

19 He shall be buried with the burial of an ass, drawn and cast forth beyond the gates of Jerusalem.

20 Go up to Lebanon, and cry; and lift up thy voice in Bashan, and cry from the passages:

for all thy lovers are destroyed.

21 I spake unto thee in thy prosperity;

but thou saidst, I will not hear.

This hath been thy manner from thy youth,

that thou obeyedst not my voice.

22 The wind shall eat up all thy pastors, and thy lovers shall go into captivity:

surely then shalt thou be ashamed and confounded for all thy wickedness.

23 O inhabitant of Lebanon, that makest thy nest in the cedars, how gracious shalt thou be when pangs come upon thee, the pain as of a woman in travail!

24 As I live, saith the Lord, though Coniah the son of Jehoiakim king of Judah were the signet upon my right hand, yet would I pluck thee thence; 25 And I will give thee into the hand of them that seek thy life, and into the hand of them whose face thou fearest, even into the hand of Nebuchadrezzar king of Babylon, and into the hand of the Chaldeans. 26 And I will cast thee out, and thy mother that bare thee, into another country, where ye were not born; and there shall ye die.

27 But to the land whereunto they desire to return, thither shall they not return. 28 Is this man Coniah a despised broken idol? is he a vessel wherein is no pleasure? wherefore are they cast out, he and his seed, and are cast into a land which they know not? 29 O earth, earth, earth, hear the word of the Lord. 30 Thus saith the Lord, Write ye this man childless, a man that shall not prosper in his days:for no man of his seed shall prosper, sitting upon the throne of David, and ruling any more in Judah.

Jeremiah 33

1 Moreover the word of the Lord came unto Jeremiah the second time, while he was yet shut up in the court of the prison, saying, 2 Thus saith the Lord the maker thereof, the Lord that formed it, to establish it; the Lord is his name; 3 Call unto me, and I will answer thee, and shew thee great and mighty things, which thou knowest not. 4 For thus saith the Lord, the God of Israel, concerning the houses of this city, and concerning the houses of the kings of Judah, which are thrown down by the mounts, and by the sword; 5 They come to fight with the Chaldeans, but it is to fill them with the dead bodies of men, whom I have slain in mine anger and in my fury, and for all whose wickedness I have hid my face from this city. 6 Behold, I will bring it health and cure, and I will cure them, and will reveal unto them the abundance of peace and truth. 7 And I will cause the captivity of Judah and the captivity of Israel to return, and will build them, as at the first. 8 And I will cleanse them from all their iniquity, whereby they have sinned against me; and I will pardon all their iniquities, whereby they have sinned, and whereby they have transgressed against me.
9 And it shall be to me a name of joy, a praise and an honour before all the nations of the earth, which shall hear all the good that I do unto them:and they shall fear and tremble for all the goodness and for all the prosperity that I procure unto it. 10 Thus saith the Lord; Again there shall be heard in this place, which ye say

shall be desolate without man and without beast, even in the cities of Judah, and in the streets of Jerusalem, that are desolate, without man, and without inhabitant, and without beast, 11 The voice of joy, and the voice of gladness, the voice of the bridegroom, and the voice of the bride, the voice of them that shall say, Praise the Lord of hosts:for the Lord is good; for his mercy endureth for ever:and of them that shall bring the sacrifice of praise into the house of the Lord. For I will cause to return the captivity of the land, as at the first, saith the Lord. 12 Thus saith the Lord of hosts; Again in this place, which is desolate without man and without beast, and in all the cities thereof, shall be an habitation of shepherds causing their flocks to lie down. 13 In the cities of the mountains, in the cities of the vale, and in the cities of the south, and in the land of Benjamin, and in the places about Jerusalem, and in the cities of Judah, shall the flocks pass again under the hands of him that telleth them, saith the Lord. 14 Behold, the days come, saith the Lord, that I will perform that good thing which I have promised unto the house of Israel and to the house of Judah.

15 In those days, and at that time, will I cause the Branch of righteousness to grow up unto David; and he shall execute judgment and righteousness in the land. 16 In those days shall Judah be saved, and Jerusalem shall dwell safely:and this is the name wherewith she shall be called, The Lord our righteousness.

17 For thus saith the Lord; David shall never want a man to sit upon the throne of the house of Israel; 18 Neither shall the priests the Levites want a man before me to offer burnt offerings, and to kindle meat offerings, and to do sacrifice continually.

19 And the word of the Lord came unto Jeremiah, saying, 20 Thus saith the Lord; If ye can break my covenant of the day, and my covenant of the night, and that there should not be day and night in their season; 21 Then may also my covenant be broken with David my servant, that he should not have a son to reign upon his throne; and with the Levites the priests, my ministers. 22 As the host of heaven cannot be numbered, neither the sand of the sea measured:so will I multiply the seed of David my servant, and the Levites that

minister unto me. 23 Moreover the word of the Lord came to Jeremiah, saying, 24 Considerest thou not what this people have spoken, saying, The two families which the Lord hath chosen, he hath even cast them off? thus they have despised my people, that they should be no more a nation before them. 25 Thus saith the Lord; If my covenant be not with day and night, and if I have not appointed the ordinances of heaven and earth; 26 Then will I cast away the seed of Jacob, and David my servant, so that I will not take any of his seed to be rulers over the seed of Abraham, Isaac, and Jacob:for I will cause their captivity to return, and have mercy on them.

Lamentations 3

1 I am the man that hath seen affliction by the rod of his wrath.

2 He hath led me, and brought me into darkness, but not into light.

3 Surely against me is he turned; he turneth his hand against me all the day.

4 My flesh and my skin hath he made old; he hath broken my bones.

5 He hath builded against me, and compassed me with gall and travail.

6 He hath set me in dark places, as they that be dead of old.

7 He hath hedged me about, that I cannot get out:he hath made my chain heavy.

8 Also when I cry and shout, he shutteth out my prayer.

9 He hath inclosed my ways with hewn stone, he hath made my paths crooked.

10 He was unto me as a bear lying in wait, and as a lion in secret places.

11 He hath turned aside my ways, and pulled me in pieces:he hath made me desolate.

12 He hath bent his bow, and set me as a mark for the arrow.

13 He hath caused the arrows of his quiver to enter into my reins.

14 I was a derision to all my people; and their song all the day.

15 He hath filled me with bitterness, he hath made me drunken with

wormwood.

16 He hath also broken my teeth with gravel stones, he hath covered me with ashes.

17 And thou hast removed my soul far off from peace:I forgat prosperity.

18 And I said, My strength and my hope is perished from the Lord:

19 Remembering mine affliction and my misery, the wormwood and the gall.

20 My soul hath them still in remembrance, and is humbled in me.

21 This I recall to my mind, therefore have I hope.

22 It is of the Lord 's mercies that we are not consumed, because his compassions fail not.

23 They are new every morning:great is thy faithfulness.

24 The Lord is my portion, saith my soul; therefore will I hope in him.

25 The Lord is good unto them that wait for him, to the soul that seeketh him.

26 It is good that a man should both hope and quietly wait for the salvation of the Lord.

27 It is good for a man that he bear the yoke in his youth.

28 He sitteth alone and keepeth silence, because he hath borne it upon him.

29 He putteth his mouth in the dust; if so be there may be hope.

30 He giveth his cheek to him that smiteth him:he is filled full with reproach.

31 For the Lord will not cast off for ever:

32 But though he cause grief, yet will he have compassion according to the multitude of his mercies.

33 For he doth not afflict willingly nor grieve the children of men.

34 To crush under his feet all the prisoners of the earth,

35 To turn aside the right of a man before the face of the most High,

36 To subvert a man in his cause, the Lord approveth not.

37 Who is he that saith, and it cometh to pass, when the Lord commandeth it not?

38 Out of the mouth of the most High proceedeth not evil and good?

39 Wherefore doth a living man complain, a man for the punishment of his sins?

40 Let us search and try our ways, and turn again to the Lord.

41 Let us lift up our heart with our hands unto God in the heavens.

42 We have transgressed and have rebelled:thou hast not pardoned.

43 Thou hast covered with anger, and persecuted us:thou hast slain, thou hast not pitied.

44 Thou hast covered thyself with a cloud, that our prayer should not pass through.

45 Thou hast made us as the offscouring and refuse in the midst of the people.

46 All our enemies have opened their mouths against us.

47 Fear and a snare is come upon us, desolation and destruction.

48 Mine eye runneth down with rivers of water for the destruction of the daughter of my people.

49 Mine eye trickleth down, and ceaseth not, without any intermission,

50 Till the Lord look down, and behold from heaven.

51 Mine eye affecteth mine heart because of all the daughters of my city.

52 Mine enemies chased me sore, like a bird, without cause.

53 They have cut off my life in the dungeon, and cast a stone upon me.

54 Waters flowed over mine head; then I said, I am cut off.

55 I called upon thy name, O Lord, out of the low dungeon.

56 Thou hast heard my voice:hide not thine ear at my breathing, at my cry.

57 Thou drewest near in the day that I called upon thee:thou saidst, Fear not.

58 O Lord, thou hast pleaded the causes of my soul; thou hast redeemed my life.

59 O Lord, thou hast seen my wrong:judge thou my cause.

60 Thou hast seen all their vengeance and all their imaginations

against me.

61 Thou hast heard their reproach, O Lord, and all their imaginations against me;

62 The lips of those that rose up against me, and their device against me all the day.

63 Behold their sitting down, and their rising up; I am their musick.

64 Render unto them a recompence, O Lord, according to the work of their hands.

65 Give them sorrow of heart, thy curse unto them.

66 Persecute and destroy them in anger from under the heavens of the Lord.

Zechariah 1

1 In the eighth month, in the second year of Darius, came the word of the Lord unto Zechariah, the son of Berechiah, the son of Iddo the prophet, saying,

2 The Lord hath been sore displeased with your fathers.

3 Therefore say thou unto them, Thus saith the Lord of hosts;

Turn ye unto me, saith the Lord of hosts,

and I will turn unto you, saith the Lord of hosts.

4 Be ye not as your fathers, unto whom the former prophets have cried, saying,

Thus saith the Lord of hosts; Turn ye now from your evil ways, and from your evil doings:

but they did not hear, nor hearken unto me, saith the Lord.

5 Your fathers, where are they?

and the prophets, do they live for ever?

6 But my words and my statutes, which I commanded my servants the prophets,

did they not take hold of your fathers?

and they returned and said, Like as the Lord of hosts thought to do unto us,

according to our ways, and according to our doings, so hath he dealt with us.

7 Upon the four and twentieth day of the eleventh month, which is the
month Sebat, in the second year of Darius, came the word of the Lord
unto Zechariah, the son of Berechiah, the son of Iddo the prophet,
saying, 8 I saw by night, and behold a man riding upon a red horse,
and he stood among the myrtle trees that were in the bottom; and
behind him were there red horses, speckled, and white. 9 Then said I,
O my lord, what are these? And the angel that talked with me said
unto me, I will shew thee what these be. 10 And the man that stood
among the myrtle trees answered and said, These are they whom the
Lord hath sent to walk to and fro through the earth. 11 And they
answered the angel of the Lord that stood among the myrtle trees, and
said, We have walked to and fro through the earth, and, behold, all the
earth sitteth still, and is at rest.

12 Then the angel of the Lord answered and said, O Lord of hosts,
how long wilt thou not have mercy on Jerusalem and on the cities of
Judah, against which thou hast had indignation these threescore and
ten years? 13 And the Lord answered the angel that talked with me
with good words and comfortable words. 14 So the angel that
communed with me said unto me, Cry thou, saying,
Thus saith the Lord of hosts;
I am jealous for Jerusalem and for Zion with a great jealousy.
15 And I am very sore displeased with the heathen that are at ease:for
I was but a little displeased, and they helped forward the affliction.
16 Therefore thus saith the Lord; I am returned to Jerusalem with
mercies:
my house shall be built in it, saith the Lord of hosts,
and a line shall be stretched forth upon Jerusalem.
17 Cry yet, saying, Thus saith the Lord of hosts;
My cities through prosperity shall yet be spread abroad;
and the Lord shall yet comfort Zion,
and shall yet choose Jerusalem.
18 Then lifted I up mine eyes, and saw, and behold four horns. 19
And I said unto the angel that talked with me, What be these? And he

answered me, These are the horns which have scattered Judah, Israel, and Jerusalem. 20 And the Lord shewed me four carpenters. 21 Then said I, What come these to do? And he spake, saying, These are the horns which have scattered Judah, so that no man did lift up his head:but these are come to fray them, to cast out the horns of the Gentiles, which lifted up their horn over the land of Judah to scatter it.

Zechariah 7
1 And it came to pass in the fourth year of king Darius, that the word of the Lord came unto Zechariah in the fourth day of the ninth month, even in Chisleu; 2 When they had sent unto the house of God Sherezer and Regemmelech, and their men, to pray before the Lord, 3 And to speak unto the priests which were in the house of the Lord of hosts, and to the prophets, saying, Should I weep in the fifth month, separating myself, as I have done these so many years?
4 Then came the word of the Lord of hosts unto me, saying, 5 Speak unto all the people of the land, and to the priests, saying, When ye fasted and mourned in the fifth and seventh month, even those seventy years, did ye at all fast unto me, even to me? 6 And when ye did eat, and when ye did drink, did not ye eat for yourselves, and drink for yourselves? **7 Should ye not hear the words which the Lord hath cried by the former prophets, when Jerusalem was inhabited and in prosperity, and the cities thereof round about her, when men inhabited the south and the plain?**
8 And the word of the Lord came unto Zechariah, saying,
9 Thus speaketh the Lord of hosts, saying,
Execute true judgment, and shew mercy and compassions every man to his brother:
10 And oppress not the widow, nor the fatherless, the stranger, nor the poor;
and let none of you imagine evil against his brother in your heart.
11 But they refused to hearken, and pulled away the shoulder, and stopped their ears, that they should not hear.
12 Yea, they made their hearts as an adamant stone, lest they should

hear the law,

and the words which the Lord of hosts hath sent in his spirit by the former prophets:

therefore came a great wrath from the Lord of hosts.

13 Therefore it is come to pass, that as he cried, and they would not hear;

so they cried, and I would not hear, saith the Lord of hosts:

14 But I scattered them with a whirlwind among all the nations whom they knew not.

Thus the land was desolate after them, that no man passed through nor returned:

for they laid the pleasant land desolate.

Chapter 3

Chapters on Prosper

PROS'PER, v.t. L.prospero, from prosperus, from the Gr. to carry to or toward; to bear. To favor; to render successful. All things concur to prosper our design.
PROS'PER, v.i. To be successful; to succeed.
The Lord made all that he did to prosper in his hand. Gen.39.
He that covereth his sins, shall not prosper. Prov.28.
1. To grow or increase; to thrive; to make gain; as, to prosper in business. Our agriculture, commerce and manufactures now prosper.

PROSPER

Genesis 24

1 And Abraham was old, and well stricken in age:and the Lord had blessed Abraham in all things. 2 And Abraham said unto his eldest servant of his house, that ruled over all that he had, Put, I pray thee, thy hand under my thigh:3 And I will make thee swear by the Lord, the God of heaven, and the God of the earth, that thou shalt not take a wife unto my son of the daughters of the Canaanites, among whom I dwell:4 But thou shalt go unto my country, and to my kindred, and take a wife unto my son Isaac. 5 And the servant said unto him, Peradventure the woman will not be willing to follow me unto this land:must I needs bring thy son again unto the land from whence thou camest? 6 And Abraham said unto him, Beware thou that thou bring not my son thither again.

7 The Lord God of heaven, which took me from my father's house, and from the land of my kindred, and which spake unto me, and that sware unto me, saying, Unto thy seed will I give this land; he shall send his angel before thee, and thou shalt take a wife unto my son from thence. 8 And if the woman will not be willing to follow thee, then thou shalt be clear from this my oath:only bring not my son thither again. 9 And the servant put his hand under the thigh of Abraham his master, and sware to him concerning that matter.
10 And the servant took ten camels of the camels of his master, and departed; for all the goods of his master were in his hand:and he arose, and went to Mesopotamia, unto the city of Nahor. 11 And he made his camels to kneel down without the city by a well of water at the time of the evening, even the time that women go out to draw water. 12 And he said, O Lord God of my master
Abraham, I pray thee, send me good speed this day, and shew kindness unto my master Abraham. 13 Behold, I stand here by the well of water; and the daughters of the men of the city come out to draw water:14 And let it come to pass, that the damsel to whom I shall say, Let down thy pitcher, I pray thee, that I may drink; and she shall say, Drink, and I will give thy camels drink also:let the same be she that thou hast appointed for thy servant Isaac; and thereby shall I know that thou hast shewed kindness unto my master.
15 And it came to pass, before he had done speaking, that, behold, Rebekah came out, who was born to Bethuel, son of Milcah, the wife of Nahor, Abraham's brother, with her pitcher upon her shoulder. 16 And the damsel was very fair to look upon, a virgin, neither had any man known her:and she went down to the well, and filled her pitcher, and came up. 17 And the servant ran to meet her, and said, Let me, I pray thee, drink a little water of thy pitcher. 18 And she said, Drink, my lord:and she hasted, and let down her pitcher upon her hand, and gave him drink. 19 And when she had done giving him drink, she said, I will draw water for thy camels also, until they have done drinking. 20 And she hasted, and emptied her pitcher into the trough, and ran again unto the well to draw water, and drew for all his camels.

21 And the man wondering at her held his peace, to wit whether the Lord had made his journey prosperous or not. 22 And it came to pass, as the camels had done drinking, that the man took a golden earring of half a shekel weight, and two bracelets for her hands of ten shekels weight of gold; 23 And said, Whose daughter art thou? tell me, I pray thee:is there room in thy father's house for us to lodge in? 24 And she said unto him, I am the daughter of Bethuel the son of Milcah, which she bare unto Nahor. 25 She said moreover unto him, We have both straw and provender enough, and room to lodge in. 26 And the man bowed down his head, and worshipped the Lord. 27 And he said, Blessed be the Lord God of my master Abraham, who hath not left destitute my master of his mercy and his truth:I being in the way, the Lord led me to the house of my master's brethren. 28 And the damsel ran, and told them of her mother's house these things.

29 And Rebekah had a brother, and his name was Laban:and Laban ran out unto the man, unto the well. 30 And it came to pass, when he saw the earring and bracelets upon his sister's hands, and when he heard the words of Rebekah his sister, saying, Thus spake the man unto me; that he came unto the man; and, behold, he stood by the camels at the well. 31 And he said, Come in, thou blessed of the Lord; wherefore standest thou without? for I have prepared the house, and room for the camels.

32 And the man came into the house:and he ungirded his camels, and gave straw and provender for the camels, and water to wash his feet, and the men's feet that were with him. 33 And there was set meat before him to eat:but he said, I will not eat, until I have told mine errand. And he said, Speak on. 34 And he said, I am Abraham's servant. 35 And the Lord hath blessed my master greatly; and he is become great:and he hath given him flocks, and herds, and silver, and gold, and menservants, and maidservants, and camels, and asses. 36 And Sarah my master's wife bare a son to my master when she was old:and unto him hath he given all that he hath. 37 And my master made me swear, saying, Thou shalt not take a wife to my son of the daughters of the Canaanites, in whose land I dwell:38 But thou shalt

go unto my father's house, and to my kindred, and take a wife unto my son. 39 And I said unto my master, Peradventure the woman will not follow me. **40 And he said unto me, The Lord, before whom I walk, will send his angel with thee, and prosper thy way; and thou shalt take a wife for my son of my kindred, and of my father's house:**41 Then shalt thou be clear from this my oath, when thou comest to my kindred; and if they give not thee one, thou shalt be clear from my oath. **42 And I came this day unto the well, and said, O Lord God of my master Abraham, if now thou do prosper my way which I go:**43 Behold, I stand by the well of water; and it shall come to pass, that when the virgin cometh forth to draw water, and I say to her, Give me, I pray thee, a little water of thy pitcher to drink; 44 And she say to me, Both drink thou, and I will also draw for thy camels:let the same be the woman whom the Lord hath appointed out for my master's son. 45 And before I had done speaking in mine heart, behold, Rebekah came forth with her pitcher on her shoulder; and she went down unto the well, and drew water:and I said unto her, Let me drink, I pray thee. 46 And she made haste, and let down her pitcher from her shoulder, and said, Drink, and I will give thy camels drink also:so I drank, and she made the camels drink also. 47 And I asked her, and said, Whose daughter art thou? And she said, The daughter of Bethuel, Nahor's son, whom Milcah bare unto him:and I put the earring upon her face, and the bracelets upon her hands. 48 And I bowed down my head, and worshipped the Lord, and blessed the Lord God of my master Abraham, which had led me in the right way to take my master's brother's daughter unto his son. 49 And now if ye will deal kindly and truly with my master, tell me:and if not, tell me; that I may turn to the right hand, or to the left. 50 Then Laban and Bethuel answered and said, The thing proceedeth from the Lord:we cannot speak unto thee bad or good. 51 Behold, Rebekah is before thee, take her, and go, and let her be thy master's son's wife, as the Lord hath spoken. 52 And it came to pass, that, when Abraham's servant heard their words, he worshipped the Lord, bowing himself to the earth. 53 And the servant brought forth jewels of silver, and jewels of gold, and raiment, and gave them to Rebekah:he gave also to her brother and to her mother precious things. 54 And they did eat and drink, he and the men that were with him, and tarried all night; and they rose up in the morning, and he said, Send me away unto my master. 55 And her brother and her mother said, Let the damsel abide with us a few days, at the least ten; after that she shall go. 56 And he said unto them, Hinder me not, seeing the Lord hath prospered my way; send me away that I may go to my master. 57 And they said, We will call the damsel, and enquire at her mouth. 58 And they called Rebekah, and said unto her, Wilt thou go with this man? And she said, I will go. 59 And they sent away Rebekah their sister, and her nurse, and Abraham's servant, and his men. 60 And they blessed Rebekah, and said unto her, Thou art our sister, be thou the mother of thousands of millions, and let thy seed possess the gate of those which hate them.

61 And Rebekah arose, and her damsels, and they rode upon the camels, and followed the man:and the servant took Rebekah, and went his way. 62 And Isaac came from the way of the well Lahairoi; for he dwelt in the south country. 63 And Isaac went out to meditate in the field at the eventide:and he lifted up his eyes, and saw, and, behold, the camels were coming. 64 And Rebekah lifted up her eyes, and when she saw Isaac, she lighted off the camel. 65 For she had said unto the servant, What man is this that walketh in the field to meet us? And the servant had said, It is my master:therefore she took a vail, and covered herself. 66 And the servant told Isaac all things that he had done. 67 And Isaac brought her into his mother Sarah's tent, and took Rebekah, and she became his wife; and he loved her:and Isaac was comforted after his mother's death.

Genesis 39

1 And Joseph was brought down to Egypt; and Potiphar, an officer of Pharaoh, captain of the guard, an Egyptian, bought him of the hands of the Ishmeelites, which had brought him down thither. 2 And the

Lord was with Joseph, and he was a prosperous man; and he was in the house of his master the Egyptian. **3 And his master saw that the Lord was with him, and that the Lord made all that he did to prosper in his hand. 4 And Joseph found grace in his sight, and he served him:and he made him overseer over his house, and all that he had he put into his hand.** 5 And it came to pass from the time that he had made him overseer in his house, and over all that he had, that the Lord blessed the Egyptian's house for Joseph's sake; and the blessing of the Lord was upon all that he had in the house, and in the field. 6 And he left all that he had in Joseph's hand; and he knew not ought he had, save the bread which he did eat. And Joseph was a goodly person, and well favoured.

7 And it came to pass after these things, that his master's wife cast her eyes upon Joseph; and she said, Lie with me. 8 But he refused, and said unto his master's wife, Behold, my master wotteth not what is with me in the house, and he hath committed all that he hath to my hand; 9 There is none greater in this house than I; neither hath he kept back any thing from me but thee, because thou art his wife:how then can I do this great wickedness, and sin against God? 10 And it came to pass, as she spake to Joseph day by day, that he hearkened not unto her, to lie by her, or to be with her. 11 And it came to pass about this time, that Joseph went into the house to do his business; and there was none of the men of the house there within. 12 And she caught him by his garment, saying, Lie with me:and he left his garment in her hand, and fled, and got him out. 13 And it came to pass, when she saw that he had left his garment in her hand, and was fled forth, 14 That she called unto the men of her house, and spake unto them, saying, See, he hath brought in an Hebrew unto us to mock us; he came in unto me to lie with me, and I cried with a loud voice:15 And it came to pass, when he heard that I lifted up my voice and cried, that he left his garment with me, and fled, and got him out. 16 And she laid up his garment by her, until his lord came home. 17 And she spake unto him according to these words, saying, The Hebrew servant, which thou hast brought unto us, came in unto me to mock me:18 And it came to

pass, as I lifted up my voice and cried, that he left his garment with me, and fled out. 19 And it came to pass, when his master heard the words of his wife, which she spake unto him, saying, After this manner did thy servant to me; that his wrath was kindled. 20 And Joseph's master took him, and put him into the prison, a place where the king's prisoners were bound:and he was there in the prison. 21 But the Lord was with Joseph, and shewed him mercy, and gave him favour in the sight of the keeper of the prison. 22 And the keeper of the prison committed to Joseph's hand all the prisoners that were in the prison; and whatsoever they did there, he was the doer of it. **23 The keeper of the prison looked not to any thing that was under his hand; because the Lord was with him, and that which he did, the Lord made it to prosper.**

Numbers 14

1 And all the congregation lifted up their voice, and cried; and the people wept that night. 2 And all the children of Israel murmured against Moses and against Aaron:and the whole congregation said unto them, Would God that we had died in the land of Egypt! or would God we had died in this wilderness! 3 And wherefore hath the Lord brought us unto this land, to fall by the sword, that our wives and our children should be a prey? were it not better for us to return into Egypt? 4 And they said one to another, Let us make a captain, and let us return into Egypt. 5 Then Moses and Aaron fell on their faces before all the assembly of the congregation of the children of Israel.

6 And Joshua the son of Nun, and Caleb the son of Jephunneh, which were of them that searched the land, rent their clothes:7 And they spake unto all the company of the children of Israel, saying, The land, which we passed through to search it, is an exceeding good land. 8 If the Lord delight in us, then he will bring us into this land, and give it us; a land which floweth with milk and honey. 9 Only rebel not ye against the Lord, neither fear ye the people of the land; for they are

bread for us:their defence is departed from them, and the Lord is with us:fear them not. 10 But all the congregation bade stone them with stones. And the glory of the Lord appeared in the tabernacle of the congregation before all the children of Israel.

11 And the Lord said unto Moses, How long will this people provoke me? and how long will it be ere they believe me, for all the signs which I have shewed among them? 12 I will smite them with the pestilence, and disinherit them, and will make of thee a greater nation and mightier than they.

13 And Moses said unto the Lord, Then the Egyptians shall hear it, (for thou broughtest up this people in thy might from among them;) 14 And they will tell it to the inhabitants of this land:for they have heard that thou Lord art among this people, that thou Lord art seen face to face, and that thy cloud standeth over them, and that thou goest before them, by day time in a pillar of a cloud, and in a pillar of fire by night.

15 Now if thou shalt kill all this people as one man, then the nations which have heard the fame of thee will speak, saying, 16 Because the Lord was not able to bring this people into the land which he sware unto them, therefore he hath slain them in the wilderness. 17 And now, I beseech thee, let the power of my Lord be great, according as thou hast spoken, saying, 18 The Lord is longsuffering, and of great mercy, forgiving iniquity and transgression, and by no means clearing the guilty, visiting the iniquity of the fathers upon the children unto the third and fourth generation. 19 Pardon, I beseech thee, the iniquity of this people according unto the greatness of thy mercy, and as thou hast forgiven this people, from Egypt even until now. 20 And the Lord said, I have pardoned according to thy word:21 But as truly as I live, all the earth shall be filled with the glory of the Lord. 22 Because all those men which have seen my glory, and my miracles, which I did in Egypt and in the wilderness, and have tempted me now these ten times, and have not hearkened to my voice; 23 Surely they shall not see the land which I sware unto their fathers, neither shall any of them that provoked me see it:24 But my servant Caleb, because he

had another spirit with him, and hath followed me fully, him will I bring into the land whereinto he went; and his seed shall possess it. 25 (Now the Amalekites and the Canaanites dwelt in the valley.) To morrow turn you, and get you into the wilderness by the way of the Red sea.

26 And the Lord spake unto Moses and unto Aaron, saying, 27 How long shall I bear with this evil congregation, which murmur against me? I have heard the murmurings of the children of Israel, which they murmur against me. 28 Say unto them, As truly as I live, saith the Lord, as ye have spoken in mine ears, so will I do to you:29 Your carcases shall fall in this wilderness; and all that were numbered of you, according to your whole number, from twenty years old and upward, which have murmured against me, 30 Doubtless ye shall not come into the land, concerning which I sware to make you dwell therein, save Caleb the son of Jephunneh, and Joshua the son of Nun. 31 But your little ones, which ye said should be a prey, them will I bring in, and they shall know the land which ye have despised. 32 But as for you, your carcases, they shall fall in this wilderness. 33 And your children shall wander in the wilderness forty years, and bear your whoredoms, until your carcases be wasted in the wilderness. 34 After the number of the days in which ye searched the land, even forty days, each day for a year, shall ye bear your iniquities, even forty years, and ye shall know my breach of promise. 35 I the Lord have said, I will surely do it unto all this evil congregation, that are gathered together against me:in this wilderness they shall be consumed, and there they shall die. 36 And the men, which Moses sent to search the land, who returned, and made all the congregation to murmur against him, by bringing up a slander upon the land, 37 Even those men that did bring up the evil report upon the land, died by the plague before the Lord. 38 But Joshua the son of Nun, and Caleb the son of Jephunneh, which were of the men that went to search the land, lived still. 39 And Moses told these sayings unto all the children of Israel:and the people mourned greatly.

40 And they rose up early in the morning, and gat them up into the

top of the mountain, saying, Lo, we be here, and will go up unto the place which the Lord hath promised:for we have sinned. **41 And Moses said, Wherefore now do ye transgress the commandment of the Lord? but it shall not prosper.** 42 Go not up, for the Lord is not among you; that ye be not smitten before your enemies. 43 For the Amalekites and the Canaanites are there before you, and ye shall fall by the sword:because ye are turned away from the Lord, therefore the Lord will not be with you. 44 But they presumed to go up unto the hill top:nevertheless the ark of the covenant of the Lord, and Moses, departed not out of the camp. 45 Then the Amalekites came down, and the Canaanites which dwelt in that hill, and smote them, and discomfited them, even unto Hormah.

Deuteronomy 28

1 And it shall come to pass, if thou shalt hearken diligently unto the voice of the Lord thy God, to observe and to do all his commandments which I command thee this day, that the Lord thy God will set thee on high above all nations of the earth:2 And all these blessings shall come on thee, and overtake thee, if thou shalt hearken unto the voice of the Lord thy God. 3 Blessed shalt thou be in the city, and blessed shalt thou be in the field. 4 Blessed shall be the fruit of thy body, and the fruit of thy ground, and the fruit of thy cattle, the increase of thy kine, and the flocks of thy sheep. 5 Blessed shall be thy basket and thy store. 6 Blessed shalt thou be when thou comest in, and blessed shalt thou be when thou goest out. 7 The Lord shall cause thine enemies that rise up against thee to be smitten before thy face:they shall come out against thee one way, and flee before thee seven ways. 8 The Lord shall command the blessing upon thee in thy storehouses, and in all that thou settest thine hand unto; and he shall bless thee in the land which the Lord thy God giveth thee. 9 The Lord shall establish thee an holy people unto himself, as he hath sworn unto thee, if thou shalt keep the commandments of the Lord thy God, and walk in his ways. 10 And all people of the earth shall see

that thou art called by the name of the Lord; and they shall be afraid of thee. 11 And the Lord shall make thee plenteous in goods, in the fruit of thy body, and in the fruit of thy cattle, and in the fruit of thy ground, in the land which the Lord sware unto thy fathers to give thee. 12 The Lord shall open unto thee his good treasure, the heaven to give the rain unto thy land in his season, and to bless all the work of thine hand:and thou shalt lend unto many nations, and thou shalt not borrow. 13 And the Lord shall make thee the head, and not the tail; and thou shalt be above only, and thou shalt not be beneath; if that thou hearken unto the commandments of the Lord thy God, which I command thee this day, to observe and to do them:14 And thou shalt not go aside from any of the words which I command thee this day, to the right hand, or to the left, to go after other gods to serve them. 15 But it shall come to pass, if thou wilt not hearken unto the voice of the Lord thy God, to observe to do all his commandments and his statutes which I command thee this day; that all these curses shall come upon thee, and overtake thee:16 Cursed shalt thou be in the city, and cursed shalt thou be in the field. 17 Cursed shall be thy basket and thy store. 18 Cursed shall be the fruit of thy body, and the fruit of thy land, the increase of thy kine, and the flocks of thy sheep. 19 Cursed shalt thou be when thou comest in, and cursed shalt thou be when thou goest out. 20 The Lord shall send upon thee cursing, vexation, and rebuke, in all that thou settest thine hand unto for to do, until thou be destroyed, and until thou perish quickly; because of the wickedness of thy doings, whereby thou hast forsaken me. 21 The Lord shall make the pestilence cleave unto thee, until he have consumed thee from off the land, whither thou goest to possess it. 22 The Lord shall smite thee with a consumption, and with a fever, and with an inflammation, and with an extreme burning, and with the sword, and with blasting, and with mildew; and they shall pursue thee until thou perish. 23 And thy heaven that is over thy head shall be brass, and the earth that is under thee shall be iron. 24 The Lord shall make the rain of thy land powder and dust:from heaven shall it come down upon thee, until thou be destroyed. 25 The Lord shall cause thee to be smitten before thine enemies:thou shalt go out one way against them, and flee seven ways before them:and shalt be removed into all the kingdoms of the earth. 26 And thy carcase shall be meat unto all fowls of the air, and unto the beasts of the earth, and no man shall fray them away. 27 The Lord will smite thee with the botch of Egypt, and with the emerods, and with the scab, and with the itch, whereof thou canst not be healed. 28 The Lord shall smite thee with madness, and blindness, and astonishment of heart:**29 And thou shalt grope at noonday, as the blind gropeth in darkness, and thou shalt not prosper in thy ways:and thou shalt be only oppressed and spoiled evermore, and no man shall save thee.** 30 Thou shalt betroth a wife, and another man shall lie with her:thou shalt build an house, and thou shalt not dwell therein:thou shalt plant a vineyard, and shalt not gather the grapes thereof. 31 Thine ox shall be slain before thine eyes, and thou shalt not eat thereof:thine ass shall be violently taken away from before thy face, and shall not be restored to thee:thy sheep shall be given unto thine enemies, and thou shalt have none to rescue them. 32 Thy sons and thy daughters shall be given unto another people, and thine eyes shall look, and fail with longing for them all the day long:and there shall be no might in thine hand. 33 The fruit of thy land, and all thy labours, shall a nation which thou knowest not eat up; and thou shalt be only oppressed and crushed alway:34 So that thou shalt be mad for the sight of thine eyes which thou shalt see. 35 The Lord shall smite thee in the knees, and in the legs, with a sore botch that cannot be healed, from the sole of thy foot unto the top of thy head. 36 The Lord shall bring thee, and thy king which thou shalt set over thee, unto a nation which neither thou nor thy fathers have known; and there shalt thou serve other gods, wood and stone. 37 And thou shalt become an astonishment, a proverb, and a byword, among all nations whither the Lord shall lead thee. 38 Thou shalt carry much seed out into the field, and shalt gather but little in; for the locust shall consume it. 39 Thou shalt plant vineyards, and dress them, but shalt neither drink of the wine, nor gather the grapes; for the worms shall eat them. 40 Thou shalt have olive trees throughout all thy coasts, but thou shalt not anoint thyself with the oil; for thine olive shall cast his fruit. 41 Thou shalt beget sons and daughters, but thou shalt not enjoy them; for they shall go into captivity. 42 All thy trees and fruit of thy land shall the locust consume. 43 The stranger that is within thee shall get up above thee very high; and thou shalt come down very low. 44 He shall lend to thee, and thou shalt not lend to him:he shall be the head, and thou shalt be the tail. 45 Moreover all these curses shall come upon thee, and shall pursue thee, and overtake thee, till thou be destroyed; because thou hearkenedst not unto the voice of the Lord thy God, to keep his commandments and his statutes which he commanded thee:46 And they shall be upon thee for a sign and for a wonder, and upon thy seed for ever. 47 Because thou servedst not the Lord thy God with joyfulness, and with gladness of heart, for the abundance of all things; 48 Therefore shalt thou serve thine enemies which the Lord shall send against thee, in hunger, and in thirst, and in nakedness, and in want of all things:and he shall put a yoke of iron upon thy neck, until he have destroyed thee. 49 The Lord shall bring a nation against thee from far, from the end of the earth, as swift as the eagle flieth; a nation whose tongue thou shalt not understand; 50 A nation of fierce countenance, which shall not regard the person of the old, nor shew favour to the young:51 And he shall eat the fruit of thy cattle, and the fruit of thy land, until thou be destroyed:which also shall not leave thee either corn, wine, or oil, or the increase of thy kine, or flocks of thy sheep, until he have destroyed thee. 52 And he shall besiege thee in all thy gates, until thy high and fenced walls come down, wherein thou trustedst, throughout all thy land:and he shall besiege thee in all thy gates throughout all thy land, which the Lord thy God hath given thee. 53 And thou shalt eat the fruit of thine own body, the flesh of thy sons and of thy daughters, which the Lord thy God hath given thee, in the siege, and in the straitness, wherewith thine enemies shall distress thee:54 So that the man that is tender among you, and very delicate, his eye shall be evil toward his brother, and toward the wife of his bosom, and toward the remnant of his children which he shall leave:55 So that he will not give to any of them of the flesh of his children whom he shall eat:because he hath nothing left him in the siege, and in the straitness, wherewith thine enemies shall distress thee in all thy gates. 56 The tender and delicate woman among you, which would not adventure to set the sole of her foot upon the ground for delicateness and tenderness, her eye shall be evil toward the husband of her bosom, and toward her son, and toward her daughter, 57 And toward her young one that cometh out from between her feet, and toward her children which she shall bear:for she shall eat them for want of all things secretly in the siege and straitness, wherewith thine enemy shall distress thee in thy gates. 58 If thou wilt not observe to do all the words of this law that are written in this book, that thou mayest fear this glorious and fearful name, the Lord thy God; 59 Then the Lord will make thy plagues wonderful, and the plagues of thy seed, even great plagues, and of long continuance, and sore sicknesses, and of long continuance. 60 Moreover he will bring upon thee all the diseases of Egypt, which thou wast afraid of; and they shall cleave unto thee. 61 Also every sickness, and every plague, which is not written in the book of this law, them will the Lord bring upon thee, until thou be destroyed. 62 And ye shall be left few in number, whereas ye were as the stars of heaven for multitude; because thou wouldest not obey the voice of the Lord thy God. 63 And it shall come to pass, that as the Lord rejoiced over you to do you good, and to multiply you; so the Lord will rejoice over you to destroy you, and to bring you to nought; and ye shall be plucked from off the land whither thou goest to possess it. 64 And the Lord shall scatter thee among all people, from the one end of the earth even unto the other; and there thou shalt serve other gods, which neither thou nor thy fathers have known, even wood and stone. 65 And among these nations shalt thou find no ease, neither shall the sole of thy foot have rest:but the Lord shall give thee there a trembling heart, and failing of eyes, and sorrow of mind:66 And thy life shall hang in doubt before thee; and thou shalt fear day and night, and shalt have none assurance of thy life:67 In the morning thou shalt say, Would God it were even! and at even thou shalt say, Would God it were morning! for the fear of thine heart wherewith thou shalt fear, and for the sight of thine eyes which thou shalt see. 68 And the Lord shall bring thee into Egypt again with ships, by the way whereof I spake unto thee, Thou shalt see it no more again:and there ye shall be sold unto your enemies for bondmen and bondwomen, and no man shall buy you.

Deuteronomy 29

1 These are the words of the covenant, which the Lord commanded Moses to make with the children of Israel in the land of Moab, beside the covenant which he made with them in Horeb.

2 And Moses called unto all Israel, and said unto them, Ye have seen all that the Lord did before your eyes in the land of Egypt unto Pharaoh, and unto all his servants, and unto all his land; 3 The great temptations which thine eyes have seen, the signs, and those great miracles:4 Yet the Lord hath not given you an heart to perceive, and eyes to see, and ears to hear, unto this day. 5 And I have led you forty years in the wilderness:your clothes are not waxen old upon you, and thy shoe is not waxen old upon thy foot. 6 Ye have not eaten bread, neither have ye drunk wine or strong drink:that ye might know that I am the Lord your God. 7 And when ye came unto this place, Sihon the king of Heshbon, and Og the king of Bashan, came out against us unto battle, and we smote them:8 And we took their land, and gave it for an inheritance unto the Reubenites, and to the Gadites, and to the half tribe of Manasseh. **9 Keep therefore the words of this covenant, and do them, that ye may prosper in all that ye do.**

10 Ye stand this day all of you before the Lord your God; your captains of your tribes, your elders, and your officers, with all the men of Israel, 11 Your little ones, your wives, and thy stranger that is in thy camp, from the hewer of thy wood unto the drawer of thy water:12 That thou shouldest enter into covenant with the Lord thy God, and into his oath, which the Lord thy God maketh with thee this day:13 That he may establish thee to day for a people unto himself,

and that he may be unto thee a God, as he hath said unto thee, and as he hath sworn unto thy fathers, to Abraham, to Isaac, and to Jacob. 14 Neither with you only do I make this covenant and this oath; 15 But with him that standeth here with us this day before the Lord our God, and also with him that is not here with us this day:16 (For ye know how we have dwelt in the land of Egypt; and how we came through the nations which ye passed by; 17 And ye have seen their abominations, and their idols, wood and stone, silver and gold, which were among them:) 18 Lest there should be among you man, or woman, or family, or tribe, whose heart turneth away this day from the Lord our God, to go and serve the gods of these nations; lest there should be among you a root that beareth gall and wormwood; 19 And it come to pass, when he heareth the words of this curse, that he bless himself in his heart, saying, I shall have peace, though I walk in the imagination of mine heart, to add drunkenness to thirst:20 The Lord will not spare him, but then the anger of the Lord and his jealousy shall smoke against that man, and all the curses that are written in this book shall lie upon him, and the Lord shall blot out his name from under heaven. 21 And the Lord shall separate him unto evil out of all the tribes of Israel, according to all the curses of the covenant that are written in this book of the law:22 So that the generation to come of your children that shall rise up after you, and the stranger that shall come from a far land, shall say, when they see the plagues of that land, and the sicknesses which the Lord hath laid upon it; 23 And that the whole land thereof is brimstone, and salt, and burning, that it is not sown, nor beareth, nor any grass groweth therein, like the overthrow of Sodom, and Gomorrah, Admah, and Zeboim, which the Lord overthrew in his anger, and in his wrath:24 Even all nations shall say, Wherefore hath the Lord done thus unto this land? what meaneth the heat of this great anger? 25 Then men shall say, Because they have forsaken the covenant of the Lord God of their fathers, which he made with them when he brought them forth out of the land of Egypt:26 For they went and served other gods, and worshipped them, gods whom they knew not, and whom he had not given unto them:27

And the anger of the Lord was kindled against this land, to bring upon it all the curses that are written in this book:28 And the Lord rooted them out of their land in anger, and in wrath, and in great indignation, and cast them into another land, as it is this day. 29 The secret things belong unto the Lord our God:but those things which are revealed belong unto us and to our children for ever, that we may do all the words of this law.

Joshua 1

1 Now after the death of Moses the servant of the Lord it came to pass, that the Lord spake unto Joshua the son of Nun, Moses 'minister, saying, 2 Moses my servant is dead; now therefore arise, go over this Jordan, thou, and all this people, unto the land which I do give to them, even to the children of Israel. 3 Every place that the sole of your foot shall tread upon, that have I given unto you, as I said unto Moses. 4 From the wilderness and this Lebanon even unto the great river, the river Euphrates, all the land of the Hittites, and unto the great sea toward the going down of the sun, shall be your coast. 5 There shall not any man be able to stand before thee all the days of thy life:as I was with Moses, so I will be with thee:I will not fail thee, nor forsake thee. 6 Be strong and of a good courage:for unto this people shalt thou divide for an inheritance the land, which I sware unto their fathers to give them. **7 Only be thou strong and very courageous, that thou mayest observe to do according to all the law, which Moses my servant commanded thee:turn not from it to the right hand or to the left, that thou mayest prosper whithersoever thou goest.** 8 This book of the law shall not depart out of thy mouth; but thou shalt meditate therein day and night, that thou mayest observe to do according to all that is written therein:for then thou shalt make thy way prosperous, and then thou shalt have good success. 9 Have not I commanded thee? Be strong and of a good courage; be not afraid, neither be thou dismayed:for the Lord thy God is with thee whithersoever thou goest.

10 Then Joshua commanded the officers of the people, saying, 11

Pass through the host, and command the people, saying, Prepare you victuals; for within three days ye shall pass over this Jordan, to go in to possess the land, which the Lord your God giveth you to possess it. 12 And to the Reubenites, and to the Gadites, and to half the tribe of Manasseh, spake Joshua, saying, 13 Remember the word which Moses the servant of the Lord commanded you, saying, The Lord your God hath given you rest, and hath given you this land. 14 Your wives, your little ones, and your cattle, shall remain in the land which Moses gave you on this side Jordan; but ye shall pass before your brethren armed, all the mighty men of valour, and help them; 15 Until the Lord have given your brethren rest, as he hath given you, and they also have possessed the land which the Lord your God giveth them:then ye shall return unto the land of your possession, and enjoy it, which Moses the Lord' s servant gave you on this side Jordan toward the sunrising.

16 And they answered Joshua, saying, All that thou commandest us we will do, and whithersoever thou sendest us, we will go. 17 According as we hearkened unto Moses in all things, so will we hearken unto thee:only the Lord thy God be with thee, as he was with Moses. 18 Whosoever he be that doth rebel against thy commandment, and will not hearken unto thy words in all that thou commandest him, he shall be put to death:only be strong and of a good courage.

1 Kings 2

1 Now the days of David drew nigh that he should die; and he charged Solomon his son, saying, 2 I go the way of all the earth:be thou strong therefore, and shew thyself a man; **3 And keep the charge of the Lord thy God, to walk in his ways, to keep his statutes, and his commandments, and his judgments, and his testimonies, as it is written in the law of Moses, that thou mayest prosper in all that thou doest, and whithersoever thou turnest thyself:**4 That the Lord may continue his word which he spake

concerning me, saying, If thy children take heed to their way, to walk before me in truth with all their heart and with all their soul, there shall not fail thee (said he) a man on the throne of Israel. 5 Moreover thou knowest also what Joab the son of Zeruiah did to me, and what he did to the two captains of the hosts of Israel, unto Abner the son of Ner, and unto Amasa the son of Jether, whom he slew, and shed the blood of war in peace, and put the blood of war upon his girdle that was about his loins, and in his shoes that were on his feet. 6 Do therefore according to thy wisdom, and let not his hoar head go down to the grave in peace. 7 But shew kindness unto the sons of Barzillai the Gileadite, and let them be of those that eat at thy table:for so they came to me when I fled because of Absalom thy brother. 8 And, behold, thou hast with thee Shimei the son of Gera, a Benjamite of Bahurim, which cursed me with a grievous curse in the day when I went to Mahanaim:but he came down to meet me at Jordan, and I sware to him by the Lord, saying, I will not put thee to death with the sword. 9 Now therefore hold him not guiltless:for thou art a wise man, and knowest what thou oughtest to do unto him; but his hoar head bring thou down to the grave with blood. 10 So David slept with his fathers, and was buried in the city of David. 11 And the days that David reigned over Israel were forty years:seven years reigned he in Hebron, and thirty and three years reigned he in Jerusalem.

12 Then sat Solomon upon the throne of David his father; and his kingdom was established greatly.

13 And Adonijah the son of Haggith came to Bathsheba the mother of Solomon. And she said, Comest thou peaceably? And he said, Peaceably. 14 He said moreover, I have somewhat to say unto thee. And she said, Say on. 15 And he said, Thou knowest that the kingdom was mine, and that all Israel set their faces on me, that I should reign:howbeit the kingdom is turned about, and is become my brother's:for it was his from the Lord. 16 And now I ask one petition of thee, deny me not. And she said unto him, Say on. 17 And he said, Speak, I pray thee, unto Solomon the king, (for he will not say thee nay,) that he give me Abishag the Shunammite to wife. 18 And

Bathsheba said, Well; I will speak for thee unto the king.
19 Bathsheba therefore went unto king Solomon, to speak unto him
for Adonijah. And the king rose up to meet her, and bowed himself
unto her, and sat down on his throne, and caused a seat to be set for
the king's mother; and she sat on his right hand. 20 Then she said, I
desire one small petition of thee; I pray thee, say me not nay. And the
king said unto her, Ask on, my mother:for I will not say thee nay. 21
And she said, Let Abishag the Shunammite be given to Adonijah thy
brother to wife. 22 And king Solomon answered and said unto his
mother, And why dost thou ask Abishag the Shunammite for
Adonijah? ask for him the kingdom also; for he is mine elder brother;
even for him, and for Abiathar the priest, and for Joab the son of
Zeruiah. 23 Then king Solomon sware by the Lord, saying, God do so
to me, and more also, if Adonijah have not spoken this word against
his own life. 24 Now therefore, as the Lord liveth, which hath
established me, and set me on the throne of David my father, and who
hath made me an house, as he promised, Adonijah shall be put to
death this day. 25 And king Solomon sent by the hand of Benaiah the
son of Jehoiada; and he fell upon him that he died.
26 And unto Abiathar the priest said the king, Get thee to Anathoth,
unto thine own fields; for thou art worthy of death:but I will not at
this time put thee to death, because thou barest the ark of the Lord
God before David my father, and because thou hast been afflicted in
all wherein my father was afflicted. 27 So Solomon thrust out
Abiathar from being priest unto the Lord; that he might fulfil the word
of the Lord, which he spake concerning the house of Eli in Shiloh.
28 Then tidings came to Joab:for Joab had turned after Adonijah,
though he turned not after Absalom. And Joab fled unto the
tabernacle of the Lord, and caught hold on the horns of the altar. 29
And it was told king Solomon that Joab was fled unto the tabernacle
of the Lord; and, behold, he is by the altar. Then Solomon sent
Benaiah the son of Jehoiada, saying, Go, fall upon him. 30 And
Benaiah came to the tabernacle of the Lord, and said unto him, Thus
saith the king, Come forth. And he said, Nay; but I will die here. And

Benaiah brought the king word again, saying, Thus said Joab, and thus he answered me. 31 And the king said unto him, Do as he hath said, and fall upon him, and bury him; that thou mayest take away the innocent blood, which Joab shed, from me, and from the house of my father. 32 And the Lord shall return his blood upon his own head, who fell upon two men more righteous and better than he, and slew them with the sword, my father David not knowing thereof, to wit, Abner the son of Ner, captain of the host of Israel, and Amasa the son of Jether, captain of the host of Judah. 33 Their blood shall therefore return upon the head of Joab, and upon the head of his seed for ever:but upon David, and upon his seed, and upon his house, and upon his throne, shall there be peace for ever from the Lord. 34 So Benaiah the son of Jehoiada went up, and fell upon him, and slew him:and he was buried in his own house in the wilderness.
35 And the king put Benaiah the son of Jehoiada in his room over the host:and Zadok the priest did the king put in the room of Abiathar. 36 And the king sent and called for Shimei, and said unto him, Build thee an house in Jerusalem, and dwell there, and go not forth thence any whither. 37 For it shall be, that on the day thou goest out, and passest over the brook Kidron, thou shalt know for certain that thou shalt surely die:thy blood shall be upon thine own head. 38 And Shimei said unto the king, The saying is good:as my lord the king hath said, so will thy servant do. And Shimei dwelt in Jerusalem many days. 39 And it came to pass at the end of three years, that two of the servants of Shimei ran away unto Achish son of Maachah king of Gath. And they told Shimei, saying, Behold, thy servants be in Gath. 40 And Shimei arose, and saddled his ass, and went to Gath to Achish to seek his servants:and Shimei went, and brought his servants from Gath. 41 And it was told Solomon that Shimei had gone from Jerusalem to Gath, and was come again. 42 And the king sent and called for Shimei, and said unto him, Did I not make thee to swear by the Lord, and protested unto thee, saying, Know for a certain, on the day thou goest out, and walkest abroad any whither, that thou shalt surely die? and thou saidst unto me, The word that I have heard is

good. 43 Why then hast thou not kept the oath of the Lord, and the commandment that I have charged thee with? 44 The king said moreover to Shimei, Thou knowest all the wickedness which thine heart is privy to, that thou didst to David my father:therefore the Lord shall return thy wickedness upon thine own head; 45 And king Solomon shall be blessed, and the throne of David shall be established before the Lord for ever. 46 So the king commanded Benaiah the son of Jehoiada; which went out, and fell upon him, that he died. And the kingdom was established in the hand of Solomon.

1 Kings 22

1 And they continued three years without war between Syria and Israel. 2 And it came to pass in the third year, that Jehoshaphat the king of Judah came down to the king of Israel. 3 And the king of Israel said unto his servants, Know ye that Ramoth in Gilead is ours, and we be still, and take it not out of the hand of the king of Syria? 4 And he said unto Jehoshaphat, Wilt thou go with me to battle to Ramothgilead? And Jehoshaphat said to the king of Israel, I am as thou art, my people as thy people, my horses as thy horses. 5 And Jehoshaphat said unto the king of Israel, Enquire, I pray thee, at the word of the Lord to day. 6 Then the king of Israel gathered the prophets together, about four hundred men, and said unto them, Shall I go against Ramothgilead to battle, or shall I forbear? And they said, Go up; for the Lord shall deliver it into the hand of the king. 7 And Jehoshaphat said, Is there not here a prophet of the Lord besides, that we might enquire of him? 8 And the king of Israel said unto Jehoshaphat, There is yet one man, Micaiah the son of Imlah, by whom we may enquire of the Lord:but I hate him; for he doth not prophesy good concerning me, but evil. And Jehoshaphat said, Let not the king say so. 9 Then the king of Israel called an officer, and said, Hasten hither Micaiah the son of Imlah. 10 And the king of Israel and Jehoshaphat the king of Judah sat each on his throne, having put on their robes, in a void place in the entrance of the gate of Samaria; and

all the prophets prophesied before them. 11 And Zedekiah the son of Chenaanah made him horns of iron:and he said, Thus saith the Lord, With these shalt thou push the Syrians, until thou have consumed them. **12 And all the prophets prophesied so, saying, Go up to Ramothgilead, and prosper:for the Lord shall deliver it into the king's hand.** 13 And the messenger that was gone to call Micaiah spake unto him, saying, Behold now, the words of the prophets declare good unto the king with one mouth:let thy word, I pray thee, be like the word of one of them, and speak that which is good. 14 And Micaiah said, As the Lord liveth, what the Lord saith unto me, that will I speak.

15 So he came to the king. And the king said unto him, Micaiah, shall we go against Ramothgilead to battle, or shall we forbear? And he answered him, Go, and prosper:for the Lord shall deliver it into the hand of the king. 16 And the king said unto him, How many times shall I adjure thee that thou tell me nothing but that which is true in the name of the Lord? 17 And he said, I saw all Israel scattered upon the hills, as sheep that have not a shepherd:and the Lord said, These have no master:let them return every man to his house in peace. 18 And the king of Israel said unto Jehoshaphat, Did I not tell thee that he would prophesy no good concerning me, but evil? 19 And he said, Hear thou therefore the word of the Lord:I saw the Lord sitting on his throne, and all the host of heaven standing by him on his right hand and on his left. 20 And the Lord said, Who shall persuade Ahab, that he may go up and fall at Ramothgilead? And one said on this manner, and another said on that manner. 21 And there came forth a spirit, and stood before the Lord, and said, I will persuade him. 22 And the Lord said unto him, Wherewith? And he said, I will go forth, and I will be a lying spirit in the mouth of all his prophets. And he said, Thou shalt persuade him, and prevail also:go forth, and do so. 23 Now therefore, behold, the Lord hath put a lying spirit in the mouth of all these thy prophets, and the Lord hath spoken evil concerning thee. 24 But Zedekiah the son of Chenaanah went near, and smote Micaiah on the cheek, and said, Which way went the

Spirit of the Lord from me to speak unto thee? 25 And Micaiah said, Behold, thou shalt see in that day, when thou shalt go into an inner chamber to hide thyself. 26 And the king of Israel said, Take Micaiah, and carry him back unto Amon the governor of the city, and to Joash the king's son; 27 And say, Thus saith the king, Put this fellow in the prison, and feed him with bread of affliction and with water of affliction, until I come in peace. 28 And Micaiah said, If thou return at all in peace, the Lord hath not spoken by me. And he said, Hearken, O people, every one of you. 29 So the king of Israel and Jehoshaphat the king of Judah went up to Ramothgilead. 30 And the king of Israel said unto Jehoshaphat, I will disguise myself, and enter into the battle; but put thou on thy robes. And the king of Israel disguised himself, and went into the battle. 31 But the king of Syria commanded his thirty and two captains that had rule over his chariots, saying, Fight neither with small nor great, save only with the king of Israel. 32 And it came to pass, when the captains of the chariots saw Jehoshaphat, that they said, Surely it is the king of Israel. And they turned aside to fight against him:and Jehoshaphat cried out. 33 And it came to pass, when the captains of the chariots perceived that it was not the king of Israel, that they turned back from pursuing him. 34 And a certain man drew a bow at a venture, and smote the king of Israel between the joints of the harness:wherefore he said unto the driver of his chariot, Turn thine hand, and carry me out of the host; for I am wounded. 35 And the battle increased that day:and the king was stayed up in his chariot against the Syrians, and died at even:and the blood ran out of the wound into the midst of the chariot. 36 And there went a proclamation throughout the host about the going down of the sun, saying, Every man to his city, and every man to his own country. 37 So the king died, and was brought to Samaria; and they buried the king in Samaria. 38 And one washed the chariot in the pool of Samaria; and the dogs licked up his blood; and they washed his armour; according unto the word of the Lord which he spake. 39 Now the rest of the acts of Ahab, and all that he did, and the ivory house which he made, and all the cities that he built, are they not written in the book of the chronicles of the kings of Israel? 40 So Ahab slept with his fathers; and Ahaziah his son reigned in his stead.

41 And Jehoshaphat the son of Asa began to reign over Judah in the fourth year of Ahab king of Israel. 42 Jehoshaphat was thirty and five years old when he began to reign; and he reigned twenty and five years in Jerusalem. And his mother's name was Azubah the daughter of Shilhi. 43 And he walked in all the ways of Asa his father; he turned not aside from it, doing that which was right in the eyes of the Lord:nevertheless the high places were not taken away; for the people offered and burnt incense yet in the high places. 44 And Jehoshaphat made peace with the king of Israel. 45 Now the rest of the acts of Jehoshaphat, and his might that he shewed, and how he warred, are they not written in the book of the chronicles of the kings of Judah? 46 And the remnant of the sodomites, which remained in the days of his father Asa, he took out of the land. 47 There was then no king in Edom:a deputy was king. 48 Jehoshaphat made ships of Tharshish to go to Ophir for gold:but they went not; for the ships were broken at Eziongeber. 49 Then said Ahaziah the son of Ahab unto Jehoshaphat, Let my servants go with thy servants in the ships. But Jehoshaphat would not.

50 And Jehoshaphat slept with his fathers, and was buried with his fathers in the city of David his father:and Jehoram his son reigned in his stead.

51 Ahaziah the son of Ahab began to reign over Israel in Samaria the seventeenth year of Jehoshaphat king of Judah, and reigned two years over Israel. 52 And he did evil in the sight of the Lord, and walked in the way of his father, and in the way of his mother, and in the way of Jeroboam the son of Nebat, who made Israel to sin:53 For he served Baal, and worshipped him, and provoked to anger the Lord God of Israel, according to all that his father had done.

1 Chronicles 22

1 Then David said, This is the house of the Lord God, and this is the altar of the burnt offering for Israel. 2 And David commanded to gather together the strangers that were in the land of Israel; and he set masons to hew wrought stones to build the house of God. 3 And David prepared iron in abundance for the nails for the doors of the gates, and for the joinings; and brass in abundance without weight; 4 Also cedar trees in abundance:for the Zidonians and they of Tyre brought much cedar wood to David. 5 And David said, Solomon my son is young and tender, and the house that is to be builded for the Lord must be exceeding magnifical, of fame and of glory throughout all countries:I will therefore now make preparation for it. So David prepared abundantly before his death.

6 Then he called for Solomon his son, and charged him to build an house for the Lord God of Israel. 7 And David said to Solomon, My son, as for me, it was in my mind to build an house unto the name of the Lord my God:8 But the word of the Lord came to me, saying, Thou hast shed blood abundantly, and hast made great wars:thou shalt not build an house unto my name, because thou hast shed much blood upon the earth in my sight. 9 Behold, a son shall be born to thee, who shall be a man of rest; and I will give him rest from all his enemies round about:for his name shall be Solomon, and I will give peace and quietness unto Israel in his days. 10 He shall build an house for my name; and he shall be my son, and I will be his father; and I will establish the throne of his kingdom over Israel for ever. **11 Now, my son, the Lord be with thee; and prosper thou, and build the house of the Lord thy God, as he hath said of thee. 12 Only the Lord give thee wisdom and understanding, and give thee charge concerning Israel, that thou mayest keep the law of the Lord thy God. 13 Then shalt thou prosper, if thou takest heed to fulfil the statutes and judgments which the Lord charged Moses with concerning Israel:be strong, and of good courage; dread not, nor be dismayed.** 14 Now, behold, in my trouble I have prepared for the house of the Lord an hundred thousand talents of gold, and a thousand thousand talents of silver; and of brass and iron without weight; for it

is in abundance:timber also and stone have I prepared; and thou mayest add thereto. 15 Moreover there are workmen with thee in abundance, hewers and workers of stone and timber, and all manner of cunning men for every manner of work. 16 Of the gold, the silver, and the brass, and the iron, there is no number. Arise therefore, and be doing, and the Lord be with thee.

17 David also commanded all the princes of Israel to help Solomon his son, saying, 18 Is not the Lord your God with you? and hath he not given you rest on every side? for he hath given the inhabitants of the land into mine hand; and the land is subdued before the Lord, and before his people. 19 Now set your heart and your soul to seek the Lord your God; arise therefore, and build ye the sanctuary of the Lord God, to bring the ark of the covenant of the Lord, and the holy vessels of God, into the house that is to be built to the name of the Lord.

2Chronicles 13

1 Now in the eighteenth year of king Jeroboam began Abijah to reign over Judah. 2 He reigned three years in Jerusalem. His mother's name also was Michaiah the daughter of Uriel of Gibeah. And there was war between Abijah and Jeroboam. 3 And Abijah set the battle in array with an army of valiant men of war, even four hundred thousand chosen men:Jeroboam also set the battle in array against him with eight hundred thousand chosen men, being mighty men of valour.4 And Abijah stood up upon mount Zemaraim, which is in mount Ephraim, and said, Hear me, thou Jeroboam, and all Israel; 5 Ought ye not to know that the Lord God of Israel gave the kingdom over Israel to David for ever, even to him and to his sons by a covenant of salt? 6 Yet Jeroboam the son of Nebat, the servant of Solomon the son of David, is risen up, and hath rebelled against his lord. 7 And there are gathered unto him vain men, the children of Belial, and have strengthened themselves against Rehoboam the son of Solomon, when Rehoboam was young and tenderhearted, and could not withstand them. 8 And now ye think to withstand the kingdom of the Lord in the

hand of the sons of David; and ye be a great multitude, and there are with you golden calves, which Jeroboam made you for gods. 9 Have ye not cast out the priests of the Lord, the sons of Aaron, and the Levites, and have made you priests after the manner of the nations of other lands? so that whosoever cometh to consecrate himself with a young bullock and seven rams, the same may be a priest of them that are no gods. 10 But as for us, the Lord is our God, and we have not forsaken him; and the priests, which minister unto the Lord, are the sons of Aaron, and the Levites wait upon their business:11 And they burn unto the Lord every morning and every evening burnt sacrifices and sweet incense:the shewbread also set they in order upon the pure table; and the candlestick of gold with the lamps thereof, to burn every evening:for we keep the charge of the Lord our God; but ye have forsaken him. **12 And, behold, God himself is with us for our captain, and his priests with sounding trumpets to cry alarm against you. O children of Israel, fight ye not against the Lord God of your fathers; for ye shall not prosper.** 13 But Jeroboam caused an ambushment to come about behind them:so they were before Judah, and the ambushment was behind them. 14 And when Judah looked back, behold, the battle was before and behind:and they cried unto the Lord, and the priests sounded with the trumpets. 15 Then the men of Judah gave a shout:and as the men of Judah shouted, it came to pass, that God smote Jeroboam and all Israel before Abijah and Judah. 16 And the children of Israel fled before Judah:and God delivered them into their hand. 17 And Abijah and his people slew them with a great slaughter:so there fell down slain of Israel five hundred thousand chosen men. 18 Thus the children of Israel were brought under at that time, and the children of Judah prevailed, because they relied upon the Lord God of their fathers. 19 And Abijah pursued after Jeroboam, and took cities from him, Bethel with the towns thereof, and Jeshanah with the towns thereof, and Ephrain with the towns thereof. 20 Neither did Jeroboam recover strength again in the days of Abijah:and the Lord struck him, and he died. 21 But Abijah waxed mighty, and married fourteen wives, and begat twenty and two sons, and sixteen daughters. 22 And the rest of the acts of Abijah, and his ways, and his sayings, are written in the story of the prophet Iddo.

2Chronicles 18

1 Now Jehoshaphat had riches and honour in abundance, and joined affinity with Ahab. 2 And after certain years he went down to Ahab to Samaria. And Ahab killed sheep and oxen for him in abundance, and for the people that he had with him, and persuaded him to go up with him to Ramothgilead. 3 And Ahab king of Israel said unto Jehoshaphat king of Judah, Wilt thou go with me to Ramothgilead? And he answered him, I am as thou art, and my people as thy people; and we will be with thee in the war.4 And Jehoshaphat said unto the king of Israel, Enquire, I pray thee, at the word of the Lord to day. 5 Therefore the king of Israel gathered together of prophets four hundred men, and said unto them, Shall we go to Ramothgilead to battle, or shall I forbear? And they said, Go up; for God will deliver it into the king's hand. 6 But Jehoshaphat said, Is there not here a prophet of the Lord besides, that we might enquire of him? 7 And the king of Israel said unto Jehoshaphat, There is yet one man, by whom we may enquire of the Lord:but I hate him; for he never prophesied good unto me, but always evil:the same is Micaiah the son of Imla. And Jehoshaphat said, Let not the king say so. 8 And the king of Israel called for one of his officers, and said, Fetch quickly Micaiah the son of Imla. 9 And the king of Israel and Jehoshaphat king of Judah sat either of them on his throne, clothed in their robes, and they sat in a void place at the entering in of the gate of Samaria; and all the prophets prophesied before them. 10 And Zedekiah the son of Chenaanah had made him horns of iron, and said, Thus saith the Lord, With these thou shalt push Syria until they be consumed. **11 And all the prophets prophesied so, saying, Go up to Ramothgilead, and prosper:for the Lord shall deliver it into the hand of the king. 12 And the messenger that went to call Micaiah spake to him, saying,**

Behold, the words of the prophets declare good to the king with one assent; let thy word therefore, I pray thee, be like one of theirs, and speak thou good. 13 And Micaiah said, As the Lord liveth, even what my God saith, that will I speak. 14 And when he was come to the king, the king said unto him, Micaiah, shall we go to Ramothgilead to battle, or shall I forbear? And he said, Go ye up, and prosper, and they shall be delivered into your hand. 15 And the king said to him, How many times shall I adjure thee that thou say nothing but the truth to me in the name of the Lord? 16 Then he said, I did see all Israel scattered upon the mountains, as sheep that have no shepherd:and the Lord said, These have no master; let them return therefore every man to his house in peace. 17 And the king of Israel said to Jehoshaphat, Did I not tell thee that he would not prophesy good unto me, but evil? 18 Again he said, Therefore hear the word of the Lord; I saw the Lord sitting upon his throne, and all the host of heaven standing on his right hand and on his left. 19 And the Lord said, Who shall entice Ahab king of Israel, that he may go up and fall at Ramothgilead? And one spake saying after this manner, and another saying after that manner. 20 Then there came out a spirit, and stood before the Lord, and said, I will entice him. And the Lord said unto him, Wherewith? 21 And he said, I will go out, and be a lying spirit in the mouth of all his prophets. And the Lord said, Thou shalt entice him, and thou shalt also prevail:go out, and do even so. 22 Now therefore, behold, the Lord hath put a lying spirit in the mouth of these thy prophets, and the Lord hath spoken evil against thee. 23 Then Zedekiah the son of Chenaanah came near, and smote Micaiah upon the cheek, and said, Which way went the Spirit of the Lord from me to speak unto thee? 24 And Micaiah said, Behold, thou shalt see on that day when thou shalt go into an inner chamber to hide thyself. 25 Then the king of Israel said, Take ye Micaiah, and carry him back to Amon the governor of the city, and to Joash the king's son; 26 And say, Thus saith the king, Put this fellow in the prison, and feed him with bread of affliction and with water of affliction, until I return in peace. 27 And Micaiah said, If thou certainly return in peace, then

hath not the Lord spoken by me. And he said, Hearken, all ye people.
28 So the king of Israel and Jehoshaphat the king of Judah went up to
Ramothgilead. 29 And the king of Israel said unto Jehoshaphat, I will
disguise myself, and will go to the battle; but put thou on thy robes.
So the king of Israel disguised himself; and they went to the battle. 30
Now the king of Syria had commanded the captains of the chariots
that were with him, saying, Fight ye not with small or great, save only
with the king of Israel. 31 And it came to pass, when the captains of
the chariots saw Jehoshaphat, that they said, It is the king of Israel.
Therefore they compassed about him to fight:but Jehoshaphat cried
out, and the Lord helped him; and God moved them to depart from
him. 32 For it came to pass, that, when the captains of the chariots
perceived that it was not the king of Israel, they turned back again
from pursuing him. 33 And a certain man drew a bow at a venture,
and smote the king of Israel between the joints of the
harness:therefore he said to his chariot man, Turn thine hand, that
thou mayest carry me out of the host; for I am wounded. 34 And the
battle increased that day:howbeit the king of Israel stayed himself up
in his chariot against the Syrians until the even:and about the time of
the sun going down he died.

2 Chronicles 20

1 It came to pass after this also, that the children of Moab, and the
children of Ammon, and with them other beside the Ammonites,
came against Jehoshaphat to battle. 2 Then there came some that told
Jehoshaphat, saying, There cometh a great multitude against thee
from beyond the sea on this side Syria; and, behold, they be in
Hazazontamar, which is Engedi. 3 And Jehoshaphat feared, and set
himself to seek the Lord, and proclaimed a fast throughout all Judah.
4 And Judah gathered themselves together, to ask help of the
Lord:even out of all the cities of Judah they came to seek the Lord.5
And Jehoshaphat stood in the congregation of Judah and Jerusalem, in
the house of the Lord, before the new court, 6 And said, O Lord God

of our fathers, art not thou God in heaven? and rulest not thou over all the kingdoms of the heathen? and in thine hand is there not power and might, so that none is able to withstand thee? 7 Art not thou our God, who didst drive out the inhabitants of this land before thy people Israel, and gavest it to the seed of Abraham thy friend for ever? 8 And they dwelt therein, and have built thee a sanctuary therein for thy name, saying, 9 If, when evil cometh upon us, as the sword, judgment, or pestilence, or famine, we stand before this house, and in thy presence, (for thy name is in this house,) and cry unto thee in our affliction, then thou wilt hear and help. 10 And now, behold, the children of Ammon and Moab and mount Seir, whom thou wouldest not let Israel invade, when they came out of the land of Egypt, but they turned from them, and destroyed them not; 11 Behold, I say, how they reward us, to come to cast us out of thy possession, which thou hast given us to inherit. 12 O our God, wilt thou not judge them? for we have no might against this great company that cometh against us; neither know we what to do:but our eyes are upon thee. 13 And all Judah stood before the Lord, with their little ones, their wives, and their children.14 Then upon Jahaziel the son of Zechariah, the son of Benaiah, the son of Jeiel, the son of Mattaniah, a Levite of the sons of Asaph, came the Spirit of the Lord in the midst of the congregation; 15 And he said, Hearken ye, all Judah, and ye inhabitants of Jerusalem, and thou king Jehoshaphat, Thus saith the Lord unto you, Be not afraid nor dismayed by reason of this great multitude; for the battle is not yours, but God's. 16 To morrow go ye down against them:behold, they come up by the cliff of Ziz; and ye shall find them at the end of the brook, before the wilderness of Jeruel. 17 Ye shall not need to fight in this battle:set yourselves, stand ye still, and see the salvation of the Lord with you, O Judah and Jerusalem:fear not, nor be dismayed; to morrow go out against them:for the Lord will be with you. 18 And Jehoshaphat bowed his head with his face to the ground:and all Judah and the inhabitants of Jerusalem fell before the Lord, worshipping the Lord. 19 And the Levites, of the children of the Kohathites, and of the children of the Korhites, stood up to praise the

Lord God of Israel with a loud voice on high. **20 And they rose early in the morning, and went forth into the wilderness of Tekoa:and as they went forth, Jehoshaphat stood and said, Hear me, O Judah, and ye inhabitants of Jerusalem; Believe in the Lord your God, so shall ye be established; believe his prophets, so shall ye prosper.** 21 And when he had consulted with the people, he appointed singers unto the Lord, and that should praise the beauty of holiness, as they went out before the army, and to say, Praise the Lord; for his mercy endureth for ever.22 And when they began to sing and to praise, the Lord set ambushments against the children of Ammon, Moab, and mount Seir, which were come against Judah; and they were smitten. 23 For the children of Ammon and Moab stood up against the inhabitants of mount Seir, utterly to slay and destroy them:and when they had made an end of the inhabitants of Seir, every one helped to destroy another. 24 And when Judah came toward the watch tower in the wilderness, they looked unto the multitude, and, behold, they were dead bodies fallen to the earth, and none escaped. 25 And when Jehoshaphat and his people came to take away the spoil of them, they found among them in abundance both riches with the dead bodies, and precious jewels, which they stripped off for themselves, more than they could carry away:and they were three days in gathering of the spoil, it was so much. 26 And on the fourth day they assembled themselves in the valley of Berachah; for there they blessed the Lord:therefore the name of the same place was called, The valley of Berachah, unto this day. 27 Then they returned, every man of Judah and Jerusalem, and Jehoshaphat in the forefront of them, to go again to Jerusalem with joy; for the Lord had made them to rejoice over their enemies. 28 And they came to Jerusalem with psalteries and harps and trumpets unto the house of the Lord. 29 And the fear of God was on all the kingdoms of those countries, when they had heard that the Lord fought against the enemies of Israel. 30 So the realm of Jehoshaphat was quiet:for his God gave him rest round about. 31 And Jehoshaphat reigned over Judah:he was thirty and five years old when he began to reign, and he reigned twenty and five years in Jerusalem. And his mother's name was Azubah the daughter of Shilhi. 32 And he walked in the way of Asa his father, and departed not from it, doing that which was right in the sight of the Lord. 33 Howbeit the high places were not taken away:for as yet the people had not prepared their hearts unto the God of their fathers. 34 Now the rest of the acts of Jehoshaphat, first and last, behold, they are written in the book of Jehu the son of Hanani, who is mentioned in the book of the kings of Israel. 35 And after this did Jehoshaphat king of Judah join himself with Ahaziah king of Israel, who did very wickedly:36 And he joined himself with him to make ships to go to Tarshish:and they made the ships in Eziongeber. 37 Then Eliezer the son of Dodavah of Mareshah prophesied against Jehoshaphat, saying, Because thou hast joined thyself with Ahaziah, the Lord hath broken thy works. And the ships were broken, that they were not able to go to Tarshish.

2 Chronicles 24

1 Joash was seven years old when he began to reign, and he reigned forty years in Jerusalem. His mother's name also was Zibiah of Beersheba. 2 And Joash did that which was right in the sight of the Lord all the days of Jehoiada the priest. 3 And Jehoiada took for him two wives; and he begat sons and daughters. 4 And it came to pass after this, that Joash was minded to repair the house of the Lord. 5 And he gathered together the priests and the Levites, and said to them, Go out unto the cities of Judah, and gather of all Israel money to repair the house of your God from year to year, and see that ye hasten the matter. Howbeit the Levites hastened it not. 6 And the king called for Jehoiada the chief, and said unto him, Why hast thou not required of the Levites to bring in out of Judah and out of Jerusalem the collection, according to the commandment of Moses the servant of the Lord, and of the congregation of Israel, for the tabernacle of witness? 7 For the sons of Athaliah, that wicked woman, had broken up the house of God; and also all the dedicated things of the house of the

Lord did they bestow upon Baalim. 8 And at the king's commandment they made a chest, and set it without at the gate of the house of the Lord. 9 And they made a proclamation through Judah and Jerusalem, to bring in to the Lord the collection that Moses the servant of God laid upon Israel in the wilderness. 10 And all the princes and all the people rejoiced, and brought in, and cast into the chest, until they had made an end. 11 Now it came to pass, that at what time the chest was brought unto the king's office by the hand of the Levites, and when they saw that there was much money, the king's scribe and the high priest's officer came and emptied the chest, and took it, and carried it to his place again. Thus they did day by day, and gathered money in abundance. 12 And the king and Jehoiada gave it to such as did the work of the service of the house of the Lord, and hired masons and carpenters to repair the house of the Lord, and also such as wrought iron and brass to mend the house of the Lord. 13 So the workmen wrought, and the work was perfected by them, and they set the house of God in his state, and strengthened it. 14 And when they had finished it, they brought the rest of the money before the king and Jehoiada, whereof were made vessels for the house of the Lord, even vessels to minister, and to offer withal, and spoons, and vessels of gold and silver. And they offered burnt offerings in the house of the Lord continually all the days of Jehoiada. 15 But Jehoiada waxed old, and was full of days when he died; an hundred and thirty years old was he when he died. 16 And they buried him in the city of David among the kings, because he had done good in Israel, both toward God, and toward his house. 17 Now after the death of Jehoiada came the princes of Judah, and made obeisance to the king. Then the king hearkened unto them. 18 And they left the house of the Lord God of their fathers, and served groves and idols:and wrath came upon Judah and Jerusalem for this their trespass. 19 Yet he sent prophets to them, to bring them again unto the Lord; and they testified against them:but they would not give ear. **20 And the Spirit of God came upon Zechariah the son of Jehoiada the priest, which stood above the people, and said unto them, Thus saith God, Why transgress ye**

the commandments of the Lord, that ye cannot prosper? because ye have forsaken the Lord, he hath also forsaken you. 21 And they conspired against him, and stoned him with stones at the commandment of the king in the court of the house of the Lord. 22 Thus Joash the king remembered not the kindness which Jehoiada his father had done to him, but slew his son. And when he died, he said, The Lord look upon it, and require it. 23 And it came to pass at the end of the year, that the host of Syria came up against him:and they came to Judah and Jerusalem, and destroyed all the princes of the people from among the people, and sent all the spoil of them unto the king of Damascus. 24 For the army of the Syrians came with a small company of men, and the Lord delivered a very great host into their hand, because they had forsaken the Lord God of their fathers. So they executed judgment against Joash. 25 And when they were departed from him, (for they left him in great diseases,) his own servants conspired against him for the blood of the sons of Jehoiada the priest, and slew him on his bed, and he died:and they buried him in the city of David, but they buried him not in the sepulchres of the kings. 26 And these are they that conspired against him; Zabad the son of Shimeath an Ammonitess, and Jehozabad the son of Shimrith a Moabitess. 27 Now concerning his sons, and the greatness of the burdens laid upon him, and the repairing of the house of God, behold, they are written in the story of the book of the kings. And Amaziah his son reigned in his stead.

2 Chronicles 26

1 Then all the people of Judah took Uzziah, who was sixteen years old, and made him king in the room of his father Amaziah. 2 He built Eloth, and restored it to Judah, after that the king slept with his fathers. 3 Sixteen years old was Uzziah when he began to reign, and he reigned fifty and two years in Jerusalem. His mother's name also was Jecoliah of Jerusalem. 4 And he did that which was right in the sight of the Lord, according to all that his father Amaziah did. **5 And**

he sought God in the days of Zechariah, who had understanding in the visions of God:and as long as he sought the Lord, God made him to prosper. 6 And he went forth and warred against the Philistines, and brake down the wall of Gath, and the wall of Jabneh, and the wall of Ashdod, and built cities about Ashdod, and among the Philistines. 7 And God helped him against the Philistines, and against the Arabians that dwelt in Gurbaal, and the Mehunims. 8 And the Ammonites gave gifts to Uzziah:and his name spread abroad even to the entering in of Egypt; for he strengthened himself exceedingly. 9 Moreover Uzziah built towers in Jerusalem at the corner gate, and at the valley gate, and at the turning of the wall, and fortified them. 10 Also he built towers in the desert, and digged many wells:for he had much cattle, both in the low country, and in the plains:husbandmen also, and vine dressers in the mountains, and in Carmel:for he loved husbandry. 11 Moreover Uzziah had an host of fighting men, that went out to war by bands, according to the number of their account by the hand of Jeiel the scribe and Maaseiah the ruler, under the hand of Hananiah, one of the king's captains. 12 The whole number of the chief of the fathers of the mighty men of valour were two thousand and six hundred. 13 And under their hand was an army, three hundred thousand and seven thousand and five hundred, that made war with mighty power, to help the king against the enemy. 14 And Uzziah prepared for them throughout all the host shields, and spears, and helmets, and habergeons, and bows, and slings to cast stones. 15 And he made in Jerusalem engines, invented by cunning men, to be on the towers and upon the bulwarks, to shoot arrows and great stones withal. And his name spread far abroad; for he was marvellously helped, till he was strong. 16 But when he was strong, his heart was lifted up to his destruction:for he transgressed against the Lord his God, and went into the temple of the Lord to burn incense upon the altar of incense. 17 And Azariah the priest went in after him, and with him fourscore priests of the Lord, that were valiant men:18 And they withstood Uzziah the king, and said unto him, It appertaineth not unto thee, Uzziah, to burn incense unto the Lord, but to the priests the sons of Aaron, that are consecrated to burn incense:go out of the sanctuary; for thou hast trespassed; neither shall it be for thine honour from the Lord God. 19 Then Uzziah was wroth, and had a censer in his hand to burn incense:and while he was wroth with the priests, the leprosy even rose up in his forehead before the priests in the house of the Lord, from beside the incense altar. 20 And Azariah the chief priest, and all the priests, looked upon him, and, behold, he was leprous in his forehead, and they thrust him out from thence; yea, himself hasted also to go out, because the Lord had smitten him. 21 And Uzziah the king was a leper unto the day of his death, and dwelt in a several house, being a leper; for he was cut off from the house of the Lord:and Jotham his son was over the king's house, judging the people of the land. 22 Now the rest of the acts of Uzziah, first and last, did Isaiah the prophet, the son of Amoz, write. 23 So Uzziah slept with his fathers, and they buried him with his fathers in the field of the burial which belonged to the kings; for they said, He is a leper:and Jotham his son reigned in his stead.

Nehemiah 1
1 The words of Nehemiah the son of Hachaliah. And it came to pass in the month Chisleu, in the twentieth year, as I was in Shushan the palace, 2 That Hanani, one of my brethren, came, he and certain men of Judah; and I asked them concerning the Jews that had escaped, which were left of the captivity, and concerning Jerusalem. 3 And they said unto me, The remnant that are left of the captivity there in the province are in great affliction and reproach:the wall of Jerusalem also is broken down, and the gates thereof are burned with fire. 4 And it came to pass, when I heard these words, that I sat down and wept, and mourned certain days, and fasted, and prayed before the God of heaven, 5 And said, I beseech thee, O Lord God of heaven, the great and terrible God, that keepeth covenant and mercy for them that love him and observe his commandments:6 Let thine ear now be attentive, and thine eyes open, that thou mayest hear the prayer of thy servant,

which I pray before thee now, day and night, for the children of Israel thy servants, and confess the sins of the children of Israel, which we have sinned against thee:both I and my father's house have sinned. 7 We have dealt very corruptly against thee, and have not kept the commandments, nor the statutes, nor the judgments, which thou commandedst thy servant Moses. 8 Remember, I beseech thee, the word that thou commandedst thy servant Moses, saying, If ye transgress, I will scatter you abroad among the nations:9 But if ye turn unto me, and keep my commandments, and do them; though there were of you cast out unto the uttermost part of the heaven, yet will I gather them from thence, and will bring them unto the place that I have chosen to set my name there. 10 Now these are thy servants and thy people, whom thou hast redeemed by thy great power, and by thy strong hand. **11 O Lord, I beseech thee, let now thine ear be attentive to the prayer of thy servant, and to the prayer of thy servants, who desire to fear thy name:and prosper, I pray thee, thy servant this day, and grant him mercy in the sight of this man. For I was the king's cupbearer.**

Nehemiah 2

1 And it came to pass in the month Nisan, in the twentieth year of Artaxerxes the king, that wine was before him:and I took up the wine, and gave it unto the king. Now I had not been beforetime sad in his presence. 2 Wherefore the king said unto me, Why is thy countenance sad, seeing thou art not sick? this is nothing else but sorrow of heart. Then I was very sore afraid, 3 And said unto the king, Let the king live for ever:why should not my countenance be sad, when the city, the place of my fathers 'sepulchres, lieth waste, and the gates thereof are consumed with fire? 4 Then the king said unto me, For what dost thou make request? So I prayed to the God of heaven. 5 And I said unto the king, If it please the king, and if thy servant have found favour in thy sight, that thou wouldest send me unto Judah, unto the city of my fathers' sepulchres, that I may build it. 6 And the king said

unto me, (the queen also sitting by him,) For how long shall thy journey be? and when wilt thou return? So it pleased the king to send me; and I set him a time. 7 Moreover I said unto the king, If it please the king, let letters be given me to the governors beyond the river, that they may convey me over till I come into Judah; 8 And a letter unto Asaph the keeper of the king's forest, that he may give me timber to make beams for the gates of the palace which appertained to the house, and for the wall of the city, and for the house that I shall enter into. And the king granted me, according to the good hand of my God upon me. 9 Then I came to the governors beyond the river, and gave them the king's letters. Now the king had sent captains of the army and horsemen with me. 10 When Sanballat the Horonite, and Tobiah the servant, the Ammonite, heard of it, it grieved them exceedingly that there was come a man to seek the welfare of the children of Israel. 11 So I came to Jerusalem, and was there three days. 12 And I arose in the night, I and some few men with me; neither told I any man what my God had put in my heart to do at Jerusalem:neither was there any beast with me, save the beast that I rode upon. 13 And I went out by night by the gate of the valley, even before the dragon well, and to the dung port, and viewed the walls of Jerusalem, which were broken down, and the gates thereof were consumed with fire. 14 Then I went on to the gate of the fountain, and to the king's pool:but there was no place for the beast that was under me to pass. 15 Then went I up in the night by the brook, and viewed the wall, and turned back, and entered by the gate of the valley, and so returned. 16 And the rulers knew not whither I went, or what I did; neither had I as yet told it to the Jews, nor to the priests, nor to the nobles, nor to the rulers, nor to the rest that did the work. 17 Then said I unto them, Ye see the distress that we are in, how Jerusalem lieth waste, and the gates thereof are burned with fire:come, and let us build up the wall of Jerusalem, that we be no more a reproach. 18 Then I told them of the hand of my God which was good upon me; as also the king's words that he had spoken unto me. And they said, Let us rise up and build. So they strengthened their hands for this good work. 19 But when

Sanballat the Horonite, and Tobiah the servant, the Ammonite, and
Geshem the Arabian, heard it, they laughed us to scorn, and despised
us, and said, What is this thing that ye do? will ye rebel against the
king? **20 Then answered I them, and said unto them, The God of
heaven, he will prosper us; therefore we his servants will arise
and build:but ye have no portion, nor right, nor memorial, in
Jerusalem.**

Psalms 1
1 Blessed is the man that walketh not in the counsel of the ungodly,
nor standeth in the way of sinners, nor sitteth in the seat of the
scornful. 2 But his delight is in the law of the Lord; and in his law
doth he meditate day and night. **3 And he shall be like a tree planted
by the rivers of water, that bringeth forth his fruit in his season;
his leaf also shall not wither; and whatsoever he doeth shall
prosper.**
4 The ungodly are not so: but are like the chaff which the wind
driveth away. 5 Therefore the ungodly shall not stand in the judgment,
nor sinners in the congregation of the righteous. 6 For the Lord
knoweth the way of the righteous: but the way of the ungodly shall
perish.

Psalms 73
A Psalm of Asaph. 1 Truly God is good to Israel, even to such as are
of a clean heart. 2 But as for me, my feet were almost gone; my steps
had well nigh slipped. 3 For I was envious at the foolish, when I saw
the prosperity of the wicked. 4 For there are no bands in their death:
but their strength is firm. 5 They are not in trouble as other men;
neither are they plagued like other men. 6 Therefore pride compasseth
them about as a chain; violence covereth them as a garment. 7 Their
eyes stand out with fatness: they have more than heart could wish.
8 They are corrupt, and speak wickedly concerning oppression:
they speak loftily. 9 They set their mouth against the heavens,
and their tongue walketh through the earth. 10 Therefore his people
return hither: and waters of a full cup are wrung out to them. 11 And
they say, How doth God know? and is there knowledge in the most

High? **12 Behold, these are the ungodly, who prosper in the world; they increase in riches.** 13 Verily I have cleansed my heart in vain, and washed my hands in innocency. 14 For all the day long have I been plagued, and chastened every morning. 15 If I say, I will speak thus; behold, I should offend against the generation of thy children. 16 When I thought to know this, it was too painful for me; 17 Until I went into the sanctuary of God; then understood I their end. 18 Surely thou didst set them in slippery places: thou castedst them down into destruction. 19 How are they brought into desolation, as in a moment! they are utterly consumed with terrors. 20 As a dream when one awaketh; so, O Lord, when thou awakest, thou shalt despise their image. 21 Thus my heart was grieved, and I was pricked in my reins. 22 So foolish was I, and ignorant: I was as a beast before thee. 23 Nevertheless I am continually with thee: thou hast holden me by my right hand. 24 Thou shalt guide me with thy counsel, and afterward receive me to glory. 25 Whom have I in heaven but thee? and there is none upon earth that I desire beside thee. 26 My flesh and my heart faileth: but God is the strength of my heart, and my portion for ever. 27 For, lo, they that are far from thee shall perish: thou hast destroyed all them that go a whoring from thee. 28 But it is good for me to draw near to God: I have put my trust in the Lord God, that I may declare all thy works.

Psalms 122
A Song of degrees of David.
1 I was glad when they said unto me,
Let us go into the house of the Lord.
2 Our feet shall stand
within thy gates, O Jerusalem.
3 Jerusalem is builded
as a city that is compact together:
4 Whither the tribes go up, the tribes of the Lord,
unto the testimony of Israel,
to give thanks unto the name of the Lord.
5 For there are set thrones of judgment,
the thrones of the house of David.
6 Pray for the peace of Jerusalem:
they shall prosper that love thee.

7 Peace be within thy walls,
and prosperity within thy palaces.
8 For my brethren and companions 'sakes,
I will now say, Peace be within thee.
9 Because of the house of the Lord our God
I will seek thy good.

Proverb Chapter 28
1 The wicked flee when no man pursueth:
but the righteous are bold as a lion.
2 For the transgression of a land many are the princes thereof:
but by a man of understanding and knowledge the state thereof shall
be prolonged.
3 A poor man that oppresseth the poor
is like a sweeping rain which leaveth no food.
4 They that forsake the law praise the wicked:
but such as keep the law contend with them.
5 Evil men understand not judgment:
but they that seek the Lord understand all things.
6 Better is the poor that walketh in his uprightness,
than he that is perverse in his ways, though he be rich.
7 Whoso keepeth the law is a wise son:
but he that is a companion of riotous men shameth his father.
8 He that by usury and unjust gain increaseth his substance,
he shall gather it for him that will pity the poor.
9 He that turneth away his ear from hearing the law,
even his prayer shall be abomination.
10 Whoso causeth the righteous to go astray in an evil way,
he shall fall himself into his own pit:but the upright shall have good
things in possession.
11 The rich man is wise in his own conceit;
but the poor that hath understanding searcheth him out.
12 When righteous men do rejoice, there is great glory:
but when the wicked rise, a man is hidden.
13 He that covereth his sins shall not prosper:
but whoso confesseth and forsaketh them shall have mercy.
14 Happy is the man that feareth alway:
but he that hardeneth his heart shall fall into mischief.

15 As a roaring lion, and a ranging bear;
so is a wicked ruler over the poor people.
16 The prince that wanteth understanding is also a great oppressor:
but he that hateth covetousness shall prolong his days.
17 A man that doeth violence to the blood of any person
shall flee to the pit; let no man stay him.
18 Whoso walketh uprightly shall be saved:
but he that is perverse in his ways shall fall at once.
19 He that tilleth his land shall have plenty of bread:
but he that followeth after vain persons shall have poverty enough.
20 A faithful man shall abound with blessings:
but he that maketh haste to be rich shall not be innocent.
21 To have respect of persons is not good:
for for a piece of bread that man will transgress.
22 He that hasteth to be rich hath an evil eye,
and considereth not that poverty shall come upon him.
23 He that rebuketh a man afterwards shall find more favour
than he that flattereth with the tongue.
24 Whoso robbeth his father or his mother,
and saith, It is no transgression;
the same is the companion of a destroyer.
25 He that is of a proud heart stirreth up strife:
but he that putteth his trust in the Lord shall be made fat.
26 He that trusteth in his own heart is a fool:
but whoso walketh wisely, he shall be delivered.
27 He that giveth unto the poor shall not lack:
but he that hideth his eyes shall have many a curse.
28 When the wicked rise, men hide themselves:
but when they perish, the righteous increase.

Ecclesiastes 11

1 Cast thy bread upon the waters:for thou shalt find it after many
days. 2 Give a portion to seven, and also to eight; for thou knowest
not what evil shall be upon the earth. 3 If the clouds be full of rain,
they empty themselves upon the earth:and if the tree fall toward the
south, or toward the north, in the place where the tree falleth, there it
shall be. 4 He that observeth the wind shall not sow; and he that

regardeth the clouds shall not reap. 5 As thou knowest not what is the way of the spirit, nor how the bones do grow in the womb of her that is with child:even so thou knowest not the works of God who maketh all. **6 In the morning sow thy seed, and in the evening withhold not thine hand:for thou knowest not whether shall prosper, either this or that, or whether they both shall be alike good.** 7 Truly the light is sweet, and a pleasant thing it is for the eyes to behold the sun:8 But if a man live many years, and rejoice in them all; yet let him remember the days of darkness; for they shall be many. All that cometh is vanity. 9 Rejoice, O young man, in thy youth; and let thy heart cheer thee in the days of thy youth, and walk in the ways of thine heart, and in the sight of thine eyes:but know thou, that for all these things God will bring thee into judgment. 10 Therefore remove sorrow from thy heart, and put away evil from thy flesh:for childhood and youth are vanity.

Isaiah 53
1 Who hath believed our report?
and to whom is the arm of the Lord revealed?
2 For he shall grow up before him as a tender plant,
and as a root out of a dry ground:
he hath no form nor comeliness;
and when we shall see him, there is no beauty that we should desire him.
3 He is despised and rejected of men;
a man of sorrows, and acquainted with grief:
and we hid as it were our faces from him;
he was despised, and we esteemed him not.
4 Surely he hath borne our griefs,
and carried our sorrows:
yet we did esteem him stricken,
smitten of God, and afflicted.
5 But he was wounded for our transgressions,
he was bruised for our iniquities:
the chastisement of our peace was upon him;
and with his stripes we are healed.

6 All we like sheep have gone astray;
we have turned every one to his own way;
and the Lord hath laid on him the iniquity of us all.
7 He was oppressed, and he was afflicted,
yet he opened not his mouth:
he is brought as a lamb to the slaughter,
and as a sheep before her shearers is dumb,
so he openeth not his mouth.
8 He was taken from prison and from judgment:
and who shall declare his generation?
for he was cut off out of the land of the living:
for the transgression of my people was he stricken.
9 And he made his grave with the wicked,
and with the rich in his death;
because he had done no violence,
neither was any deceit in his mouth.
**10 Yet it pleased the Lord to bruise him; he hath put him to
grief:when thou shalt make his soul an offering for sin, he shall
see his seed, he shall prolong his days, and the pleasure of the
Lord shall prosper in his hand.**
11 He shall see of the travail of his soul, and shall be satisfied:
by his knowledge shall my righteous servant justify many;
for he shall bear their iniquities.
12 Therefore will I divide him a portion with the great,
and he shall divide the spoil with the strong;
because he hath poured out his soul unto death:
and he was numbered with the transgressors;
and he bare the sin of many,
and made intercession for the transgressors.

Isaiah 54
1 Sing, O barren, thou that didst not bear;
break forth into singing, and cry aloud, thou that didst not travail with
child:
for more are the children of the desolate than the children of the
married wife, saith the Lord.
2 Enlarge the place of thy tent,
and let them stretch forth the curtains of thine habitations:

spare not, lengthen thy cords, and strengthen thy stakes;
3 For thou shalt break forth on the right hand and on the left;
and thy seed shall inherit the Gentiles,
and make the desolate cities to be inhabited.
4 Fear not; for thou shalt not be ashamed:
neither be thou confounded; for thou shalt not be put to shame:
for thou shalt forget the shame of thy youth,
and shalt not remember the reproach of thy widowhood any more.
5 For thy Maker is thine husband;
the Lord of hosts is his name;
and thy Redeemer the Holy One of Israel; The God of the whole earth
shall he be called.
6 For the Lord hath called thee as a woman forsaken and grieved in
spirit, and a wife of youth, when thou wast refused, saith thy God.
7 For a small moment have I forsaken thee;
but with great mercies will I gather thee.
8 In a little wrath I hid my face from thee for a moment;
but with everlasting kindness will I have mercy on thee,
saith the Lord thy Redeemer.
9 For this is as the waters of Noah unto me:
for as I have sworn that the waters of Noah should no more go over
the earth;
so have I sworn that I would not be wroth with thee, nor rebuke thee.
10 For the mountains shall depart,
and the hills be removed;
but my kindness shall not depart from thee,
neither shall the covenant of my peace be removed,
saith the Lord that hath mercy on thee.
11 O thou afflicted, tossed with tempest, and not comforted,
behold, I will lay thy stones with fair colours,
and lay thy foundations with sapphires.
12 And I will make thy windows of agates,
and thy gates of carbuncles,
and all thy borders of pleasant stones.
13 And all thy children shall be taught of the Lord;
and great shall be the peace of thy children.
14 In righteousness shalt thou be established:
thou shalt be far from oppression; for thou shalt not fear:
and from terror; for it shall not come near thee.

15 Behold, they shall surely gather together, but not by me:
whosoever shall gather together against thee shall fall for thy sake.
16 Behold, I have created the smith
that bloweth the coals in the fire,
and that bringeth forth an instrument for his work;
and I have created the waster to destroy.
**17 No weapon that is formed against thee shall prosper;
and every tongue that shall rise against thee in judgment thou
shalt condemn.**
This is the heritage of the servants of the Lord,
and their righteousness is of me, saith the Lord.

Isaiah 55
1 Ho, every one that thirsteth, come ye to the waters,
and he that hath no money;
come ye, buy, and eat;
yea, come, buy wine and milk without money and without price.
2 Wherefore do ye spend money for that which is not bread?
and your labour for that which satisfieth not?
hearken diligently unto me, and eat ye that which is good,
and let your soul delight itself in fatness.
3 Incline your ear, and come unto me:
hear, and your soul shall live;
and I will make an everlasting covenant with you,
even the sure mercies of David.
4 Behold, I have given him for a witness to the people,
a leader and commander to the people.
5 Behold, thou shalt call a nation that thou knowest not,
and nations that knew not thee
shall run unto thee because of the Lord thy God,
and for the Holy One of Israel; for he hath glorified thee.
6 Seek ye the Lord while he may be found,
call ye upon him while he is near:
7 Let the wicked forsake his way,
and the unrighteous man his thoughts:
and let him return unto the Lord, and he will have mercy upon him;
and to our God, for he will abundantly pardon.
8 For my thoughts are not your thoughts,

114

neither are your ways my ways, saith the Lord.
9 For as the heavens are higher than the earth,
so are my ways higher than your ways,
and my thoughts than your thoughts.
10 For as the rain cometh down,
and the snow from heaven, and returneth not thither,
but watereth the earth,
and maketh it bring forth and bud,
that it may give seed to the sower, and bread to the eater:
11 So shall my word be that goeth forth out of my mouth:
it shall not return unto me void,
but it shall accomplish that which I please,
and it shall prosper in the thing whereto I sent it.
12 For ye shall go out with joy,
and be led forth with peace:
the mountains and the hills shall break forth before you into singing,
and all the trees of the field shall clap their hands.
13 Instead of the thorn shall come up the fir tree,
and instead of the brier shall come up the myrtle tree:
and it shall be to the Lord for a name,
for an everlasting sign that shall not be cut off.

Jeremiah 2

1 Moreover the word of the Lord came to me, saying, 2 Go and cry in
the ears of Jerusalem, saying, Thus saith the Lord; I remember thee,
the kindness of thy youth, the love of thine espousals, when thou
wentest after me in the wilderness, in a land that was not sown. 3
Israel was holiness unto the Lord, and the firstfruits of his increase:all
that devour him shall offend; evil shall come upon them, saith the
Lord. 4 Hear ye the word of the Lord, O house of Jacob, and all the
families of the house of Israel: 5 Thus saith the Lord, What iniquity
have your fathers found in me, that they are gone far from me, and
have walked after vanity, and are become vain? 6 Neither said they,
Where is the Lord that brought us up out of the land of Egypt, that led
us through the wilderness, through a land of deserts and of pits,
through a land of drought, and of the shadow of death, through a land

that no man passed through, and where no man dwelt? 7 And I brought you into a plentiful country, to eat the fruit thereof and the goodness thereof; but when ye entered, ye defiled my land, and made mine heritage an abomination. 8 The priests said not, Where is the Lord? and they that handle the law knew me not:the pastors also transgressed against me, and the prophets prophesied by Baal, and walked after things that do not profit. 9 Wherefore I will yet plead with you, saith the Lord, and with your children's children will I plead. 10 For pass over the isles of Chittim, and see; and send unto Kedar, and consider diligently, and see if there be such a thing. 11 Hath a nation changed their gods, which are yet no gods? but my people have changed their glory for that which doth not profit. 12 Be astonished, O ye heavens, at this, and be horribly afraid, be ye very desolate, saith the Lord. 13 For my people have committed two evils; they have forsaken me the fountain of living waters, and hewed them out cisterns, broken cisterns, that can hold no water. 14 Is Israel a servant? is he a homeborn slave? why is he spoiled? 15 The young lions roared upon him, and yelled, and they made his land waste:his cities are burned without inhabitant. 16 Also the children of Noph and Tahapanes have broken the crown of thy head. 17 Hast thou not procured this unto thyself, in that thou hast forsaken the Lord thy God, when he led thee by the way? 18 And now what hast thou to do in the way of Egypt, to drink the waters of Sihor? or what hast thou to do in the way of Assyria, to drink the waters of the river? 19 Thine own wickedness shall correct thee, and thy backslidings shall reprove thee:know therefore and see that it is an evil thing and bitter, that thou hast forsaken the Lord thy God, and that my fear is not in thee, saith the Lord God of hosts. 20 For of old time I have broken thy yoke, and burst thy bands; and thou saidst, I will not transgress; when upon every high hill and under every green tree thou wanderest, playing the harlot. 21 Yet I had planted thee a noble vine, wholly a right seed:how then art thou turned into the degenerate plant of a strange vine unto me? 22 For though thou wash thee with nitre, and take thee much soap, yet thine iniquity is marked before me, saith the Lord God. 23

How canst thou say, I am not polluted, I have not gone after Baalim? see thy way in the valley, know what thou hast done:thou art a swift dromedary traversing her ways; 24 A wild ass used to the wilderness, that snuffeth up the wind at her pleasure; in her occasion who can turn her away? all they that seek her will not weary themselves; in her month they shall find her. 25 Withhold thy foot from being unshod, and thy throat from thirst:but thou saidst, There is no hope:no; for I have loved strangers, and after them will I go. 26 As the thief is ashamed when he is found, so is the house of Israel ashamed; they, their kings, their princes, and their priests, and their prophets, 27 Saying to a stock, Thou art my father; and to a stone, Thou hast brought me forth:for they have turned their back unto me, and not their face:but in the time of their trouble they will say, Arise, and save us. 28 But where are thy gods that thou hast made thee? let them arise, if they can save thee in the time of thy trouble:for according to the number of thy cities are thy gods, O Judah. 29 Wherefore will ye plead with me? ye all have transgressed against me, saith the Lord. 30 In vain have I smitten your children; they received no correction:your own sword hath devoured your prophets, like a destroying lion. 31 O generation, see ye the word of the Lord. Have I been a wilderness unto Israel? a land of darkness? wherefore say my people, We are lords; we will come no more unto thee? 32 Can a maid forget her ornaments, or a bride her attire? yet my people have forgotten me days without number. 33 Why trimmest thou thy way to seek love? therefore hast thou also taught the wicked ones thy ways. 34 Also in thy skirts is found the blood of the souls of the poor innocents:I have not found it by secret search, but upon all these. 35 Yet thou sayest, Because I am innocent, surely his anger shall turn from me. Behold, I will plead with thee, because thou sayest, I have not sinned. 36 Why gaddest thou about so much to change thy way? thou also shalt be ashamed of Egypt, as thou wast ashamed of Assyria. **37 Yea, thou shalt go forth from him, and thine hands upon thine head:for the Lord hath rejected thy confidences, and thou shalt not prosper in them.**

Jeremiah 5

1 Run ye to and fro through the streets of Jerusalem, and see now, and know, and seek in the broad places thereof, if ye can find a man, if there be any that executeth judgment, that seeketh the truth; and I will pardon it. 2 And though they say, The Lord liveth; surely they swear falsely. 3 O Lord, are not thine eyes upon the truth? thou hast stricken them, but they have not grieved; thou hast consumed them, but they have refused to receive correction:they have made their faces harder than a rock; they have refused to return. 4 Therefore I said, Surely these are poor; they are foolish:for they know not the way of the Lord, nor the judgment of their God. 5 I will get me unto the great men, and will speak unto them; for they have known the way of the Lord, and the judgment of their God:but these have altogether broken the yoke, and burst the bonds. 6 Wherefore a lion out of the forest shall slay them, and a wolf of the evenings shall spoil them, a leopard shall watch over their cities:every one that goeth out thence shall be torn in pieces:because their transgressions are many, and their backslidings are increased. 7 How shall I pardon thee for this? thy children have forsaken me, and sworn by them that are no gods:when I had fed them to the full, they then committed adultery, and assembled themselves by troops in the harlots 'houses. 8 They were as fed horses in the morning:every one neighed after his neighbour's wife. 9 Shall I not visit for these things? saith the Lord:and shall not my soul be avenged on such a nation as this? 10 Go ye up upon her walls, and destroy; but make not a full end:take away her battlements; for they are not the Lord' s. 11 For the house of Israel and the house of Judah have dealt very treacherously against me, saith the Lord. 12 They have belied the Lord, and said, It is not he; neither shall evil come upon us; neither shall we see sword nor famine:13 And the prophets shall become wind, and the word is not in them:thus shall it be done unto them. 14 Wherefore thus saith the Lord God of hosts, Because ye speak this word, behold, I will make my words in thy mouth fire, and this people wood, and it shall devour them. 15 Lo, I will bring a nation upon you from far, O house of Israel, saith the Lord:it is a mighty nation, it is an

ancient nation, a nation whose language thou knowest not, neither understandest what they say. 16 Their quiver is as an open sepulchre, they are all mighty men. 17 And they shall eat up thine harvest, and thy bread, which thy sons and thy daughters should eat:they shall eat up thy flocks and thine herds:they shall eat up thy vines and thy fig trees:they shall impoverish thy fenced cities, wherein thou trustedst, with the sword. 18 Nevertheless in those days, saith the Lord, I will not make a full end with you. 19 And it shall come to pass, when ye shall say, Wherefore doeth the Lord our God all these things unto us? then shalt thou answer them, Like as ye have forsaken me, and served strange gods in your land, so shall ye serve strangers in a land that is not yours. 20 Declare this in the house of Jacob, and publish it in Judah, saying, 21 Hear now this, O foolish people, and without understanding; which have eyes, and see not; which have ears, and hear not:22 Fear ye not me? saith the Lord:will ye not tremble at my presence, which have placed the sand for the bound of the sea by a perpetual decree, that it cannot pass it:and though the waves thereof toss themselves, yet can they not prevail; though they roar, yet can they not pass over it? 23 But this people hath a revolting and a rebellious heart; they are revolted and gone. 24 Neither say they in their heart, Let us now fear the Lord our God, that giveth rain, both the former and the latter, in his season:he reserveth unto us the appointed weeks of the harvest. 25 Your iniquities have turned away these things, and your sins have withholden good things from you. 26 For among my people are found wicked men:they lay wait, as he that setteth snares; they set a trap, they catch men. 27 As a cage is full of birds, so are their houses full of deceit:therefore they are become great, and waxen rich. **28 They are waxen fat, they shine:yea, they overpass the deeds of the wicked:they judge not the cause, the cause of the fatherless, yet they prosper; and the right of the needy do they not judge. 29 Shall I not visit for these things? saith the Lord:shall not my soul be avenged on such a nation as this?** 30 A wonderful and horrible thing is committed in the land; 31 The prophets prophesy falsely, and the priests bear rule by their means;

and my people love to have it so:and what will ye do in the end thereof?

Jeremiah 10

1 Hear ye the word which the Lord speaketh unto you, O house of Israel:

2 Thus saith the Lord,
Learn not the way of the heathen,
and be not dismayed at the signs of heaven;
for the heathen are dismayed at them.

3 For the customs of the people are vain:
for one cutteth a tree out of the forest,
the work of the hands of the workman, with the axe.

4 They deck it with silver and with gold;
they fasten it with nails and with hammers, that it move not.

5 They are upright as the palm tree, but speak not:
they must needs be borne, because they cannot go.
Be not afraid of them; for they cannot do evil,
neither also is it in them to do good.

6 Forasmuch as there is none like unto thee, O Lord;
thou art great, and thy name is great in might.

7 Who would not fear thee, O King of nations? for to thee doth it appertain: forasmuch as among all the wise men of the nations, and in all their kingdoms, there is none like unto thee.

8 But they are altogether brutish and foolish:
the stock is a doctrine of vanities.

9 Silver spread into plates is brought from Tarshish,
and gold from Uphaz, the work of the workman, and of the hands of the founder: blue and purple is their clothing:
they are all the work of cunning men.

10 But the Lord is the true God,
he is the living God, and an everlasting king:
at his wrath the earth shall tremble, and the nations shall not be able to abide his indignation.

11 Thus shall ye say unto them,
The gods that have not made the heavens and the earth,
even they shall perish from the earth, and from under these heavens.

12 He hath made the earth by his power,

he hath established the world by his wisdom, and hath stretched out
the heavens by his discretion.
13 When he uttereth his voice, there is a multitude of waters in the
heavens, and he causeth the vapours to ascend from the ends of the
earth;
he maketh lightnings with rain, and bringeth forth the wind out of his
treasures.
14 Every man is brutish in his knowledge:
every founder is confounded by the graven image:for his molten
image is falsehood, and there is no breath in them.
15 They are vanity, and the work of errors:
in the time of their visitation they shall perish.
16 The portion of Jacob is not like them:
for he is the former of all things; and Israel is the rod of his
inheritance: The Lord of hosts is his name.
17 Gather up thy wares out of the land,
O inhabitant of the fortress.
18 For thus saith the Lord,
Behold, I will sling out the inhabitants of the land at this once,
and will distress them, that they may find it so.
19 Woe is me for my hurt! my wound is grievous:
but I said, Truly this is a grief, and I must bear it.
20 My tabernacle is spoiled, and all my cords are broken:
my children are gone forth of me, and they are not:
there is none to stretch forth my tent any more,
and to set up my curtains.
21 For the pastors are become brutish,
and have not sought the Lord:
therefore they shall not prosper,
and all their flocks shall be scattered.
22 Behold, the noise of the bruit is come,
and a great commotion out of the north country,
to make the cities of Judah desolate,
and a den of dragons.
23 O Lord, I know that the way of man is not in himself:
it is not in man that walketh to direct his steps.
24 O Lord, correct me, but with judgment;
not in thine anger, lest thou bring me to nothing.
25 Pour out thy fury upon the heathen that know thee not,

and upon the families that call not on thy name:
for they have eaten up Jacob, and devoured him,
and consumed him, and have made his habitation.

Jeremiah 12
1 Righteous art thou, O Lord, when I plead with thee:yet let me
talk with thee of thy judgments:Wherefore doth the way of the
wicked prosper? wherefore are all they happy that deal very
treacherously? 2 Thou hast planted them, yea, they have taken
root:they grow, yea, they bring forth fruit:thou art near in their mouth,
and far from their reins. 3 But thou, O Lord, knowest me:thou hast
seen me, and tried mine heart toward thee:pull them out like sheep for
the slaughter, and prepare them for the day of slaughter. 4 How long
shall the land mourn, and the herbs of every field wither, for the
wickedness of them that dwell therein? the beasts are consumed, and
the birds; because they said, He shall not see our last end. 5 If thou
hast run with the footmen, and they have wearied thee, then how canst
thou contend with horses? and if in the land of peace, wherein thou
trustedst, they wearied thee, then how wilt thou do in the swelling of
Jordan? 6 For even thy brethren, and the house of thy father, even
they have dealt treacherously with thee; yea, they have called a
multitude after thee:believe them not, though they speak fair words
unto thee. 7 I have forsaken mine house, I have left mine heritage; I
have given the dearly beloved of my soul into the hand of her
enemies. 8 Mine heritage is unto me as a lion in the forest; it crieth
out against me:therefore have I hated it. 9 Mine heritage is unto me as
a speckled bird, the birds round about are against her; come ye,
assemble all the beasts of the field, come to devour. 10 Many pastors
have destroyed my vineyard, they have trodden my portion under
foot, they have made my pleasant portion a desolate wilderness. 11
They have made it desolate, and being desolate it mourneth unto me;
the whole land is made desolate, because no man layeth it to heart. 12
The spoilers are come upon all high places through the wilderness:for
the sword of the Lord shall devour from the one end of the land even

to the other end of the land:no flesh shall have peace. 13 They have sown wheat, but shall reap thorns:they have put themselves to pain, but shall not profit:and they shall be ashamed of your revenues because of the fierce anger of the Lord. 14 Thus saith the Lord against all mine evil neighbours, that touch the inheritance which I have caused my people Israel to inherit; Behold, I will pluck them out of their land, and pluck out the house of Judah from among them. 15 And it shall come to pass, after that I have plucked them out I will return, and have compassion on them, and will bring them again, every man to his heritage, and every man to his land. 16 And it shall come to pass, if they will diligently learn the ways of my people, to swear by my name, The Lord liveth; as they taught my people to swear by Baal; then shall they be built in the midst of my people. 17 But if they will not obey, I will utterly pluck up and destroy that nation, saith the Lord.

Jeremiah 20
1 Now Pashur the son of Immer the priest, who was also chief governor in the house of the Lord, heard that Jeremiah prophesied these things. 2 Then Pashur smote Jeremiah the prophet, and put him in the stocks that were in the high gate of Benjamin, which was by the house of the Lord. 3 And it came to pass on the morrow, that Pashur brought forth Jeremiah out of the stocks. Then said Jeremiah unto him, The Lord hath not called thy name Pashur, but Magormissabib. 4 For thus saith the Lord, Behold, I will make thee a terror to thyself, and to all thy friends:and they shall fall by the sword of their enemies, and thine eyes shall behold it:and I will give all Judah into the hand of the king of Babylon, and he shall carry them captive into Babylon, and shall slay them with the sword. 5 Moreover I will deliver all the strength of this city, and all the labours thereof, and all the precious things thereof, and all the treasures of the kings of Judah will I give into the hand of their enemies, which shall spoil them, and take them, and carry them to Babylon. 6 And thou, Pashur, and all that dwell in

thine house shall go into captivity:and thou shalt come to Babylon, and there thou shalt die, and shalt be buried there, thou, and all thy friends, to whom thou hast prophesied lies. 7 O Lord, thou hast deceived me, and I was deceived: thou art stronger than I, and hast prevailed: I am in derision daily, every one mocketh me. 8 For since I spake, I cried out, I cried violence and spoil; because the word of the Lord was made a reproach unto me, and a derision, daily. 9 Then I said, I will not make mention of him, nor speak any more in his name.But his word was in mine heart as a burning fire shut up in my bones, and I was weary with forbearing, and I could not stay. 10 For I heard the defaming of many, fear on every side. Report, say they, and we will report it. All my familiars watched for my halting, saying, Peradventure he will be enticed, and we shall prevail against him, and we shall take our revenge on him. **11 But the Lord is with me as a mighty terrible one: therefore my persecutors shall stumble, and they shall not prevail: they shall be greatly ashamed; for they shall not prosper: their everlasting confusion shall never be forgotten.** 12 But, O Lord of hosts, that triest the righteous, and seest the reins and the heart, let me see thy vengeance on them: for unto thee have I opened my cause. 13 Sing unto the Lord, praise ye the Lord:for he hath delivered the soul of the poor from the hand of evildoers. 14 Cursed be the day wherein I was born: let not the day wherein my mother bare me be blessed. 15 Cursed be the man who brought tidings to my father, saying, A man child is born unto thee; making him very glad. 16 And let that man be as the cities which the Lord overthrew, and repented not: and let him hear the cry in the morning, and the shouting at noontide; 17 Because he slew me not from the womb; or that my mother might have been my grave, and her womb to be always great with me. 18 Wherefore came I forth out of the womb to see labour and sorrow, that my days should be consumed with shame?

Jeremiah 22

1 Thus saith the Lord; Go down to the house of the king of Judah, and speak there this word, 2 And say, Hear the word of the Lord, O king of Judah, that sittest upon the throne of David, thou, and thy servants, and thy people that enter in by these gates:3 Thus saith the Lord; Execute ye judgment and righteousness, and deliver the spoiled out of the hand of the oppressor:and do no wrong, do no violence to the stranger, the fatherless, nor the widow, neither shed innocent blood in this place. 4 For if ye do this thing indeed, then shall there enter in by the gates of this house kings sitting upon the throne of David, riding in chariots and on horses, he, and his servants, and his people. 5 But if ye will not hear these words, I swear by myself, saith the Lord, that this house shall become a desolation. 6 For thus saith the Lord unto the king's house of Judah; Thou art Gilead unto me, and the head of Lebanon:yet surely I will make thee a wilderness, and cities which are not inhabited. 7 And I will prepare destroyers against thee, every one with his weapons:and they shall cut down thy choice cedars, and cast them into the fire. 8 And many nations shall pass by this city, and they shall say every man to his neighbour, Wherefore hath the Lord done thus unto this great city? 9 Then they shall answer, Because they have forsaken the covenant of the Lord their God, and worshipped other gods, and served them. 10 Weep ye not for the dead, neither bemoan him: but weep sore for him that goeth away: for he shall return no more, nor see his native country. 11 For thus saith the Lord touching Shallum the son of Josiah king of Judah, which reigned instead of Josiah his father, which went forth out of this place; He shall not return thither any more:12 But he shall die in the place whither they have led him captive, and shall see this land no more. 13 Woe unto him that buildeth his house by unrighteousness, and his chambers by wrong; that useth his neighbour's service without wages, and giveth him not for his work; 14 That saith, I will build me a wide house and large chambers, and cutteth him out windows; and it is cieled with cedar, and painted with vermilion. 15 Shalt thou reign, because thou closest thyself in cedar? did not thy father eat and drink,

and do judgment and justice, and then it was well with him? 16 He judged the cause of the poor and needy; then it was well with him: was not this to know me? saith the Lord. 17 But thine eyes and thine heart are not but for thy covetousness, and for to shed innocent blood, and for oppression, and for violence, to do it. 18 Therefore thus saith the Lord concerning Jehoiakim the son of Josiah king of Judah; They shall not lament for him, saying, Ah my brother! or, Ah sister! they shall not lament for him, saying, Ah lord! or, Ah his glory! 19 He shall be buried with the burial of an ass, drawn and cast forth beyond the gates of Jerusalem. 20 Go up to Lebanon, and cry; and lift up thy voice in Bashan, and cry from the passages: for all thy lovers are destroyed. 21 I spake unto thee in thy prosperity; but thou saidst, I will not hear. This hath been thy manner from thy youth, that thou obeyedst not my voice. 22 The wind shall eat up all thy pastors, and thy lovers shall go into captivity: surely then shalt thou be ashamed and confounded for all thy wickedness. 23 O inhabitant of Lebanon, that makest thy nest in the cedars, how gracious shalt thou be when pangs come upon thee, the pain as of a woman in travail! 24 As I live, saith the Lord, though Coniah the son of Jehoiakim king of Judah were the signet upon my right hand, yet would I pluck thee thence; 25 And I will give thee into the hand of them that seek thy life, and into the hand of them whose face thou fearest, even into the hand of Nebuchadrezzar king of Babylon, and into the hand of the Chaldeans. 26 And I will cast thee out, and thy mother that bare thee, into another country, where ye were not born; and there shall ye die. 27 But to the land whereunto they desire to return, thither shall they not return. 28 Is this man Coniah a despised broken idol? is he a vessel wherein is no pleasure? wherefore are they cast out, he and his seed, and are cast into a land which they know not? 29 O earth, earth, earth, hear the word of the Lord. **30 Thus saith the Lord, Write ye this man childless, a man that shall not prosper in his days:for no man of his seed shall prosper, sitting upon the throne of David, and ruling any more in Judah.**

Jeremiah 23

1 Woe be unto the pastors that destroy and scatter the sheep of my pasture! saith the Lord. 2 Therefore thus saith the Lord God of Israel against the pastors that feed my people; Ye have scattered my flock, and driven them away, and have not visited them:behold, I will visit upon you the evil of your doings, saith the Lord. 3 And I will gather the remnant of my flock out of all countries whither I have driven them, and will bring them again to their folds; and they shall be fruitful and increase. 4 And I will set up shepherds over them which shall feed them:and they shall fear no more, nor be dismayed, neither shall they be lacking, saith the Lord. **5 Behold, the days come, saith the Lord, that I will raise unto David a righteous Branch, and a King shall reign and prosper, and shall execute judgment and justice in the earth. 6 In his days Judah shall be saved, and Israel shall dwell safely:and this is his name whereby he shall be called, the Lord our Righteousness.** 7 Therefore, behold, the days come, saith the Lord, that they shall no more say, The Lord liveth, which brought up the children of Israel out of the land of Egypt; 8 But, The Lord liveth, which brought up and which led the seed of the house of Israel out of the north country, and from all countries whither I had driven them; and they shall dwell in their own land. 9 Mine heart within me is broken because of the prophets; all my bones shake; I am like a drunken man, and like a man whom wine hath overcome, because of the Lord, and because of the words of his holiness. 10 For the land is full of adulterers; for because of swearing the land mourneth; the pleasant places of the wilderness are dried up, and their course is evil, and their force is not right. 11 For both prophet and priest are profane; yea, in my house have I found their wickedness, saith the Lord. 12 Wherefore their way shall be unto them as slippery ways in the darkness: they shall be driven on, and fall therein: for I will bring evil upon them, even the year of their visitation, saith the Lord. 13 And I have seen folly in the prophets of Samaria; they prophesied in Baal, and caused my people Israel to err. 14 I have seen also in the prophets of Jerusalem an horrible thing: they commit

adultery, and walk in lies: they strengthen also the hands of evildoers, that none doth return from his wickedness: they are all of them unto me as Sodom, and the inhabitants thereof as Gomorrah. 15 Therefore thus saith the Lord of hosts concerning the prophets; Behold, I will feed them with wormwood, and make them drink the water of gall:for from the prophets of Jerusalem is profaneness gone forth into all the land. 16 Thus saith the Lord of hosts, Hearken not unto the words of the prophets that prophesy unto you:they make you vain:they speak a vision of their own heart, and not out of the mouth of the Lord. 17 They say still unto them that despise me, The Lord hath said, Ye shall have peace; and they say unto every one that walketh after the imagination of his own heart, No evil shall come upon you. 18 For who hath stood in the counsel of the Lord, and hath perceived and heard his word? who hath marked his word, and heard it? 19 Behold, a whirlwind of the Lord is gone forth in fury, even a grievous whirlwind:it shall fall grievously upon the head of the wicked. 20 The anger of the Lord shall not return, until he have executed, and till he have performed the thoughts of his heart:in the latter days ye shall consider it perfectly. 21 I have not sent these prophets, yet they ran:I have not spoken to them, yet they prophesied. 22 But if they had stood in my counsel, and had caused my people to hear my words, then they should have turned them from their evil way, and from the evil of their doings. 23 Am I a God at hand, saith the Lord, and not a God afar off? 24 Can any hide himself in secret places that I shall not see him? saith the Lord. Do not I fill heaven and earth? saith the Lord. 25 I have heard what the prophets said, that prophesy lies in my name, saying, I have dreamed, I have dreamed. 26 How long shall this be in the heart of the prophets that prophesy lies? yea, they are prophets of the deceit of their own heart; 27 Which think to cause my people to forget my name by their dreams which they tell every man to his neighbour, as their fathers have forgotten my name for Baal. 28 The prophet that hath a dream, let him tell a dream; and he that hath my word, let him speak my word faithfully. What is the chaff to the wheat? saith the Lord. 29 Is not my word like as a fire? saith the Lord;

and like a hammer that breaketh the rock in pieces? 30 Therefore, behold, I am against the prophets, saith the Lord, that steal my words every one from his neighbour. 31 Behold, I am against the prophets, saith the Lord, that use their tongues, and say, He saith. 32 Behold, I am against them that prophesy false dreams, saith the Lord, and do tell them, and cause my people to err by their lies, and by their lightness; yet I sent them not, nor commanded them:therefore they shall not profit this people at all, saith the Lord. 33 And when this people, or the prophet, or a priest, shall ask thee, saying, What is the burden of the Lord? thou shalt then say unto them, What burden? I will even forsake you, saith the Lord. 34 And as for the prophet, and the priest, and the people, that shall say, The burden of the Lord, I will even punish that man and his house. 35 Thus shall ye say every one to his neighbour, and every one to his brother, What hath the Lord answered? and, What hath the Lord spoken? 36 And the burden of the Lord shall ye mention no more:for every man's word shall be his burden; for ye have perverted the words of the living God, of the Lord of hosts our God. 37 Thus shalt thou say to the prophet, What hath the Lord answered thee? and, What hath the Lord spoken? 38 But since ye say, The burden of the Lord; therefore thus saith the Lord; Because ye say this word, The burden of the Lord, and I have sent unto you, saying, Ye shall not say, The burden of the Lord; 39 Therefore, behold, I, even I, will utterly forget you, and I will forsake you, and the city that I gave you and your fathers, and cast you out of my presence:40 And I will bring an everlasting reproach upon you, and a perpetual shame, which shall not be forgotten.

Jeremiah 32

1 The word that came to Jeremiah from the Lord in the tenth year of Zedekiah king of Judah, which was the eighteenth year of Nebuchadrezzar. 2 For then the king of Babylon's army besieged Jerusalem:and Jeremiah the prophet was shut up in the court of the prison, which was in the king of Judah's house. 3 For Zedekiah king

of Judah had shut him up, saying, Wherefore dost thou prophesy, and say, Thus saith the Lord, Behold, I will give this city into the hand of the king of Babylon, and he shall take it; 4 And Zedekiah king of Judah shall not escape out of the hand of the Chaldeans, but shall surely be delivered into the hand of the king of Babylon, and shall speak with him mouth to mouth, and his eyes shall behold his eyes; **5 And he shall lead Zedekiah to Babylon, and there shall he be until I visit him, saith the Lord:though ye fight with the Chaldeans, ye shall not prosper.** 6 And Jeremiah said, The word of the Lord came unto me, saying, 7 Behold, Hanameel the son of Shallum thine uncle shall come unto thee, saying, Buy thee my field that is in Anathoth:for the right of redemption is thine to buy it. 8 So Hanameel mine uncle's son came to me in the court of the prison according to the word of the Lord, and said unto me, Buy my field, I pray thee, that is in Anathoth, which is in the country of Benjamin:for the right of inheritance is thine, and the redemption is thine; buy it for thyself. Then I knew that this was the word of the Lord. 9 And I bought the field of Hanameel my uncle's son, that was in Anathoth, and weighed him the money, even seventeen shekels of silver. 10 And I subscribed the evidence, and sealed it, and took witnesses, and weighed him the money in the balances. 11 So I took the evidence of the purchase, both that which was sealed according to the law and custom, and that which was open:12 And I gave the evidence of the purchase unto Baruch the son of Neriah, the son of Maaseiah, in the sight of Hanameel mine uncle's son, and in the presence of the witnesses that subscribed the book of the purchase, before all the Jews that sat in the court of the prison. 13 And I charged Baruch before them, saying, 14 Thus saith the Lord of hosts, the God of Israel; Take these evidences, this evidence of the purchase, both which is sealed, and this evidence which is open; and put them in an earthen vessel, that they may continue many days. 15 For thus saith the Lord of hosts, the God of Israel; Houses and fields and vineyards shall be possessed again in this land. 16 Now when I had delivered the evidence of the purchase unto Baruch the son of Neriah, I prayed unto the Lord, saying, 17 Ah Lord God! behold, thou hast made the heaven and the earth by thy great power and stretched out arm, and there is nothing too hard for thee:18 Thou shewest lovingkindness unto thousands, and recompensest the iniquity of the fathers into the bosom of their children after them:the Great, the Mighty God, the Lord of hosts, is his name, 19 Great in counsel, and mighty in work:for thine eyes are open upon all the ways of the sons of men:to give every one according to his ways, and according to the fruit of his doings:20 Which hast set signs and wonders in the land of Egypt, even unto this day, and in Israel, and among other men; and hast made thee a name, as at this day; 21 And hast brought forth thy people Israel out of the land of Egypt with signs, and with wonders, and with a strong hand, and with a stretched out arm, and with great terror; 22 And hast given them this land, which thou didst swear to their fathers to give them, a land flowing with milk and honey; 23 And they came in, and possessed it; but they obeyed not thy voice, neither walked in thy law; they have done nothing of all that thou commandedst them to do:therefore thou hast caused all this evil to come upon them:24 Behold the mounts, they are come unto the city to take it; and the city is given into the hand of the Chaldeans, that fight against it, because of the sword, and of the famine, and of the pestilence:and what thou hast spoken is come to pass; and, behold, thou seest it. 25 And thou hast said unto me, O Lord God, Buy thee the field for money, and take witnesses; for the city is given into the hand of the Chaldeans. 26 Then came the word of the Lord unto Jeremiah, saying, 27 Behold, I am the Lord, the God of all flesh:is there any thing too hard for me? 28 Therefore thus saith the Lord; Behold, I will give this city into the hand of the Chaldeans, and into the hand of Nebuchadrezzar king of Babylon, and he shall take it:29 And the Chaldeans, that fight against this city, shall come and set fire on this city, and burn it with the houses, upon whose roofs they have offered incense unto Baal, and poured out drink offerings unto other gods, to provoke me to anger. 30 For the children of Israel and the children of Judah have only done evil before me from their youth:for the children of Israel have only provoked me to anger with the work of their hands, saith the Lord. 31 For this city hath been to me as a provocation of mine anger and of my fury from the day that they built it even unto this day; that I should remove it from before my face, 32 Because of all the evil of the children of Israel and of the children of Judah, which they have done to provoke me to anger, they, their kings, their princes, their priests, and their prophets, and the men of Judah, and the inhabitants of Jerusalem. 33 And they have turned unto me the back, and not the face:though I taught them, rising up early and teaching them, yet they have not hearkened to receive instruction. 34 But they set their abominations in the house, which is called by my name, to defile it. 35 And they built the high places of Baal, which are in the valley of the son of Hinnom, to cause their sons and their daughters to pass through the fire unto Molech; which I commanded them not, neither came it into my mind, that they should do this abomination, to cause Judah to sin. 36 And now therefore thus saith the Lord, the God of Israel, concerning this city, whereof ye say, It shall be delivered into the hand of the king of Babylon by the sword, and by the famine, and by the pestilence; 37 Behold, I will gather them out of all countries, whither I have driven them in mine anger, and in my fury, and in great wrath; and I will bring them again unto this place, and I will cause them to dwell safely:38 And they shall be my people, and I will be their God:39 And I will give them one heart, and one way, that they may fear me for ever, for the good of them, and of their children after them:40 And I will make an everlasting covenant with them, that I will not turn away from them, to do them good; but I will put my fear in their hearts, that they shall not depart from me. 41 Yea, I will rejoice over them to do them good, and I will plant them in this land assuredly with my whole heart and with my whole soul. 42 For thus saith the Lord; Like as I have brought all this great evil upon this people, so will I bring upon them all the good that I have promised them. 43 And fields shall be bought in this land, whereof ye say, It is desolate without man or beast; it is given into the hand of the Chaldeans. 44 Men shall buy fields for money, and subscribe evidences, and seal them, and take witnesses in the land of

Benjamin, and in the places about Jerusalem, and in the cities of
Judah, and in the cities of the mountains, and in the cities of the
valley, and in the cities of the south:for I will cause their captivity to
return, saith the Lord.

Lamentations 1

1 How doth the city sit solitary, that was full of people!
how is she become as a widow! she that was great among the nations,
and princess among the provinces, how is she become tributary!
2 She weepeth sore in the night, and her tears are on her cheeks:
among all her lovers she hath none to comfort her:
all her friends have dealt treacherously with her, they are become her
enemies. 3 Judah is gone into captivity because of affliction, and
because of great servitude: she dwelleth among the heathen, she
findeth no rest: all her persecutors overtook her between the straits.
4 The ways of Zion do mourn, because none come to the solemn
feasts: all her gates are desolate:her priests sigh, her virgins are
afflicted, and she is in bitterness. **5 Her adversaries are the chief,
her enemies prosper; for the Lord hath afflicted her for the
multitude of her transgressions: her children are gone into
captivity before the enemy.** 6 And from the daughter of Zion all her
beauty is departed:
her princes are become like harts that find no pasture, and they are
gone without strength before the pursuer. 7 Jerusalem remembered in
the days of her affliction and of her miseries all her pleasant things
that she had in the days of old, when her people fell into the hand of
the enemy, and none did help her: the adversaries saw her, and did
mock at her sabbaths. 8 Jerusalem hath grievously sinned; therefore
she is removed: all that honoured her despise her, because they have
seen her nakedness: yea, she sigheth, and turneth backward.
9 Her filthiness is in her skirts; she remembereth not her last end;
therefore she came down wonderfully:she had no comforter.
O Lord, behold my affliction:for the enemy hath magnified himself.
10 The adversary hath spread out his hand upon all her pleasant
things: for she hath seen that the heathen entered into her sanctuary,
whom thou didst command that they should not enter into thy
congregation. 11 All her people sigh, they seek bread; they have given
their pleasant things for meat to relieve the soul: see, O Lord, and

consider; for I am become vile. 12 Is it nothing to you, all ye that pass by? behold, and see if there be any sorrow like unto my sorrow, which is done unto me, wherewith the Lord hath afflicted me in the day of his fierce anger. 13 From above hath he sent fire into my bones, and it prevaileth against them: he hath spread a net for my feet, he hath turned me back: he hath made me desolate and faint all the day. 14 The yoke of my transgressions is bound by his hand: they are wreathed, and come up upon my neck:he hath made my strength to fall, the Lord hath delivered me into their hands, from whom I am not able to rise up. 15 The Lord hath trodden under foot all my mighty men in the midst of me: he hath called an assembly against me to crush my young men: the Lord hath trodden the virgin, the daughter of Judah, as in a winepress. 16 For these things I weep; mine eye, mine eye runneth down with water, because the comforter that should relieve my soul is far from me: my children are desolate, because the enemy prevailed. 17 Zion spreadeth forth her hands, and there is none to comfort her: the Lord hath commanded concerning Jacob, that his adversaries should be round about him: Jerusalem is as a menstruous woman among them. 18 The Lord is righteous; for I have rebelled against his commandment: hear, I pray you, all people, and behold my sorrow: my virgins and my young men are gone into captivity. 19 I called for my lovers, but they deceived me: my priests and mine elders gave up the ghost in the city, while they sought their meat to relieve their souls. 20 Behold, O Lord; for I am in distress:my bowels are troubled; mine heart is turned within me; for I have grievously rebelled: abroad the sword bereaveth, at home there is as death. 21 They have heard that I sigh:there is none to comfort me: all mine

Ezekiel 16

1 Again the word of the Lord came unto me, saying, 2 Son of man, cause Jerusalem to know her abominations, 3 And say, Thus saith the Lord God unto Jerusalem; Thy birth and thy nativity is of the land of Canaan; thy father was an Amorite, and thy mother an Hittite. 4 And as for thy nativity, in the day thou wast born thy navel was not cut, neither wast thou washed in water to supple thee; thou wast not salted at all, nor swaddled at all. 5 None eye pitied thee, to do any of these

unto thee, to have compassion upon thee; but thou wast cast out in the open field, to the lothing of thy person, in the day that thou wast born. 6 And when I passed by thee, and saw thee polluted in thine own blood, I said unto thee when thou wast in thy blood, Live; yea, I said unto thee when thou wast in thy blood, Live. 7 I have caused thee to multiply as the bud of the field, and thou hast increased and waxen great, and thou art come to excellent ornaments:thy breasts are fashioned, and thine hair is grown, whereas thou wast naked and bare. 8 Now when I passed by thee, and looked upon thee, behold, thy time was the time of love; and I spread my skirt over thee, and covered thy nakedness:yea, I sware unto thee, and entered into a covenant with thee, saith the Lord God, and thou becamest mine. 9 Then washed I thee with water; yea, I throughly washed away thy blood from thee, and I anointed thee with oil. 10 I clothed thee also with broidered work, and shod thee with badgers 'skin, and I girded thee about with fine linen, and I covered thee with silk. 11 I decked thee also with ornaments, and I put bracelets upon thy hands, and a chain on thy neck. 12 And I put a jewel on thy forehead, and earrings in thine ears, and a beautiful crown upon thine head. **13 Thus wast thou decked with gold and silver; and thy raiment was of fine linen, and silk, and broidered work; thou didst eat fine flour, and honey, and oil:and thou wast exceeding beautiful, and thou didst prosper into a kingdom.** 14 And thy renown went forth among the heathen for thy beauty:for it was perfect through my comeliness, which I had put upon thee, saith the Lord God.

15 But thou didst trust in thine own beauty, and playedst the harlot because of thy renown, and pouredst out thy fornications on every one that passed by; his it was. 16 And of thy garments thou didst take, and deckedst thy high places with divers colours, and playedst the harlot thereupon:the like things shall not come, neither shall it be so. 17 Thou hast also taken thy fair jewels of my gold and of my silver, which I had given thee, and madest to thyself images of men, and didst commit whoredom with them, 18 And tookest thy broidered garments, and coveredst them:and thou hast set mine oil and mine

incense before them. 19 My meat also which I gave thee, fine flour, and oil, and honey, wherewith I fed thee, thou hast even set it before them for a sweet savour:and thus it was, saith the Lord God. 20 Moreover thou hast taken thy sons and thy daughters, whom thou hast borne unto me, and these hast thou sacrificed unto them to be devoured. Is this of thy whoredoms a small matter, 21 That thou hast slain my children, and delivered them to cause them to pass through the fire for them? 22 And in all thine abominations and thy whoredoms thou hast not remembered the days of thy youth, when thou wast naked and bare, and wast polluted in thy blood. 23 And it came to pass after all thy wickedness, (woe, woe unto thee! saith the Lord God;) 24 That thou hast also built unto thee an eminent place, and hast made thee an high place in every street. 25 Thou hast built thy high place at every head of the way, and hast made thy beauty to be abhorred, and hast opened thy feet to every one that passed by, and multiplied thy whoredoms. 26 Thou hast also committed fornication with the Egyptians thy neighbours, great of flesh; and hast increased thy whoredoms, to provoke me to anger. 27 Behold, therefore I have stretched out my hand over thee, and have diminished thine ordinary food, and delivered thee unto the will of them that hate thee, the daughters of the Philistines, which are ashamed of thy lewd way. 28 Thou hast played the whore also with the Assyrians, because thou wast unsatiable; yea, thou hast played the harlot with them, and yet couldest not be satisfied. 29 Thou hast moreover multiplied thy fornication in the land of Canaan unto Chaldea; and yet thou wast not satisfied herewith. 30 How weak is thine heart, saith the Lord God, seeing thou doest all these things, the work of an imperious whorish woman; 31 In that thou buildest thine eminent place in the head of every way, and makest thine high place in every street; and hast not been as an harlot, in that thou scornest hire; 32 But as a wife that committeth adultery, which taketh strangers instead of her husband! 33 They give gifts to all whores:but thou givest thy gifts to all thy lovers, and hirest them, that they may come unto thee on every side for thy whoredom. 34 And the contrary is in thee from other women in thy whoredoms, whereas none followeth thee to commit whoredoms:and in that thou givest a reward, and no reward is given unto thee, therefore thou art contrary.

35 Wherefore, O harlot, hear the word of the Lord:36 Thus saith the Lord God; Because thy filthiness was poured out, and thy nakedness discovered through thy whoredoms with thy lovers, and with all the idols of thy abominations, and by the blood of thy children, which thou didst give unto them; 37 Behold, therefore I will gather all thy lovers, with whom thou hast taken pleasure, and all them that thou hast loved, with all them that thou hast hated; I will even gather them round about against thee, and will discover thy nakedness unto them, that they may see all thy nakedness. 38 And I will judge thee, as women that break wedlock and shed blood are judged; and I will give thee blood in fury and jealousy. 39 And I will also give thee into their hand, and they shall throw down thine eminent place, and shall break down thy high places:they shall strip thee also of thy clothes, and shall take thy fair jewels, and leave thee naked and bare. 40 They shall also bring up a company against thee, and they shall stone thee with stones, and thrust thee through with their swords. 41 And they shall burn thine houses with fire, and execute judgments upon thee in the sight of many women:and I will cause thee to cease from playing the harlot, and thou also shalt give no hire any more. 42 So will I make my fury toward thee to rest, and my jealousy shall depart from thee, and I will be quiet, and will be no more angry. 43 Because thou hast not remembered the days of thy youth, but hast fretted me in all these things; behold, therefore I also will recompense thy way upon thine head, saith the Lord God:and thou shalt not commit this lewdness above all thine abominations.

44 Behold, every one that useth proverbs shall use this proverb against thee, saying, As is the mother, so is her daughter. 45 Thou art thy mother's daughter, that lotheth her husband and her children; and thou art the sister of thy sisters, which lothed their husbands and their children:your mother was an Hittite, and your father an Amorite. 46 And thine elder sister is Samaria, she and her daughters that dwell at

thy left hand:and thy younger sister, that dwelleth at thy right hand, is Sodom and her daughters. 47 Yet hast thou not walked after their ways, nor done after their abominations:but, as if that were a very little thing, thou wast corrupted more than they in all thy ways. 48 As I live, saith the Lord God, Sodom thy sister hath not done, she nor her daughters, as thou hast done, thou and thy daughters. 49 Behold, this was the iniquity of thy sister Sodom, pride, fulness of bread, and abundance of idleness was in her and in her daughters, neither did she strengthen the hand of the poor and needy. 50 And they were haughty, and committed abomination before me:therefore I took them away as I saw good. 51 Neither hath Samaria committed half of thy sins; but thou hast multiplied thine abominations more than they, and hast justified thy sisters in all thine abominations which thou hast done. 52 Thou also, which hast judged thy sisters, bear thine own shame for thy sins that thou hast committed more abominable than they:they are more righteous than thou:yea, be thou confounded also, and bear thy shame, in that thou hast justified thy sisters. 53 When I shall bring again their captivity, the captivity of Sodom and her daughters, and the captivity of Samaria and her daughters, then will I bring again the captivity of thy captives in the midst of them:54 That thou mayest bear thine own shame, and mayest be confounded in all that thou hast done, in that thou art a comfort unto them. 55 When thy sisters, Sodom and her daughters, shall return to their former estate, and Samaria and her daughters shall return to their former estate, then thou and thy daughters shall return to your former estate. 56 For thy sister Sodom was not mentioned by thy mouth in the day of thy pride, 57 Before thy wickedness was discovered, as at the time of thy reproach of the daughters of Syria, and all that are round about her, the daughters of the Philistines, which despise thee round about. 58 Thou hast borne thy lewdness and thine abominations, saith the Lord. 59 For thus saith the Lord God; I will even deal with thee as thou hast done, which hast despised the oath in breaking the covenant.
60 Nevertheless I will remember my covenant with thee in the days of thy youth, and I will establish unto thee an everlasting covenant. 61

Then thou shalt remember thy ways, and be ashamed, when thou shalt receive thy sisters, thine elder and thy younger:and I will give them unto thee for daughters, but not by thy covenant. 62 And I will establish my covenant with thee; and thou shalt know that I am the Lord:63 That thou mayest remember, and be confounded, and never open thy mouth any more because of thy shame, when I am pacified toward thee for all that thou hast done, saith the Lord God.

Ezekiel 17
1 And the word of the Lord came unto me, saying, 2 Son of man, put forth a riddle, and speak a parable unto the house of Israel; 3 And say, Thus saith the Lord God; A great eagle with great wings, longwinged, full of feathers, which had divers colours, came unto Lebanon, and took the highest branch of the cedar:4 He cropped off the top of his young twigs, and carried it into a land of traffick; he set it in a city of merchants. 5 He took also of the seed of the land, and planted it in a fruitful field; he placed it by great waters, and set it as a willow tree. 6 And it grew, and became a spreading vine of low stature, whose branches turned toward him, and the roots thereof were under him:so it became a vine, and brought forth branches, and shot forth sprigs. 7 There was also another great eagle with great wings and many feathers:and, behold, this vine did bend her roots toward him, and shot forth her branches toward him, that he might water it by the furrows of her plantation. 8 It was planted in a good soil by great waters, that it might bring forth branches, and that it might bear fruit, that it might be a goodly vine. **9 Say thou, Thus saith the Lord God; Shall it prosper? shall he not pull up the roots thereof, and cut off the fruit thereof, that it wither? it shall wither in all the leaves of her spring, even without great power or many people to pluck it up by the roots thereof. 10 Yea, behold, being planted, shall it prosper? shall it not utterly wither, when the east wind toucheth it? it shall wither in the furrows where it grew.**
11 Moreover the word of the Lord came unto me, saying, 12 Say now to the rebellious house, Know ye not what these things mean? tell

them, Behold, the king of Babylon is come to Jerusalem, and hath taken the king thereof, and the princes thereof, and led them with him to Babylon; 13 And hath taken of the king's seed, and made a covenant with him, and hath taken an oath of him:he hath also taken the mighty of the land:14 That the kingdom might be base, that it might not lift itself up, but that by keeping of his covenant it might stand. **15 But he rebelled against him in sending his ambassadors into Egypt, that they might give him horses and much people. Shall he prosper? shall he escape that doeth such things? or shall he break the covenant, and be delivered?** 16 As I live, saith the Lord God, surely in the place where the king dwelleth that made him king, whose oath he despised, and whose covenant he brake, even with him in the midst of Babylon he shall die. 17 Neither shall Pharaoh with his mighty army and great company make for him in the war, by casting up mounts, and building forts, to cut off many persons:18 Seeing he despised the oath by breaking the covenant, when, lo, he had given his hand, and hath done all these things, he shall not escape. 19 Therefore thus saith the Lord God; As I live, surely mine oath that he hath despised, and my covenant that he hath broken, even it will I recompense upon his own head. 20 And I will spread my net upon him, and he shall be taken in my snare, and I will bring him to Babylon, and will plead with him there for his trespass that he hath trespassed against me. 21 And all his fugitives with all his bands shall fall by the sword, and they that remain shall be scattered toward all winds:and ye shall know that I the Lord have spoken it. 22 Thus saith the Lord God; I will also take of the highest branch of the high cedar, and will set it; I will crop off from the top of his young twigs a tender one, and will plant it upon an high mountain and eminent:23 In the mountain of the height of Israel will I plant it:and it shall bring forth boughs, and bear fruit, and be a goodly cedar:and under it shall dwell all fowl of every wing; in the shadow of the branches thereof shall they dwell. 24 And all the trees of the field shall know that I the Lord have brought down the high tree, have exalted the low tree, have dried up the green tree, and have made the dry tree to flourish:I the Lord have spoken and have done it.

Daniel 8

1 In the third year of the reign of king Belshazzar a vision appeared unto me, even unto me Daniel, after that which appeared unto me at the first. 2 And I saw in a vision; and it came to pass, when I saw, that I was at Shushan in the palace, which is in the province of Elam; and I saw in a vision, and I was by the river of Ulai. 3 Then I lifted up mine eyes, and saw, and, behold, there stood before the river a ram which had two horns:and the two horns were high; but one was higher than the other, and the higher came up last. 4 I saw the ram pushing westward, and northward, and southward; so that no beasts might stand before him, neither was there any that could deliver out of his hand; but he did according to his will, and became great. 5 And as I was considering, behold, an he goat came from the west on the face of the whole earth, and touched not the ground:and the goat had a notable horn between his eyes. 6 And he came to the ram that had two horns, which I had seen standing before the river, and ran unto him in the fury of his power. 7 And I saw him come close unto the ram, and he was moved with choler against him, and smote the ram, and brake his two horns:and there was no power in the ram to stand before him, but he cast him down to the ground, and stamped upon him:and there was none that could deliver the ram out of his hand. 8 Therefore the he goat waxed very great:and when he was strong, the great horn was broken; and for it came up four notable ones toward the four winds of heaven. 9 And out of one of them came forth a little horn, which waxed exceeding great, toward the south, and toward the east, and toward the pleasant land. 10 And it waxed great, even to the host of heaven; and it cast down some of the host and of the stars to the ground, and stamped upon them. 11 Yea, he magnified himself even to the prince of the host, and by him the daily sacrifice was taken away, and the place of his sanctuary was cast down. 12 And an host was given him against the daily sacrifice by reason of transgression, and it cast down the truth to the ground; and it practised, and

prospered.

13 Then I heard one saint speaking, and another saint said unto that certain saint which spake, How long shall be the vision concerning the daily sacrifice, and the transgression of desolation, to give both the sanctuary and the host to be trodden under foot? 14 And he said unto me, Unto two thousand and three hundred days; then shall the sanctuary be cleansed.

15 And it came to pass, when I, even I Daniel, had seen the vision, and sought for the meaning, then, behold, there stood before me as the appearance of a man. 16 And I heard a man's voice between the banks of Ulai, which called, and said, Gabriel, make this man to understand the vision. 17 So he came near where I stood:and when he came, I was afraid, and fell upon my face:but he said unto me, Understand, O son of man:for at the time of the end shall be the vision. 18 Now as he was speaking with me, I was in a deep sleep on my face toward the ground:but he touched me, and set me upright. 19 And he said, Behold, I will make thee know what shall be in the last end of the indignation:for at the time appointed the end shall be. 20 The ram which thou sawest having two horns are the kings of Media and Persia. 21 And the rough goat is the king of Grecia:and the great horn that is between his eyes is the first king. 22 Now that being broken, whereas four stood up for it, four kingdoms shall stand up out of the nation, but not in his power. 23 And in the latter time of their kingdom, when the transgressors are come to the full, a king of fierce countenance, and understanding dark sentences, shall stand up. 24 And his power shall be mighty, but not by his own power:and he shall destroy wonderfully, and shall prosper, and practise, and shall destroy the mighty and the holy people. **25 And through his policy also he shall cause craft to prosper in his hand; and he shall magnify himself in his heart, and by peace shall destroy many:he shall also stand up against the Prince of princes; but he shall be broken without hand.** 26 And the vision of the evening and the morning which was told is true:wherefore shut thou up the vision; for it shall be for many days. 27 And I Daniel fainted, and was sick certain days;

afterward I rose up, and did the king's business; and I was astonished at the vision, but none understood it.

Daniel 11

1 Also I in the first year of Darius the Mede, even I, stood to confirm and to strengthen him.

2 And now will I shew thee the truth. Behold, there shall stand up yet three kings in Persia; and the fourth shall be far richer than they all:and by his strength through his riches he shall stir up all against the realm of Grecia. 3 And a mighty king shall stand up, that shall rule with great dominion, and do according to his will. 4 And when he shall stand up, his kingdom shall be broken, and shall be divided toward the four winds of heaven; and not to his posterity, nor according to his dominion which he ruled:for his kingdom shall be plucked up, even for others beside those.

5 And the king of the south shall be strong, and one of his princes; and he shall be strong above him, and have dominion; his dominion shall be a great dominion. 6 And in the end of years they shall join themselves together; for the king's daughter of the south shall come to the king of the north to make an agreement:but she shall not retain the power of the arm; neither shall he stand, nor his arm:but she shall be given up, and they that brought her, and he that begat her, and he that strengthened her in these times. 7 But out of a branch of her roots shall one stand up in his estate, which shall come with an army, and shall enter into the fortress of the king of the north, and shall deal against them, and shall prevail:8 And shall also carry captives into Egypt their gods, with their princes, and with their precious vessels of silver and of gold; and he shall continue more years than the king of the north. 9 So the king of the south shall come into his kingdom, and shall return into his own land. 10 But his sons shall be stirred up, and shall assemble a multitude of great forces:and one shall certainly come, and overflow, and pass through:then shall he return, and be stirred up, even to his fortress. 11 And the king of the south shall be

moved with choler, and shall come forth and fight with him, even with the king of the north:and he shall set forth a great multitude; but the multitude shall be given into his hand. 12 And when he hath taken away the multitude, his heart shall be lifted up; and he shall cast down many ten thousands:but he shall not be strengthened by it. 13 For the king of the north shall return, and shall set forth a multitude greater than the former, and shall certainly come after certain years with a great army and with much riches. 14 And in those times there shall many stand up against the king of the south:also the robbers of thy people shall exalt themselves to establish the vision; but they shall fall. 15 So the king of the north shall come, and cast up a mount, and take the most fenced cities:and the arms of the south shall not withstand, neither his chosen people, neither shall there be any strength to withstand. 16 But he that cometh against him shall do according to his own will, and none shall stand before him:and he shall stand in the glorious land, which by his hand shall be consumed. 17 He shall also set his face to enter with the strength of his whole kingdom, and upright ones with him; thus shall he do:and he shall give him the daughter of women, corrupting her:but she shall not stand on his side, neither be for him. 18 After this shall he turn his face unto the isles, and shall take many:but a prince for his own behalf shall cause the reproach offered by him to cease; without his own reproach he shall cause it to turn upon him. 19 Then he shall turn his face toward the fort of his own land:but he shall stumble and fall, and not be found. 20 Then shall stand up in his estate a raiser of taxes in the glory of the kingdom:but within few days he shall be destroyed, neither in anger, nor in battle. 21 And in his estate shall stand up a vile person, to whom they shall not give the honour of the kingdom:but he shall come in peaceably, and obtain the kingdom by flatteries. 22 And with the arms of a flood shall they be overflown from before him, and shall be broken; yea, also the prince of the covenant. 23 And after the league made with him he shall work deceitfully:for he shall come up, and shall become strong with a small people. 24 He shall enter peaceably even upon the fattest places of the province; and he shall do that which his fathers have not done, nor his fathers 'fathers; he shall scatter among them the prey, and spoil, and riches:yea, and he shall forecast his devices against the strong holds, even for a time. 25 And he shall stir up his power and his courage against the king of the south with a great army; and the king of the south shall be stirred up to battle with a very great and mighty army; but he shall not stand:for they shall forecast devices against him. 26 Yea, they that feed of the portion of his meat shall destroy him, and his army shall overflow:and many shall fall down slain. **27 And both these kings' hearts shall be to do mischief, and they shall speak lies at one table; but it shall not prosper:for yet the end shall be at the time appointed.** 28 Then shall he return into his land with great riches; and his heart shall be against the holy covenant; and he shall do exploits, and return to his own land. 29 At the time appointed he shall return, and come toward the south; but it shall not be as the former, or as the latter.

30 For the ships of Chittim shall come against him:therefore he shall be grieved, and return, and have indignation against the holy covenant:so shall he do; he shall even return, and have intelligence with them that forsake the holy covenant. 31 And arms shall stand on his part, and they shall pollute the sanctuary of strength, and shall take away the daily sacrifice, and they shall place the abomination that maketh desolate. 32 And such as do wickedly against the covenant shall he corrupt by flatteries:but the people that do know their God shall be strong, and do exploits. 33 And they that understand among the people shall instruct many:yet they shall fall by the sword, and by flame, by captivity, and by spoil, many days. 34 Now when they shall fall, they shall be holpen with a little help:but many shall cleave to them with flatteries. 35 And some of them of understanding shall fall, to try them, and to purge, and to make them white, even to the time of the end:because it is yet for a time appointed. **36 And the king shall do according to his will; and he shall exalt himself, and magnify himself above every god, and shall speak marvellous things against the God of gods, and shall prosper till the indignation be**

accomplished:for that that is determined shall be done. 37 Neither shall he regard the God of his fathers, nor the desire of women, nor regard any god:for he shall magnify himself above all. 38 But in his estate shall he honour the God of forces:and a god whom his fathers knew not shall he honour with gold, and silver, and with precious stones, and pleasant things. 39 Thus shall he do in the most strong holds with a strange god, whom he shall acknowledge and increase with glory:and he shall cause them to rule over many, and shall divide the land for gain. 40 And at the time of the end shall the king of the south push at him:and the king of the north shall come against him like a whirlwind, with chariots, and with horsemen, and with many ships; and he shall enter into the countries, and shall overflow and pass over. 41 He shall enter also into the glorious land, and many countries shall be overthrown:but these shall escape out of his hand, even Edom, and Moab, and the chief of the children of Ammon. 42 He shall stretch forth his hand also upon the countries:and the land of Egypt shall not escape. 43 But he shall have power over the treasures of gold and of silver, and over all the precious things of Egypt:and the Libyans and the Ethiopians shall be at his steps. 44 But tidings out of the east and out of the north shall trouble him:therefore he shall go forth with great fury to destroy, and utterly to make away many. 45 And he shall plant the tabernacles of his palace between the seas in the glorious holy mountain; yet he shall come to his end, and none shall help him.

3 John

1 The elder unto the wellbeloved Gaius, whom I love in the truth. **2 Beloved, I wish above all things that thou mayest prosper and be in health, even as thy soul prospereth.** 3 For I rejoiced greatly, when the brethren came and testified of the truth that is in thee, even as thou walkest in the truth. 4 I have no greater joy than to hear that my children walk in truth. 5 Beloved, thou doest faithfully whatsoever

thou doest to the brethren, and to strangers; 6 Which have borne witness of thy charity before the church:whom if thou bring forward on their journey after a godly sort, thou shalt do well:7 Because that for his name's sake they went forth, taking nothing of the Gentiles. 8 We therefore ought to receive such, that we might be fellowhelpers to the truth. 9 I wrote unto the church:but Diotrephes, who loveth to have the preeminence among them, receiveth us not. 10 Wherefore, if I come, I will remember his deeds which he doeth, prating against us with malicious words:and not content therewith, neither doth he himself receive the brethren, and forbiddeth them that would, and casteth them out of the church. 11 Beloved, follow not that which is evil, but that which is good. He that doeth good is of God:but he that doeth evil hath not seen God.12 Demetrius hath good report of all men, and of the truth itself:yea, and we also bear record; and ye know that our record is true.13 I had many things to write, but I will not with ink and pen write unto thee:14 But I trust I shall shortly see thee, and we shall speak face to face. Peace be to thee. Our friends salute thee. Greet the friends by name.

Wisdom Keys – Faith is a Spirit

Chapter 4

Chapters on Prospereth

PROSPERETH

Ezra 5

1 Then the prophets, Haggai the prophet, and Zechariah the son of Iddo, prophesied unto the Jews that were in Judah and Jerusalem in the name of the God of Israel, even unto them. 2 Then rose up Zerubbabel the son of Shealtiel, and Jeshua the son of Jozadak, and began to build the house of God which is at Jerusalem:and with them were the prophets of God helping them.

3 At the same time came to them Tatnai, governor on this side the river, and Shetharboznai, and their companions, and said thus unto them, Who hath commanded you to build this house, and to make up this wall? 4 Then said we unto them after this manner, What are the names of the men that make this building? 5 But the eye of their God was upon the elders of the Jews, that they could not cause them to cease, till the matter came to Darius:and then they returned answer by letter concerning this matter.

6 The copy of the letter that Tatnai, governor on this side the river, and Shetharboznai, and his companions the Apharsachites, which were on this side the river, sent unto Darius the king:7 They sent a letter unto him, wherein was written thus; Unto Darius the king, all peace. **8 Be it known unto the king, that we went into the province of Judea, to the house of the great God, which is builded with great stones, and timber is laid in the walls, and this work goeth fast on, and prospereth in their hands.** 9 Then asked we those elders, and said unto them thus, Who commanded you to build this

house, and to make up these walls? 10 We asked their names also, to certify thee, that we might write the names of the men that were the chief of them. 11 And thus they returned us answer, saying, We are the servants of the God of heaven and earth, and build the house that was builded these many years ago, which a great king of Israel builded and set up. 12 But after that our fathers had provoked the God of heaven unto wrath, he gave them into the hand of Nebuchadnezzar the king of Babylon, the Chaldean, who destroyed this house, and carried the people away into Babylon. 13 But in the first year of Cyrus the king of Babylon the same king Cyrus made a decree to build this house of God. 14 And the vessels also of gold and silver of the house of God, which Nebuchadnezzar took out of the temple that was in Jerusalem, and brought them into the temple of Babylon, those did Cyrus the king take out of the temple of Babylon, and they were delivered unto one, whose name was Sheshbazzar, whom he had made governor; 15 And said unto him, Take these vessels, go, carry them into the temple that is in Jerusalem, and let the house of God be builded in his place. 16 Then came the same Sheshbazzar, and laid the foundation of the house of God which is in Jerusalem:and since that time even until now hath it been in building, and yet it is not finished. 17 Now therefore, if it seem good to the king, let there be search made in the king's treasure house, which is there at Babylon, whether it be so, that a decree was made of Cyrus the king to build this house of God at Jerusalem, and let the king send his pleasure to us concerning this matter.

Psalms 37.

1 Fret not thyself because of evildoers,
neither be thou envious against the workers of iniquity.
2 For they shall soon be cut down like the grass,
and wither as the green herb.
3 Trust in the Lord, and do good;
so shalt thou dwell in the land, and verily thou shalt be fed.

4 Delight thyself also in the Lord;
and he shall give thee the desires of thine heart.
5 Commit thy way unto the Lord;
trust also in him; and he shall bring it to pass.
6 And he shall bring forth thy righteousness as the light,
and thy judgment as the noonday.
7 Rest in the Lord, and wait patiently for him:
fret not thyself because of him who prospereth in his way,
because of the man who bringeth wicked devices to pass.
8 Cease from anger, and forsake wrath:
fret not thyself in any wise to do evil.
9 For evildoers shall be cut off:
but those that wait upon the Lord, they shall inherit the earth.
10 For yet a little while, and the wicked shall not be:
yea, thou shalt diligently consider his place, and it shall not be.
11 But the meek shall inherit the earth;
and shall delight themselves in the abundance of peace.
12 The wicked plotteth against the just,
and gnasheth upon him with his teeth.
13 The Lord shall laugh at him:
for he seeth that his day is coming.
14 The wicked have drawn out the sword, and have bent their bow,
to cast down the poor and needy,
and to slay such as be of upright conversation.
15 Their sword shall enter into their own heart,
and their bows shall be broken.
16 A little that a righteous man hath
is better than the riches of many wicked.
17 For the arms of the wicked shall be broken:
but the Lord upholdeth the righteous.
18 The Lord knoweth the days of the upright:
and their inheritance shall be for ever.
19 They shall not be ashamed in the evil time:
and in the days of famine they shall be satisfied.

20 But the wicked shall perish,
and the enemies of the Lord shall be as the fat of lambs:
they shall consume; into smoke shall they consume away.
21 The wicked borroweth, and payeth not again:
but the righteous sheweth mercy, and giveth.
22 For such as be blessed of him shall inherit the earth;
and they that be cursed of him shall be cut off.
23 The steps of a good man are ordered by the Lord:
and he delighteth in his way.
24 Though he fall, he shall not be utterly cast down:
for the Lord upholdeth him with his hand.
25 I have been young, and now am old;
yet have I not seen the righteous forsaken,
nor his seed begging bread.
26 He is ever merciful, and lendeth;
and his seed is blessed.
27 Depart from evil, and do good;
and dwell for evermore.
28 For the Lord loveth judgment,
and forsaketh not his saints;
they are preserved for ever:
but the seed of the wicked shall be cut off.
29 The righteous shall inherit the land,
and dwell therein for ever.
30 The mouth of the righteous speaketh wisdom,
and his tongue talketh of judgment.
31 The law of his God is in his heart;
none of his steps shall slide.
32 The wicked watcheth the righteous,
and seeketh to slay him.
33 The Lord will not leave him in his hand,
nor condemn him when he is judged.
34 Wait on the Lord, and keep his way,
and he shall exalt thee to inherit the land:

when the wicked are cut off, thou shalt see it.

35 I have seen the wicked in great power,

and spreading himself like a green bay tree.

36 Yet he passed away, and, lo, he was not:

yea, I sought him, but he could not be found.

37 Mark the perfect man, and behold the upright:

for the end of that man is peace.

38 But the transgressors shall be destroyed together:

the end of the wicked shall be cut off.

39 But the salvation of the righteous is of the Lord:

he is their strength in the time of trouble.

40 And the Lord shall help them,

and deliver them:he shall deliver them from the wicked,

and save them, because they trust in him.

Proverbs 17

1 Better is a dry morsel, and quietness therewith,

than an house full of sacrifices with strife.

2 A wise servant shall have rule over a son that causeth shame,

and shall have part of the inheritance among the brethren.

3 The fining pot is for silver, and the furnace for gold:

but the Lord trieth the hearts.

4 A wicked doer giveth heed to false lips;

and a liar giveth ear to a naughty tongue.

5 Whoso mocketh the poor reproacheth his Maker:

and he that is glad at calamities shall not be unpunished.

6 Children's children are the crown of old men;

and the glory of children are their fathers.

7 Excellent speech becometh not a fool:

much less do lying lips a prince.

8 A gift is as a precious stone in the eyes of him that hath it:

whithersoever it turneth, it prospereth.

9 He that covereth a transgression seeketh love;

but he that repeateth a matter separateth very friends.

10 A reproof entereth more into a wise man
than an hundred stripes into a fool.

11 An evil man seeketh only rebellion:
therefore a cruel messenger shall be sent against him.

12 Let a bear robbed of her whelps meet a man,
rather than a fool in his folly.

13 Whoso rewardeth evil for good,
evil shall not depart from his house.

14 The beginning of strife is as when one letteth out water:
therefore leave off contention, before it be meddled with.

15 He that justifieth the wicked, and he that condemneth the just,
even they both are abomination to the Lord.

16 Wherefore is there a price in the hand of a fool
to get wisdom, seeing he hath no heart to it?

17 A friend loveth at all times,
and a brother is born for adversity.

18 A man void of understanding striketh hands,
and becometh surety in the presence of his friend.

19 He loveth transgression that loveth strife:
and he that exalteth his gate seeketh destruction.

20 He that hath a froward heart findeth no good:
and he that hath a perverse tongue falleth into mischief.

21 He that begetteth a fool doeth it to his sorrow:
and the father of a fool hath no joy.

22 A merry heart doeth good like a medicine:
but a broken spirit drieth the bones.

23 A wicked man taketh a gift out of the bosom
to pervert the ways of judgment.

24 Wisdom is before him that hath understanding;
but the eyes of a fool are in the ends of the earth.

25 A foolish son is a grief to his father,
and bitterness to her that bare him.

26 Also to punish the just is not good,

nor to strike princes for equity.

27 He that hath knowledge spareth his words:
and a man of understanding is of an excellent spirit.

28 Even a fool, when he holdeth his peace, is counted wise:
and he that shutteth his lips is esteemed a man of understanding.

3 John

1 The elder unto the well beloved Gaius, whom I love in the truth.
**2 Beloved, I wish above all things that thou mayest prosper and
be in health, even as thy soul prospereth.** 3 For I rejoiced greatly,
when the brethren came and testified of the truth that is in thee, even
as thou walkest in the truth. 4 I have no greater joy than to hear that
my children walk in truth.

5 Beloved, thou doest faithfully whatsoever thou doest to the
brethren, and to strangers; 6 Which have borne witness of thy charity
before the church:whom if thou bring forward on their journey after a
godly sort, thou shalt do well:7 Because that for his name's sake they
went forth, taking nothing of the Gentiles. 8 We therefore ought to
receive such, that we might be fellowhelpers to the truth.

9 I wrote unto the church:but Diotrephes, who loveth to have the
preeminence among them, receiveth us not. 10 Wherefore, if I come, I
will remember his deeds which he doeth, prating against us with
malicious words:and not content therewith, neither doth he himself
receive the brethren, and forbiddeth them that would, and casteth
them out of the church.

11 Beloved, follow not that which is evil, but that which is good. He
that doeth good is of God:but he that doeth evil hath not seen God.

12 Demetrius hath good report of all men, and of the truth itself:yea,
and we also bear record; and ye know that our record is true.

13 I had many things to write, but I will not with ink and pen write
unto thee:14 But I trust I shall shortly see thee, and we shall speak
face to face. Peace be to thee. Our friends salute thee. Greet the
friends by name.

Wisdom Keys – Christ Body is God Word

Chapters 5

Chapters on Prospered

PROSPERED

Genesis 24

1 And Abraham was old, and well stricken in age:and the Lord had blessed Abraham in all things. 2 And Abraham said unto his eldest servant of his house, that ruled over all that he had, Put, I pray thee, thy hand under my thigh:3 And I will make thee swear by the Lord, the God of heaven, and the God of the earth, that thou shalt not take a wife unto my son of the daughters of the Canaanites, among whom I dwell:4 But thou shalt go unto my country, and to my kindred, and take a wife unto my son Isaac. 5 And the servant said unto him, Peradventure the woman will not be willing to follow me unto this land:must I needs bring thy son again unto the land from whence thou camest? 6 And Abraham said unto him, Beware thou that thou bring not my son thither again.

7 The Lord God of heaven, which took me from my father's house, and from the land of my kindred, and which spake unto me, and that sware unto me, saying, Unto thy seed will I give this land; he shall send his angel before thee, and thou shalt take a wife unto my son from thence. 8 And if the woman will not be willing to follow thee, then thou shalt be clear from this my oath:only bring not my son thither again. 9 And the servant put his hand under the thigh of Abraham his master, and sware to him concerning that matter.

10 And the servant took ten camels of the camels of his master, and departed; for all the goods of his master were in his hand:and he

arose, and went to Mesopotamia, unto the city of Nahor. 11 And he made his camels to kneel down without the city by a well of water at the time of the evening, even the time that women go out to draw water. 12 And he said, O Lord God of my master Abraham, I pray thee, send me good speed this day, and shew kindness unto my master Abraham. 13 Behold, I stand here by the well of water; and the daughters of the men of the city come out to draw water:14 And let it come to pass, that the damsel to whom I shall say, Let down thy pitcher, I pray thee, that I may drink; and she shall say, Drink, and I will give thy camels drink also:let the same be she that thou hast appointed for thy servant Isaac; and thereby shall I know that thou hast shewed kindness unto my master.

15 And it came to pass, before he had done speaking, that, behold, Rebekah came out, who was born to Bethuel, son of Milcah, the wife of Nahor, Abraham's brother, with her pitcher upon her shoulder. 16 And the damsel was very fair to look upon, a virgin, neither had any man known her:and she went down to the well, and filled her pitcher, and came up. 17 And the servant ran to meet her, and said, Let me, I pray thee, drink a little water of thy pitcher. 18 And she said, Drink, my lord:and she hasted, and let down her pitcher upon her hand, and gave him drink. 19 And when she had done giving him drink, she said, I will draw water for thy camels also, until they have done drinking. 20 And she hasted, and emptied her pitcher into the trough, and ran again unto the well to draw water, and drew for all his camels. 21 And the man wondering at her held his peace, to wit whether the Lord had made his journey prosperous or not. 22 And it came to pass, as the camels had done drinking, that the man took a golden earring of half a shekel weight, and two bracelets for her hands of ten shekels weight of gold; 23 And said, Whose daughter art thou? tell me, I pray thee:is there room in thy father's house for us to lodge in? 24 And she said unto him, I am the daughter of Bethuel the son of Milcah, which she bare unto Nahor. 25 She said moreover unto him, We have both straw and provender enough, and room to lodge in. 26 And the man bowed down his head, and worshipped the Lord. 27 And he said,

Blessed be the Lord God of my master Abraham, who hath not left destitute my master of his mercy and his truth:I being in the way, the Lord led me to the house of my master's brethren. 28 And the damsel ran, and told them of her mother's house these things.

29 And Rebekah had a brother, and his name was Laban:and Laban ran out unto the man, unto the well. 30 And it came to pass, when he saw the earring and bracelets upon his sister's hands, and when he heard the words of Rebekah his sister, saying, Thus spake the man unto me; that he came unto the man; and, behold, he stood by the camels at the well. 31 And he said, Come in, thou blessed of the Lord; wherefore standest thou without? for I have prepared the house, and room for the camels.

32 And the man came into the house:and he ungirded his camels, and gave straw and provender for the camels, and water to wash his feet, and the men's feet that were with him. 33 And there was set meat before him to eat:but he said, I will not eat, until I have told mine errand. And he said, Speak on. 34 And he said, I am Abraham's servant. 35 And the Lord hath blessed my master greatly; and he is become great:and he hath given him flocks, and herds, and silver, and gold, and menservants, and maidservants, and camels, and asses. 36 And Sarah my master's wife bare a son to my master when she was old:and unto him hath he given all that he hath. 37 And my master made me swear, saying, Thou shalt not take a wife to my son of the daughters of the Canaanites, in whose land I dwell:38 But thou shalt go unto my father's house, and to my kindred, and take a wife unto my son. 39 And I said unto my master, Peradventure the woman will not follow me. 40 And he said unto me, The Lord, before whom I walk, will send his angel with thee, and prosper thy way; and thou shalt take a wife for my son of my kindred, and of my father's house:41 Then shalt thou be clear from this my oath, when thou comest to my kindred; and if they give not thee one, thou shalt be clear from my oath. 42 And I came this day unto the well, and said, O Lord God of my master Abraham, if now thou do prosper my way which I go:43 Behold, I stand by the well of water; and it shall come

to pass, that when the virgin cometh forth to draw water, and I say to her, Give me, I pray thee, a little water of thy pitcher to drink; 44 And she say to me, Both drink thou, and I will also draw for thy camels:let the same be the woman whom the Lord hath appointed out for my master's son. 45 And before I had done speaking in mine heart, behold, Rebekah came forth with her pitcher on her shoulder; and she went down unto the well, and drew water:and I said unto her, Let me drink, I pray thee. 46 And she made haste, and let down her pitcher from her shoulder, and said, Drink, and I will give thy camels drink also:so I drank, and she made the camels drink also. 47 And I asked her, and said, Whose daughter art thou? And she said, The daughter of Bethuel, Nahor's son, whom Milcah bare unto him:and I put the earring upon her face, and the bracelets upon her hands. 48 And I bowed down my head, and worshipped the Lord, and blessed the Lord God of my master Abraham, which had led me in the right way to take my master's brother's daughter unto his son. 49 And now if ye will deal kindly and truly with my master, tell me:and if not, tell me; that I may turn to the right hand, or to the left. 50 Then Laban and Bethuel answered and said, The thing proceedeth from the Lord:we cannot speak unto thee bad or good. 51 Behold, Rebekah is before thee, take her, and go, and let her be thy master's son's wife, as the Lord hath spoken. 52 And it came to pass, that, when Abraham's servant heard their words, he worshipped the Lord, bowing himself to the earth. 53 And the servant brought forth jewels of silver, and jewels of gold, and raiment, and gave them to Rebekah:he gave also to her brother and to her mother precious things. 54 And they did eat and drink, he and the men that were with him, and tarried all night; and they rose up in the morning, and he said, Send me away unto my master. 55 And her brother and her mother said, Let the damsel abide with us a few days, at the least ten; after that she shall go. **56 And he said unto them, Hinder me not, seeing the Lord hath prospered my way; send me away that I may go to my master.** 57 And they said, We will call the damsel, and enquire at her mouth. 58 And they called Rebekah, and said unto her, Wilt thou go with this man? And she said, I will go. 59 And they sent away Rebekah their sister, and her nurse, and Abraham's servant, and his men. 60 And they blessed Rebekah, and said unto her, Thou art our sister, be thou the mother of thousands of millions, and let thy seed possess the gate of those which hate them.

61 And Rebekah arose, and her damsels, and they rode upon the camels, and followed the man:and the servant took Rebekah, and went his way. 62 And Isaac came from the way of the well Lahairoi; for he dwelt in the south country. 63 And Isaac went out to meditate in the field at the eventide:and he lifted up his eyes, and saw, and, behold, the camels were coming. 64 And Rebekah lifted up her eyes, and when she saw Isaac, she lighted off the camel. 65 For she had said unto the servant, What man is this that walketh in the field to meet us? And the servant had said, It is my master:therefore she took a vail, and covered herself. 66 And the servant told Isaac all things that he had done. 67 And Isaac brought her into his mother Sarah's tent, and took Rebekah, and she became his wife; and he loved her:and Isaac was comforted after his mother's death.

Judges 4

1 And the children of Israel again did evil in the sight of the Lord, when Ehud was dead. 2 And the Lord sold them into the hand of Jabin king of Canaan, that reigned in Hazor; the captain of whose host was Sisera, which dwelt in Harosheth of the Gentiles. 3 And the children of Israel cried unto the Lord:for he had nine hundred chariots of iron; and twenty years he mightily oppressed the children of Israel.

4 And Deborah, a prophetess, the wife of Lapidoth, she judged Israel at that time. 5 And she dwelt under the palm tree of Deborah between Ramah and Bethel in mount Ephraim:and the children of Israel came up to her for judgment. 6 And she sent and called Barak the son of Abinoam out of Kedeshnaphtali, and said unto him, Hath not the Lord God of Israel commanded, saying, Go and draw toward mount Tabor, and take with thee ten thousand men of the children of Naphtali and

of the children of Zebulun? 7 And I will draw unto thee to the river Kishon Sisera, the captain of Jabin's army, with his chariots and his multitude; and I will deliver him into thine hand. 8 And Barak said unto her, If thou wilt go with me, then I will go:but if thou wilt not go with me, then I will not go. 9 And she said, I will surely go with thee:notwithstanding the journey that thou takest shall not be for thine honour; for the Lord shall sell Sisera into the hand of a woman. And Deborah arose, and went with Barak to Kedesh.

10 And Barak called Zebulun and Naphtali to Kedesh; and he went up with ten thousand men at his feet:and Deborah went up with him. 11 Now Heber the Kenite, which was of the children of Hobab the father in law of Moses, had severed himself from the Kenites, and pitched his tent unto the plain of Zaanaim, which is by Kedesh. 12 And they shewed Sisera that Barak the son of Abinoam was gone up to mount Tabor. 13 And Sisera gathered together all his chariots, even nine hundred chariots of iron, and all the people that were with him, from Harosheth of the Gentiles unto the river of Kishon. 14 And Deborah said unto Barak, Up; for this is the day in which the Lord hath delivered Sisera into thine hand:is not the Lord gone out before thee? So Barak went down from mount Tabor, and ten thousand men after him. 15 And the Lord discomfited Sisera, and all his chariots, and all his host, with the edge of the sword before Barak; so that Sisera lighted down off his chariot, and fled away on his feet. 16 But Barak pursued after the chariots, and after the host, unto Harosheth of the Gentiles:and all the host of Sisera fell upon the edge of the sword; and there was not a man left. 17 Howbeit Sisera fled away on his feet to the tent of Jael the wife of Heber the Kenite:for there was peace between Jabin the king of Hazor and the house of Heber the Kenite. 18 And Jael went out to meet Sisera, and said unto him, Turn in, my lord, turn in to me; fear not. And when he had turned in unto her into the tent, she covered him with a mantle. 19 And he said unto her, Give me, I pray thee, a little water to drink; for I am thirsty. And she opened a bottle of milk, and gave him drink, and covered him. 20 Again he said unto her, Stand in the door of the tent, and it shall be,

when any man doth come and enquire of thee, and say, Is there any man here? that thou shalt say, No. 21 Then Jael Heber's wife took a nail of the tent, and took an hammer in her hand, and went softly unto him, and smote the nail into his temples, and fastened it into the ground:for he was fast asleep and weary. So he died. 22 And, behold, as Barak pursued Sisera, Jael came out to meet him, and said unto him, Come, and I will shew thee the man whom thou seekest. And when he came into her tent, behold, Sisera lay dead, and the nail was in his temples. 23 So God subdued on that day Jabin the king of Canaan before the children of Israel. **24 And the hand of the children of Israel prospered, and prevailed against Jabin the king of Canaan, until they had destroyed Jabin king of Canaan.**

2 Samuel 11

1 And it came to pass, after the year was expired, at the time when kings go forth to battle, that David sent Joab, and his servants with him, and all Israel; and they destroyed the children of Ammon, and besieged Rabbah. But David tarried still at Jerusalem.
2 And it came to pass in an eveningtide, that David arose from off his bed, and walked upon the roof of the king's house:and from the roof he saw a woman washing herself; and the woman was very beautiful to look upon. 3 And David sent and enquired after the woman. And one said, Is not this Bathsheba, the daughter of Eliam, the wife of Uriah the Hittite? 4 And David sent messengers, and took her; and she came in unto him, and he lay with her; for she was purified from her uncleanness:and she returned unto her house. 5 And the woman conceived, and sent and told David, and said, I am with child.
6 And David sent to Joab, saying, Send me Uriah the Hittite. And Joab sent Uriah to David. **7 And when Uriah was come unto him, David demanded of him how Joab did, and how the people did, and how the war prospered.** 8 And David said to Uriah, Go down to thy house, and wash thy feet. And Uriah departed out of the king's house, and there followed him a mess of meat from the king. 9 But

Uriah slept at the door of the king's house with all the servants of his lord, and went not down to his house. 10 And when they had told David, saying, Uriah went not down unto his house, David said unto Uriah, Camest thou not from thy journey? why then didst thou not go down unto thine house? 11 And Uriah said unto David, The ark, and Israel, and Judah, abide in tents; and my lord Joab, and the servants of my lord, are encamped in the open fields; shall I then go into mine house, to eat and to drink, and to lie with my wife? as thou livest, and as thy soul liveth, I will not do this thing. 12 And David said to Uriah, Tarry here to day also, and to morrow I will let thee depart. So Uriah abode in Jerusalem that day, and the morrow. 13 And when David had called him, he did eat and drink before him; and he made him drunk:and at even he went out to lie on his bed with the servants of his lord, but went not down to his house.

14 And it came to pass in the morning, that David wrote a letter to Joab, and sent it by the hand of Uriah. 15 And he wrote in the letter, saying, Set ye Uriah in the forefront of the hottest battle, and retire ye from him, that he may be smitten, and die. 16 And it came to pass, when Joab observed the city, that he assigned Uriah unto a place where he knew that valiant men were. 17 And the men of the city went out, and fought with Joab:and there fell some of the people of the servants of David; and Uriah the Hittite died also.

18 Then Joab sent and told David all the things concerning the war; 19 And charged the messenger, saying, When thou hast made an end of telling the matters of the war unto the king, 20 And if so be that the king's wrath arise, and he say unto thee, Wherefore approached ye so nigh unto the city when ye did fight? knew ye not that they would shoot from the wall? 21 Who smote Abimelech the son of Jerubbesheth? did not a woman cast a piece of a millstone upon him from the wall, that he died in Thebez? why went ye nigh the wall? then say thou, Thy servant Uriah the Hittite is dead also.

22 So the messenger went, and came and shewed David all that Joab had sent him for. 23 And the messenger said unto David, Surely the men prevailed against us, and came out unto us into the field, and we

were upon them even unto the entering of the gate. 24 And the shooters shot from off the wall upon thy servants; and some of the king's servants be dead, and thy servant Uriah the Hittite is dead also. 25 Then David said unto the messenger, Thus shalt thou say unto Joab, Let not this thing displease thee, for the sword devoureth one as well as another:make thy battle more strong against the city, and overthrow it:and encourage thou him.

26 And when the wife of Uriah heard that Uriah her husband was dead, she mourned for her husband. 27 And when the mourning was past, David sent and fetched her to his house, and she became his wife, and bare him a son. But the thing that David had done displeased the Lord.

2 Kings 18

1 Now it came to pass in the third year of Hoshea son of Elah king of Israel, that Hezekiah the son of Ahaz king of Judah began to reign. 2 Twenty and five years old was he when he began to reign; and he reigned twenty and nine years in Jerusalem. His mother's name also was Abi, the daughter of Zachariah. 3 And he did that which was right in the sight of the Lord, according to all that David his father did. 4 He removed the high places, and brake the images, and cut down the groves, and brake in pieces the brasen serpent that Moses had made:for unto those days the children of Israel did burn incense to it:and he called it Nehushtan. 5 He trusted in the Lord God of Israel; so that after him was none like him among all the kings of Judah, nor any that were before him. 6 For he clave to the Lord, and departed not from following him, but kept his commandments, which the Lord commanded Moses. **7 And the Lord was with him; and he prospered whithersoever he went forth:and he rebelled against the king of Assyria, and served him not.** 8 He smote the Philistines, even unto Gaza, and the borders thereof, from the tower of the watchmen to the fenced city.

9 And it came to pass in the fourth year of king Hezekiah, which was

the seventh year of Hoshea son of Elah king of Israel, that
Shalmaneser king of Assyria came up against Samaria, and besieged
it. 10 And at the end of three years they took it:even in the sixth year
of Hezekiah, that is the ninth year of Hoshea king of Israel, Samaria
was taken. 11 And the king of Assyria did carry away Israel unto
Assyria, and put them in Halah and in Habor by the river of Gozan,
and in the cities of the Medes:12 Because they obeyed not the voice
of the Lord their God, but transgressed his covenant, and all that
Moses the servant of the Lord commanded, and would not hear them,
nor do them.

13 Now in the fourteenth year of king Hezekiah did Sennacherib king
of Assyria come up against all the fenced cities of Judah, and took
them. 14 And Hezekiah king of Judah sent to the king of Assyria to
Lachish, saying, I have offended; return from me:that which thou
puttest on me will I bear. And the king of Assyria appointed unto
Hezekiah king of Judah three hundred talents of silver and thirty
talents of gold. 15 And Hezekiah gave him all the silver that was
found in the house of the Lord, and in the treasures of the king's
house. 16 At that time did Hezekiah cut off the gold from the doors of
the temple of the Lord, and from the pillars which Hezekiah king of
Judah had overlaid, and gave it to the king of Assyria.

17 And the king of Assyria sent Tartan and Rabsaris and Rabshakeh
from Lachish to king Hezekiah with a great host against Jerusalem.
And they went up and came to Jerusalem. And when they were come
up, they came and stood by the conduit of the upper pool, which is in
the highway of the fuller's field. 18 And when they had called to the
king, there came out to them Eliakim the son of Hilkiah, which was
over the household, and Shebna the scribe, and Joah the son of Asaph
the recorder. 19 And Rabshakeh said unto them, Speak ye now to
Hezekiah, Thus saith the great king, the king of Assyria, What
confidence is this wherein thou trustest? 20 Thou sayest, (but they are
but vain words,) I have counsel and strength for the war. Now on
whom dost thou trust, that thou rebellest against me? 21 Now, behold,
thou trustest upon the staff of this bruised reed, even upon Egypt, on

which if a man lean, it will go into his hand, and pierce it:so is
Pharaoh king of Egypt unto all that trust on him. 22 But if ye say unto
me, We trust in the Lord our God:is not that he, whose high places
and whose altars Hezekiah hath taken away, and hath said to Judah
and Jerusalem, Ye shall worship before this altar in Jerusalem? 23
Now therefore, I pray thee, give pledges to my lord the king of
Assyria, and I will deliver thee two thousand horses, if thou be able
on thy part to set riders upon them. 24 How then wilt thou turn away
the face of one captain of the least of my master's servants, and put
thy trust on Egypt for chariots and for horsemen? 25 Am I now come
up without the Lord against this place to destroy it? The Lord said to
me, Go up against this land, and destroy it. 26 Then said Eliakim the
son of Hilkiah, and Shebna, and Joah, unto Rabshakeh, Speak, I pray
thee, to thy servants in the Syrian language; for we understand it:and
talk not with us in the Jews 'language in the ears of the people that are
on the wall. 27 But Rabshakeh said unto them, Hath my master sent
me to thy master, and to thee, to speak these words? hath he not sent
me to the men which sit on the wall, that they may eat their own dung,
and drink their own piss with you? 28 Then Rabshakeh stood and
cried with a loud voice in the Jews' language, and spake, saying, Hear
the word of the great king, the king of Assyria:29 Thus saith the king,
Let not Hezekiah deceive you:for he shall not be able to deliver you
out of his hand:30 Neither let Hezekiah make you trust in the Lord,
saying, The Lord will surely deliver us, and this city shall not be
delivered into the hand of the king of Assyria. 31 Hearken not to
Hezekiah:for thus saith the king of Assyria, Make an agreement with
me by a present, and come out to me, and then eat ye every man of his
own vine, and every one of his fig tree, and drink ye every one the
waters of his cistern:32 Until I come and take you away to a land like
your own land, a land of corn and wine, a land of bread and
vineyards, a land of oil olive and of honey, that ye may live, and not
die:and hearken not unto Hezekiah, when he persuadeth you, saying,
The Lord will deliver us. 33 Hath any of the gods of the nations
delivered at all his land out of the hand of the king of Assyria? 34

Where are the gods of Hamath, and of Arpad? where are the gods of Sepharvaim, Hena, and Ivah? have they delivered Samaria out of mine hand? 35 Who are they among all the gods of the countries, that have delivered their country out of mine hand, that the Lord should deliver Jerusalem out of mine hand? 36 But the people held their peace, and answered him not a word:for the king's commandment was, saying, Answer him not. 37 Then came Eliakim the son of Hilkiah, which was over the household, and Shebna the scribe, and Joah the son of Asaph the recorder, to Hezekiah with their clothes rent, and told him the words of Rabshakeh.

1 Chronicles 29

1 Furthermore David the king said unto all the congregation, Solomon my son, whom alone God hath chosen, is yet young and tender, and the work is great:for the palace is not for man, but for the Lord God. 2 Now I have prepared with all my might for the house of my God the gold for things to be made of gold, and the silver for things of silver, and the brass for things of brass, the iron for things of iron, and wood for things of wood; onyx stones, and stones to be set, glistering stones, and of divers colours, and all manner of precious stones, and marble stones in abundance. 3 Moreover, because I have set my affection to the house of my God, I have of mine own proper good, of gold and silver, which I have given to the house of my God, over and above all that I have prepared for the holy house, 4 Even three thousand talents of gold, of the gold of Ophir, and seven thousand talents of refined silver, to overlay the walls of the houses withal:5 The gold for things of gold, and the silver for things of silver, and for all manner of work to be made by the hands of artificers. And who then is willing to consecrate his service this day unto the Lord? 6 Then the chief of the fathers and princes of the tribes of Israel, and the captains of thousands and of hundreds, with the rulers of the king's work, offered willingly, 7 And gave for the service of the house

of God of gold five thousand talents and ten thousand drams, and of silver ten thousand talents, and of brass eighteen thousand talents, and one hundred thousand talents of iron. 8 And they with whom precious stones were found gave them to the treasure of the house of the Lord, by the hand of Jehiel the Gershonite. 9 Then the people rejoiced, for that they offered willingly, because with perfect heart they offered willingly to the Lord:and David the king also rejoiced with great joy. 10 Wherefore David blessed the Lord before all the congregation:and David said, Blessed be thou, Lord God of Israel our father, for ever and ever. 11 Thine, O Lord, is the greatness, and the power, and the glory, and the victory, and the majesty:for all that is in the heaven and in the earth is thine; thine is the kingdom, O Lord, and thou art exalted as head above all. 12 Both riches and honour come of thee, and thou reignest over all; and in thine hand is power and might; and in thine hand it is to make great, and to give strength unto all. 13 Now therefore, our God, we thank thee, and praise thy glorious name. 14 But who am I, and what is my people, that we should be able to offer so willingly after this sort? for all things come of thee, and of thine own have we given thee. 15 For we are strangers before thee, and sojourners, as were all our fathers:our days on the earth are as a shadow, and there is none abiding. 16 O Lord our God, all this store that we have prepared to build thee an house for thine holy name cometh of thine hand, and is all thine own. 17 I know also, my God, that thou triest the heart, and hast pleasure in uprightness. As for me, in the uprightness of mine heart I have willingly offered all these things:and now have I seen with joy thy people, which are present here, to offer willingly unto thee. 18 O Lord God of Abraham, Isaac, and of Israel, our fathers, keep this for ever in the imagination of the thoughts of the heart of thy people, and prepare their heart unto thee:19 And give unto Solomon my son a perfect heart, to keep thy commandments, thy testimonies, and thy statutes, and to do all these things, and to build the palace, for the which I have made provision. 20 And David said to all the congregation, Now bless the Lord your God. And all the congregation blessed the Lord God of their fathers, and bowed down their heads, and worshipped the Lord, and the king. 21 And they sacrificed sacrifices unto the Lord, and offered burnt offerings unto the Lord, on the morrow after that day, even a thousand bullocks, a thousand rams, and a thousand lambs, with their drink offerings, and sacrifices in abundance for all Israel:22 And did eat and drink before the Lord on that day with great gladness. And they made Solomon the son of David king the second time, and anointed him unto the Lord to be the chief governor, and Zadok to be priest. **23 Then Solomon sat on the throne of the Lord as king instead of David his father, and prospered; and all Israel obeyed him.** 24 And all the princes, and the mighty men, and all the sons likewise of king David, submitted themselves unto Solomon the king. 25 And the Lord magnified Solomon exceedingly in the sight of all Israel, and bestowed upon him such royal majesty as had not been on any king before him in Israel.

26 Thus David the son of Jesse reigned over all Israel. 27 And the time that he reigned over Israel was forty years; seven years reigned he in Hebron, and thirty and three years reigned he in Jerusalem. 28 And he died in a good old age, full of days, riches, and honour:and Solomon his son reigned in his stead. 29 Now the acts of David the king, first and last, behold, they are written in the book of Samuel the seer, and in the book of Nathan the prophet, and in the book of Gad the seer, 30 With all his reign and his might, and the times that went over him, and over Israel, and over all the kingdoms of the countries.

2 Chronicles 14

1 So Abijah slept with his fathers, and they buried him in the city of David:and Asa his son reigned in his stead. In his days the land was quiet ten years. 2 And Asa did that which was good and right in the eyes of the Lord his God:3 For he took away the altars of the strange gods, and the high places, and brake down the images, and cut down the groves:4 And commanded Judah to seek the Lord God of their fathers, and to do the law and the commandment. 5 Also he took away

out of all the cities of Judah the high places and the images:and the kingdom was quiet before him.

6 And he built fenced cities in Judah:for the land had rest, and he had no war in those years; because the Lord had given him rest. **7 Therefore he said unto Judah, Let us build these cities, and make about them walls, and towers, gates, and bars, while the land is yet before us; because we have sought the Lord our God, we have sought him, and he hath given us rest on every side. So they built and prospered.** 8 And Asa had an army of men that bare targets and spears, out of Judah three hundred thousand; and out of Benjamin, that bare shields and drew bows, two hundred and fourscore thousand:all these were mighty men of valour.

9 And there came out against them Zerah the Ethiopian with an host of a thousand thousand, and three hundred chariots; and came unto Mareshah. 10 Then Asa went out against him, and they set the battle in array in the valley of Zephathah at Mareshah. 11 And Asa cried unto the Lord his God, and said, Lord, it is nothing with thee to help, whether with many, or with them that have no power:help us, O Lord our God; for we rest on thee, and in thy name we go against this multitude. O Lord, thou art our God; let not man prevail against thee. 12 So the Lord smote the Ethiopians before Asa, and before Judah; and the Ethiopians fled. 13 And Asa and the people that were with him pursued them unto Gerar:and the Ethiopians were overthrown, that they could not recover themselves; for they were destroyed before the Lord, and before his host; and they carried away very much spoil. 14 And they smote all the cities round about Gerar; for the fear of the Lord came upon them:and they spoiled all the cities; for there was exceeding much spoil in them. 15 They smote also the tents of cattle, and carried away sheep and camels in abundance, and returned to Jerusalem.

2 Chronicles 31

1 Now when all this was finished, all Israel that were present went out

to the cities of Judah, and brake the images in pieces, and cut down
the groves, and threw down the high places and the altars out of all
Judah and Benjamin, in Ephraim also and Manasseh, until they had
utterly destroyed them all. Then all the children of Israel returned,
every man to his possession, into their own cities.
2 And Hezekiah appointed the courses of the priests and the Levites
after their courses, every man according to his service, the priests and
Levites for burnt offerings and for peace offerings, to minister, and to
give thanks, and to praise in the gates of the tents of the Lord. 3 He
appointed also the king's portion of his substance for the burnt
offerings, to wit, for the morning and evening burnt offerings, and the
burnt offerings for the sabbaths, and for the new moons, and for the
set feasts, as it is written in the law of the Lord. 4 Moreover he
commanded the people that dwelt in Jerusalem to give the portion of
the priests and the Levites, that they might be encouraged in the law
of the Lord.
5 And as soon as the commandment came abroad, the children of
Israel brought in abundance the firstfruits of corn, wine, and oil, and
honey, and of all the increase of the field; and the tithe of all things
brought they in abundantly. 6 And concerning the children of Israel
and Judah, that dwelt in the cities of Judah, they also brought in the
tithe of oxen and sheep, and the tithe of holy things which were
consecrated unto the Lord their God, and laid them by heaps. 7 In the
third month they began to lay the foundation of the heaps, and
finished them in the seventh month. 8 And when Hezekiah and the
princes came and saw the heaps, they blessed the Lord, and his people
Israel. 9 Then Hezekiah questioned with the priests and the Levites
concerning the heaps. 10 And Azariah the chief priest of the house of
Zadok answered him, and said, Since the people began to bring the
offerings into the house of the Lord, we have had enough to eat, and
have left plenty:for the Lord hath blessed his people; and that which is
left is this great store.
11 Then Hezekiah commanded to prepare chambers in the house of
the Lord; and they prepared them, 12 And brought in the offerings

and the tithes and the dedicated things faithfully:over which Cononiah the Levite was ruler, and Shimei his brother was the next. 13 And Jehiel, and Azaziah, and Nahath, and Asahel, and Jerimoth, and Jozabad, and Eliel, and Ismachiah, and Mahath, and Benaiah, were overseers under the hand of Cononiah and Shimei his brother, at the commandment of Hezekiah the king, and Azariah the ruler of the house of God. 14 And Kore the son of Imnah the Levite, the porter toward the east, was over the freewill offerings of God, to distribute the oblations of the Lord, and the most holy things. 15 And next him were Eden, and Miniamin, and Jeshua, and Shemaiah, Amariah, and Shecaniah, in the cities of the priests, in their set office, to give to their brethren by courses, as well to the great as to the small:16 Beside their genealogy of males, from three years old and upward, even unto every one that entereth into the house of the Lord, his daily portion for their service in their charges according to their courses; 17 Both to the genealogy of the priests by the house of their fathers, and the Levites from twenty years old and upward, in their charges by their courses; 18 And to the genealogy of all their little ones, their wives, and their sons, and their daughters, through all the congregation:for in their set office they sanctified themselves in holiness:19 Also of the sons of Aaron the priests, which were in the fields of the suburbs of their cities, in every several city, the men that were expressed by name, to give portions to all the males among the priests, and to all that were reckoned by genealogies among the Levites.

20 And thus did Hezekiah throughout all Judah, and wrought that which was good and right and truth before the Lord his God. **21 And in every work that he began in the service of the house of God, and in the law, and in the commandments, to seek his God, he did it with all his heart, and prospered.**

Chronicles 32

1 After these things, and the establishment thereof, Sennacherib king of Assyria came, and entered into Judah, and encamped against the fenced cities, and thought to win them for himself. 2 And when Hezekiah saw that Sennacherib was come, and that he was purposed to fight against Jerusalem, 3 He took counsel with his princes and his mighty men to stop the waters of the fountains which were without the city:and they did help him. 4 So there was gathered much people together, who stopped all the fountains, and the brook that ran through the midst of the land, saying, Why should the kings of Assyria come, and find much water? 5 Also he strengthened himself, and built up all the wall that was broken, and raised it up to the towers, and another wall without, and repaired Millo in the city of David, and made darts and shields in abundance. 6 And he set captains of war over the people, and gathered them together to him in the street of the gate of the city, and spake comfortably to them, saying, 7 Be strong and courageous, be not afraid nor dismayed for the king of Assyria, nor for all the multitude that is with him:for there be more with us than with him:8 With him is an arm of flesh; but with us is the Lord our God to help us, and to fight our battles. And the people rested themselves upon the words of Hezekiah king of Judah.

9 After this did Sennacherib king of Assyria send his servants to Jerusalem, (but he himself laid siege against Lachish, and all his power with him,) unto Hezekiah king of Judah, and unto all Judah that were at Jerusalem, saying, 10 Thus saith Sennacherib king of Assyria, Whereon do ye trust, that ye abide in the siege in Jerusalem? 11 Doth not Hezekiah persuade you to give over yourselves to die by famine and by thirst, saying, The Lord our God shall deliver us out of the hand of the king of Assyria? 12 Hath not the same Hezekiah taken away his high places and his altars, and commanded Judah and Jerusalem, saying, Ye shall worship before one altar, and burn incense upon it? 13 Know ye not what I and my fathers have done unto all the people of other lands? were the gods of the nations of those lands any ways able to deliver their lands out of mine hand? 14 Who was there

among all the gods of those nations that my fathers utterly destroyed, that could deliver his people out of mine hand, that your God should be able to deliver you out of mine hand? 15 Now therefore let not Hezekiah deceive you, nor persuade you on this manner, neither yet believe him:for no god of any nation or kingdom was able to deliver his people out of mine hand, and out of the hand of my fathers:how much less shall your God deliver you out of mine hand? 16 And his servants spake yet more against the Lord God, and against his servant Hezekiah. 17 He wrote also letters to rail on the Lord God of Israel, and to speak against him, saying, As the gods of the nations of other lands have not delivered their people out of mine hand, so shall not the God of Hezekiah deliver his people out of mine hand. 18 Then they cried with a loud voice in the Jews 'speech unto the people of Jerusalem that were on the wall, to affright them, and to trouble them; that they might take the city. 19 And they spake against the God of Jerusalem, as against the gods of the people of the earth, which were the work of the hands of man. 20 And for this cause Hezekiah the king, and the prophet Isaiah the son of Amoz, prayed and cried to heaven.

21 And the Lord sent an angel, which cut off all the mighty men of valour, and the leaders and captains in the camp of the king of Assyria. So he returned with shame of face to his own land. And when he was come into the house of his god, they that came forth of his own bowels slew him there with the sword. 22 Thus the Lord saved Hezekiah and the inhabitants of Jerusalem from the hand of Sennacherib the king of Assyria, and from the hand of all other, and guided them on every side. 23 And many brought gifts unto the Lord to Jerusalem, and presents to Hezekiah king of Judah:so that he was magnified in the sight of all nations from thenceforth.

24 In those days Hezekiah was sick to the death, and prayed unto the Lord:and he spake unto him, and he gave him a sign. 25 But Hezekiah rendered not again according to the benefit done unto him; for his heart was lifted up:therefore there was wrath upon him, and upon Judah and Jerusalem. 26 Notwithstanding Hezekiah humbled himself

for the pride of his heart, both he and the inhabitants of Jerusalem, so that the wrath of the Lord came not upon them in the days of Hezekiah.

27 And Hezekiah had exceeding much riches and honour:and he made himself treasuries for silver, and for gold, and for precious stones, and for spices, and for shields, and for all manner of pleasant jewels; 28 Storehouses also for the increase of corn, and wine, and oil; and stalls for all manner of beasts, and cotes for flocks. 29 Moreover he provided him cities, and possessions of flocks and herds in abundance:for God had given him substance very much. **30 This same Hezekiah also stopped the upper watercourse of Gihon, and brought it straight down to the west side of the city of David. And Hezekiah prospered in all his works.**

31 Howbeit in the business of the ambassadors of the princes of Babylon, who sent unto him to enquire of the wonder that was done in the land, God left him, to try him, that he might know all that was in his heart.

32 Now the rest of the acts of Hezekiah, and his goodness, behold, they are written in the vision of Isaiah the prophet, the son of Amoz, and in the book of the kings of Judah and Israel. 33 And Hezekiah slept with his fathers, and they buried him in the chiefest of the sepulchres of the sons of David:and all Judah and the inhabitants of Jerusalem did him honour at his death. And Manasseh his son reigned in his stead.

Ezra 6

1 Then Darius the king made a decree, and search was made in the house of the rolls, where the treasures were laid up in Babylon. 2 And there was found at Achmetha, in the palace that is in the province of the Medes, a roll, and therein was a record thus written:3 In the first year of Cyrus the king the same Cyrus the king made a decree concerning the house of God at Jerusalem, Let the house be builded, the place where they offered sacrifices, and let the foundations thereof

be strongly laid; the height thereof threescore cubits, and the breadth thereof threescore cubits; 4 With three rows of great stones, and a row of new timber:and let the expenses be given out of the king's house:5 And also let the golden and silver vessels of the house of God, which Nebuchadnezzar took forth out of the temple which is at Jerusalem, and brought unto Babylon, be restored, and brought again unto the temple which is at Jerusalem, every one to his place, and place them in the house of God. 6 Now therefore, Tatnai, governor beyond the river, Shetharboznai, and your companions the Apharsachites, which are beyond the river, be ye far from thence:7 Let the work of this house of God alone; let the governor of the Jews and the elders of the Jews build this house of God in his place. 8 Moreover I make a decree what ye shall do to the elders of these Jews for the building of this house of God:that of the king's goods, even of the tribute beyond the river, forthwith expenses be given unto these men, that they be not hindered. 9 And that which they have need of, both young bullocks, and rams, and lambs, for the burnt offerings of the God of heaven, wheat, salt, wine, and oil, according to the appointment of the priests which are at Jerusalem, let it be given them day by day without fail:10 That they may offer sacrifices of sweet savours unto the God of heaven, and pray for the life of the king, and of his sons. 11 Also I have made a decree, that whosoever shall alter this word, let timber be pulled down from his house, and being set up, let him be hanged thereon; and let his house be made a dunghill for this. 12 And the God that hath caused his name to dwell there destroy all kings and people, that shall put to their hand to alter and to destroy this house of God which is at Jerusalem. I Darius have made a decree; let it be done with speed.

13 Then Tatnai, governor on this side the river, Shetharboznai, and their companions, according to that which Darius the king had sent, so they did speedily. **14 And the elders of the Jews builded, and they prospered through the prophesying of Haggai the prophet and Zechariah the son of Iddo. And they builded, and finished it, according to the commandment of the God of Israel, and**

177

according to the commandment of Cyrus, and Darius, and Artaxerxes king of Persia. 15 And this house was finished on the third day of the month Adar, which was in the sixth year of the reign of Darius the king.

16 And the children of Israel, the priests, and the Levites, and the rest of the children of the captivity, kept the dedication of this house of God with joy, 17 And offered at the dedication of this house of God an hundred bullocks, two hundred rams, four hundred lambs; and for a sin offering for all Israel, twelve he goats, according to the number of the tribes of Israel. 18 And they set the priests in their divisions, and the Levites in their courses, for the service of God, which is at Jerusalem; as it is written in the book of Moses. 19 And the children of the captivity kept the passover upon the fourteenth day of the first month. 20 For the priests and the Levites were purified together, all of them were pure, and killed the passover for all the children of the captivity, and for their brethren the priests, and for themselves. 21 And the children of Israel, which were come again out of captivity, and all such as had separated themselves unto them from the filthiness of the heathen of the land, to seek the Lord God of Israel, did eat, 22 And kept the feast of unleavened bread seven days with joy:for the Lord had made them joyful, and turned the heart of the king of Assyria unto them, to strengthen their hands in the work of the house of God, the God of Israel.

Job 9

1 Then Job answered and said,
2 I know it is so of a truth:
but how should man be just with God?
3 If he will contend with him,
he cannot answer him one of a thousand.
4 He is wise in heart, and mighty in strength:
who hath hardened himself against him, and hath prospered?
5 Which removeth the mountains, and they know not:

which overturneth them in his anger.

6 Which shaketh the earth out of her place,
and the pillars thereof tremble.

7 Which commandeth the sun, and it riseth not;
and sealeth up the stars.

8 Which alone spreadeth out the heavens,
and treadeth upon the waves of the sea.

9 Which maketh Arcturus, Orion,
and Pleiades, and the chambers of the south.

10 Which doeth great things past finding out;
yea, and wonders without number.

11 Lo, he goeth by me, and I see him not:
he passeth on also, but I perceive him not.

12 Behold, he taketh away, who can hinder him?
who will say unto him, What doest thou?

13 If God will not withdraw his anger,
the proud helpers do stoop under him.

14 How much less shall I answer him,
and choose out my words to reason with him?

15 Whom, though I were righteous, yet would I not answer,
but I would make supplication to my judge.

16 If I had called, and he had answered me;
yet would I not believe that he had hearkened unto my voice.

17 For he breaketh me with a tempest,
and multiplieth my wounds without cause.

18 He will not suffer me to take my breath,
but filleth me with bitterness.

19 If I speak of strength, lo, he is strong:
and if of judgment, who shall set me a time to plead?

20 If I justify myself, mine own mouth shall condemn me:
if I say, I am perfect, it shall also prove me perverse.

21 Though I were perfect, yet would I not know my soul:
I would despise my life.

22 This is one thing, therefore I said it,

He destroyeth the perfect and the wicked.

23 If the scourge slay suddenly,

he will laugh at the trial of the innocent.

24 The earth is given into the hand of the wicked:

he covereth the faces of the judges thereof;

if not, where, and who is he?

25 Now my days are swifter than a post:

they flee away, they see no good.

26 They are passed away as the swift ships:

as the eagle that hasteth to the prey.

27 If I say, I will forget my complaint,

I will leave off my heaviness, and comfort myself:

28 I am afraid of all my sorrows,

I know that thou wilt not hold me innocent.

29 If I be wicked,

why then labour I in vain?

30 If I wash myself with snow water,

and make my hands never so clean;

31 Yet shalt thou plunge me in the ditch,

and mine own clothes shall abhor me.

32 For he is not a man, as I am, that I should answer him,

and we should come together in judgment.

33 Neither is there any daysman betwixt us,

that might lay his hand upon us both.

34 Let him take his rod away from me,

and let not his fear terrify me:

35 Then would I speak, and not fear him;

but it is not so with me.

Daniel 6

1 It pleased Darius to set over the kingdom an hundred and twenty princes, which should be over the whole kingdom; 2 And over these three presidents; of whom Daniel was first:that the princes might give accounts unto them, and the king should have no damage. 3 Then this

Daniel was preferred above the presidents and princes, because an excellent spirit was in him; and the king thought to set him over the whole realm.

4 Then the presidents and princes sought to find occasion against Daniel concerning the kingdom; but they could find none occasion nor fault; forasmuch as he was faithful, neither was there any error or fault found in him. 5 Then said these men, We shall not find any occasion against this Daniel, except we find it against him concerning the law of his God. 6 Then these presidents and princes assembled together to the king, and said thus unto him, King Darius, live for ever. 7 All the presidents of the kingdom, the governors, and the princes, the counsellors, and the captains, have consulted together to establish a royal statute, and to make a firm decree, that whosoever shall ask a petition of any God or man for thirty days, save of thee, O king, he shall be cast into the den of lions. 8 Now, O king, establish the decree, and sign the writing, that it be not changed, according to the law of the Medes and Persians, which altereth not. 9 Wherefore king Darius signed the writing and the decree.

10 Now when Daniel knew that the writing was signed, he went into his house; and his windows being open in his chamber toward Jerusalem, he kneeled upon his knees three times a day, and prayed, and gave thanks before his God, as he did aforetime. 11 Then these men assembled, and found Daniel praying and making supplication before his God. 12 Then they came near, and spake before the king concerning the king's decree; Hast thou not signed a decree, that every man that shall ask a petition of any God or man within thirty days, save of thee, O king, shall be cast into the den of lions? The king answered and said, The thing is true, according to the law of the Medes and Persians, which altereth not. 13 Then answered they and said before the king, That Daniel, which is of the children of the captivity of Judah, regardeth not thee, O king, nor the decree that thou hast signed, but maketh his petition three times a day. 14 Then the king, when he heard these words, was sore displeased with himself, and set his heart on Daniel to deliver him:and he laboured till the going down of the sun to deliver him. 15 Then these men assembled unto the king, and said unto the king, Know, O king, that the law of the Medes and Persians is, That no decree nor statute which the king establisheth may be changed. 16 Then the king commanded, and they brought Daniel, and cast him into the den of lions. Now the king

spake and said unto Daniel, Thy God whom thou servest continually, he will deliver thee. 17 And a stone was brought, and laid upon the mouth of the den; and the king sealed it with his own signet, and with the signet of his lords; that the purpose might not be changed concerning Daniel.

18 Then the king went to his palace, and passed the night fasting:neither were instruments of musick brought before him:and his sleep went from him. 19 Then the king arose very early in the morning, and went in haste unto the den of lions. 20 And when he came to the den, he cried with a lamentable voice unto Daniel:and the king spake and said to Daniel, O Daniel, servant of the living God, is thy God, whom thou servest continually, able to deliver thee from the lions? 21 Then said Daniel unto the king, O king, live for ever. 22 My God hath sent his angel, and hath shut the lions 'mouths, that they have not hurt me:forasmuch as before him innocency was found in me; and also before thee, O king, have I done no hurt. 23 Then was the king exceeding glad for him, and commanded that they should take Daniel up out of the den. So Daniel was taken up out of the den, and no manner of hurt was found upon him, because he believed in his God.

24 And the king commanded, and they brought those men which had accused Daniel, and they cast them into the den of lions, them, their children, and their wives; and the lions had the mastery of them, and brake all their bones in pieces or ever they came at the bottom of the den.

25 Then king Darius wrote unto all people, nations, and languages, that dwell in all the earth; Peace be multiplied unto you. 26 I make a decree, That in every dominion of my kingdom men tremble and fear before the God of Daniel:for he is the living God, and stedfast for ever, and his kingdom that which shall not be destroyed, and his dominion shall be even unto the end. 27 He delivereth and rescueth, and he worketh signs and wonders in heaven and in earth, who hath delivered Daniel from the power of the lions. **28 So this Daniel prospered in the reign of Darius, and in the reign of Cyrus the Persian.**

Daniel 8
1 In the third year of the reign of king Belshazzar a vision appeared unto me, even unto me Daniel, after that which appeared unto me at the first. 2 And I saw in a vision; and it came to pass, when I saw, that I was at Shushan in the palace, which is in the province of Elam; and I saw in a vision, and I was by the river of Ulai. 3 Then I lifted up mine eyes, and saw, and, behold, there stood before the river a ram which had two horns:and the two horns were high; but one was higher than the other, and the higher came up last. 4 I saw the ram pushing westward, and northward, and southward; so that no beasts might stand before him, neither was there any that could deliver out of his hand; but he did according to his will, and became great. 5 And as I was considering, behold, an he goat came from the west on the face of the whole earth, and touched not the ground:and the goat had a notable horn between his eyes. 6 And he came to the ram that had two horns, which I had seen standing before the river, and ran unto him in the fury of his power. 7 And I saw him come close unto the ram, and he was moved with choler against him, and smote the ram, and brake his two horns:and there was no power in the ram to stand before him, but he cast him down to the ground, and stamped upon him:and there was none that could deliver the ram out of his hand. 8 Therefore the he goat waxed very great:and when he was strong, the great horn was broken; and for it came up four notable ones toward the four winds of heaven. 9 And out of one of them came forth a little horn, which waxed exceeding great, toward the south, and toward the east, and toward the pleasant land. 10 And it waxed great, even to the host of heaven; and it cast down some of the host and of the stars to the ground, and stamped upon them. 11 Yea, he magnified himself even to the prince of the host, and by him the daily sacrifice was taken away, and the place of his sanctuary was cast down. **12 And an host was given him against the daily sacrifice by reason of transgression, and it cast down the truth to the ground; and it practised, and prospered.** 13 Then I heard one saint speaking, and another saint said unto that certain saint which spake, How long shall

be the vision concerning the daily sacrifice, and the transgression of desolation, to give both the sanctuary and the host to be trodden under foot? 14 And he said unto me, Unto two thousand and three hundred days; then shall the sanctuary be cleansed. 15 And it came to pass, when I, even I Daniel, had seen the vision, and sought for the meaning, then, behold, there stood before me as the appearance of a man. 16 And I heard a man's voice between the banks of Ulai, which called, and said, Gabriel, make this man to understand the vision. 17 So he came near where I stood:and when he came, I was afraid, and fell upon my face:but he said unto me, Understand, O son of man:for at the time of the end shall be the vision. 18 Now as he was speaking with me, I was in a deep sleep on my face toward the ground:but he touched me, and set me upright. 19 And he said, Behold, I will make thee know what shall be in the last end of the indignation:for at the time appointed the end shall be. 20 The ram which thou sawest having two horns are the kings of Media and Persia. 21 And the rough goat is the king of Grecia:and the great horn that is between his eyes is the first king. 22 Now that being broken, whereas four stood up for it, four kingdoms shall stand up out of the nation, but not in his power. 23 And in the latter time of their kingdom, when the transgressors are come to the full, a king of fierce countenance, and understanding dark sentences, shall stand up. 24 And his power shall be mighty, but not by his own power:and he shall destroy wonderfully, and shall prosper, and practise, and shall destroy the mighty and the holy people. 25 And through his policy also he shall cause craft to prosper in his hand; and he shall magnify himself in his heart, and by peace shall destroy many:he shall also stand up against the Prince of princes; but he shall be broken without hand. 26 And the vision of the evening and the morning which was told is true:wherefore shut thou up the vision; for it shall be for many days. 27 And I Daniel fainted, and was sick certain days; afterward I rose up, and did the king's business; and I was astonished at the vision, but none understood it.

1 Corinthians 16

1 Now concerning the collection for the saints, as I have given order to the churches of Galatia, even so do ye. **2 Upon the first day of the week let every one of you lay by him in store, as God hath prospered him, that there be no gatherings when I come.** 3 And when I come, whomsoever ye shall approve by your letters, them will I send to bring your liberality unto Jerusalem. 4 And if it be meet that I go also, they shall go with me.

5 Now I will come unto you, when I shall pass through Macedonia:for I do pass through Macedonia. 6 And it may be that I will abide, yea, and winter with you, that ye may bring me on my journey whithersoever I go. 7 For I will not see you now by the way; but I trust to tarry a while with you, if the Lord permit.

8 But I will tarry at Ephesus until Pentecost. 9 For a great door and effectual is opened unto me, and there are many adversaries.

10 Now if Timotheus come, see that he may be with you without fear:for he worketh the work of the Lord, as I also do. 11 Let no man therefore despise him:but conduct him forth in peace, that he may come unto me:for I look for him with the brethren.

12 As touching our brother Apollos, I greatly desired him to come unto you with the brethren:but his will was not at all to come at this time; but he will come when he shall have convenient time.

13 Watch ye, stand fast in the faith, quit you like men, be strong. 14 Let all your things be done with charity.

15 I beseech you, brethren, (ye know the house of Stephanas, that it is the firstfruits of Achaia, and that they have addicted themselves to the ministry of the saints,) 16 That ye submit yourselves unto such, and to every one that helpeth with us, and laboureth.

17 I am glad of the coming of Stephanas and Fortunatus and Achaicus:for that which was lacking on your part they have supplied. 18 For they have refreshed my spirit and yours:therefore acknowledge ye them that are such.

19 The churches of Asia salute you. Aquila and Priscilla salute you much in the Lord, with the church that is in their house. 20 All the

brethren greet you. Greet ye one another with an holy kiss.

21 The salutation of me Paul with mine own hand.

22 If any man love not the Lord Jesus Christ, let him be Anathema Maranatha.

23 The grace of our Lord Jesus Christ be with you. 24 My love be with you all in Christ Jesus. Amen.

The first [epistle to the Corinthians was written from Philippi by Stephanas and Fortunatus and Achaicus and Timotheus.]

Chapter 6

Chapters on Prosperous

PROSPEROUS

Genesis 24

1 And Abraham was old, and well stricken in age:and the Lord had blessed Abraham in all things. 2 And Abraham said unto his eldest servant of his house, that ruled over all that he had, Put, I pray thee, thy hand under my thigh:3 And I will make thee swear by the Lord, the God of heaven, and the God of the earth, that thou shalt not take a wife unto my son of the daughters of the Canaanites, among whom I dwell:4 But thou shalt go unto my country, and to my kindred, and take a wife unto my son Isaac. 5 And the servant said unto him, Peradventure the woman will not be willing to follow me unto this land:must I needs bring thy son again unto the land from whence thou camest? 6 And Abraham said unto him, Beware thou that thou bring not my son thither again.

7 The Lord God of heaven, which took me from my father's house, and from the land of my kindred, and which spake unto me, and that sware unto me, saying, Unto thy seed will I give this land; he shall send his angel before thee, and thou shalt take a wife unto my son from thence. 8 And if the woman will not be willing to follow thee, then thou shalt be clear from this my oath:only bring not my son thither again. 9 And the servant put his hand under the thigh of Abraham his master, and sware to him concerning that matter.

10 And the servant took ten camels of the camels of his master, and departed; for all the goods of his master were in his hand:and he arose, and went to Mesopotamia, unto the city of Nahor. 11 And he made his camels to kneel down without the city by a well of water at the time of the evening, even the time that women go out to draw

water. 12 And he said, O Lord God of my master Abraham, I pray thee, send me good speed this day, and shew kindness unto my master Abraham. 13 Behold, I stand here by the well of water; and the daughters of the men of the city come out to draw water:14 And let it come to pass, that the damsel to whom I shall say, Let down thy pitcher, I pray thee, that I may drink; and she shall say, Drink, and I will give thy camels drink also:let the same be she that thou hast appointed for thy servant Isaac; and thereby shall I know that thou hast shewed kindness unto my master.

15 And it came to pass, before he had done speaking, that, behold, Rebekah came out, who was born to Bethuel, son of Milcah, the wife of Nahor, Abraham's brother, with her pitcher upon her shoulder. 16 And the damsel was very fair to look upon, a virgin, neither had any man known her:and she went down to the well, and filled her pitcher, and came up. 17 And the servant ran to meet her, and said, Let me, I pray thee, drink a little water of thy pitcher. 18 And she said, Drink, my lord:and she hasted, and let down her pitcher upon her hand, and gave him drink. 19 And when she had done giving him drink, she said, I will draw water for thy camels also, until they have done drinking. 20 And she hasted, and emptied her pitcher into the trough, and ran again unto the well to draw water, and drew for all his camels. **21 And the man wondering at her held his peace, to wit whether the Lord had made his journey prosperous or not.** 22 And it came to pass, as the camels had done drinking, that the man took a golden earring of half a shekel weight, and two bracelets for her hands of ten shekels weight of gold; 23 And said, Whose daughter art thou? tell me, I pray thee:is there room in thy father's house for us to lodge in? 24 And she said unto him, I am the daughter of Bethuel the son of Milcah, which she bare unto Nahor. 25 She said moreover unto him, We have both straw and provender enough, and room to lodge in. 26 And the man bowed down his head, and worshipped the Lord. 27 And he said, Blessed be the Lord God of my master Abraham, who hath not left destitute my master of his mercy and his truth:I being in the way, the Lord led me to the house of my master's brethren. 28 And

the damsel ran, and told them of her mother's house these things.
29 And Rebekah had a brother, and his name was Laban:and Laban
ran out unto the man, unto the well. 30 And it came to pass, when he
saw the earring and bracelets upon his sister's hands, and when he
heard the words of Rebekah his sister, saying, Thus spake the man
unto me; that he came unto the man; and, behold, he stood by the
camels at the well. 31 And he said, Come in, thou blessed of the Lord;
wherefore standest thou without? for I have prepared the house, and
room for the camels.
32 And the man came into the house:and he ungirded his camels, and
gave straw and provender for the camels, and water to wash his feet,
and the men's feet that were with him. 33 And there was set meat
before him to eat:but he said, I will not eat, until I have told mine
errand. And he said, Speak on. 34 And he said, I am Abraham's
servant. 35 And the Lord hath blessed my master greatly; and he is
become great:and he hath given him flocks, and herds, and silver, and
gold, and menservants, and maidservants, and camels, and asses. 36
And Sarah my master's wife bare a son to my master when she was
old:and unto him hath he given all that he hath. 37 And my master
made me swear, saying, Thou shalt not take a wife to my son of the
daughters of the Canaanites, in whose land I dwell:38 But thou shalt
go unto my father's house, and to my kindred, and take a wife unto
my son. 39 And I said unto my master, Peradventure the woman will
not follow me. 40 And he said unto me, The Lord, before whom I
walk, will send his angel with thee, and prosper thy way; and thou
shalt take a wife for my son of my kindred, and of my father's
house:41 Then shalt thou be clear from this my oath, when thou
comest to my kindred; and if they give not thee one, thou shalt be
clear from my oath. 42 And I came this day unto the well, and said, O
Lord God of my master Abraham, if now thou do prosper my way
which I go:43 Behold, I stand by the well of water; and it shall come
to pass, that when the virgin cometh forth to draw water, and I say to
her, Give me, I pray thee, a little water of thy pitcher to drink; 44 And
she say to me, Both drink thou, and I will also draw for thy camels:let

the same be the woman whom the Lord hath appointed out for my master's son. 45 And before I had done speaking in mine heart, behold, Rebekah came forth with her pitcher on her shoulder; and she went down unto the well, and drew water:and I said unto her, Let me drink, I pray thee. 46 And she made haste, and let down her pitcher from her shoulder, and said, Drink, and I will give thy camels drink also:so I drank, and she made the camels drink also. 47 And I asked her, and said, Whose daughter art thou? And she said, The daughter of Bethuel, Nahor's son, whom Milcah bare unto him:and I put the earring upon her face, and the bracelets upon her hands. 48 And I bowed down my head, and worshipped the Lord, and blessed the Lord God of my master Abraham, which had led me in the right way to take my master's brother's daughter unto his son. 49 And now if ye will deal kindly and truly with my master, tell me:and if not, tell me; that I may turn to the right hand, or to the left. 50 Then Laban and Bethuel answered and said, The thing proceedeth from the Lord:we cannot speak unto thee bad or good. 51 Behold, Rebekah is before thee, take her, and go, and let her be thy master's son's wife, as the Lord hath spoken. 52 And it came to pass, that, when Abraham's servant heard their words, he worshipped the Lord, bowing himself to the earth. 53 And the servant brought forth jewels of silver, and jewels of gold, and raiment, and gave them to Rebekah:he gave also to her brother and to her mother precious things. 54 And they did eat and drink, he and the men that were with him, and tarried all night; and they rose up in the morning, and he said, Send me away unto my master. 55 And her brother and her mother said, Let the damsel abide with us a few days, at the least ten; after that she shall go. 56 And he said unto them, Hinder me not, seeing the Lord hath prospered my way; send me away that I may go to my master. 57 And they said, We will call the damsel, and enquire at her mouth. 58 And they called Rebekah, and said unto her, Wilt thou go with this man? And she said, I will go. 59 And they sent away Rebekah their sister, and her nurse, and Abraham's servant, and his men. 60 And they blessed Rebekah, and said unto her, Thou art our sister, be thou the mother of thousands of millions, and let thy seed possess the gate of those which hate them.

61 And Rebekah arose, and her damsels, and they rode upon the camels, and followed the man:and the servant took Rebekah, and went his way. 62 And Isaac came from the way of the well Lahairoi; for he dwelt in the south country. 63 And Isaac went out to meditate in the field at the eventide:and he lifted up his eyes, and saw, and, behold, the camels were coming. 64 And Rebekah lifted up her eyes, and when she saw Isaac, she lighted off the camel. 65 For she had said unto the servant, What man is this that walketh in the field to meet us? And the servant had said, It is my master:therefore she took a vail, and covered herself. 66 And the servant told Isaac all things that he had done. 67 And Isaac brought her into his mother Sarah's tent, and took Rebekah, and she became his wife; and he loved her:and Isaac was comforted after his mother's death.

Genesis 39

1 And Joseph was brought down to Egypt; and Potiphar, an officer of Pharaoh, captain of the guard, an Egyptian, bought him of the hands of the Ishmeelites, which had brought him down thither. **2 And the Lord was with Joseph, and he was a prosperous man; and he was in the house of his master the Egyptian.** 3 And his master saw that the Lord was with him, and that the Lord made all that he did to prosper in his hand. 4 And Joseph found grace in his sight, and he served him:and he made him overseer over his house, and all that he had he put into his hand. 5 And it came to pass from the time that he had made him overseer in his house, and over all that he had, that the Lord blessed the Egyptian's house for Joseph's sake; and the blessing of the Lord was upon all that he had in the house, and in the field. 6 And he left all that he had in Joseph's hand; and he knew not ought he had, save the bread which he did eat. And Joseph was a goodly person, and well favoured.

7 And it came to pass after these things, that his master's wife cast her

eyes upon Joseph; and she said, Lie with me. 8 But he refused, and said unto his master's wife, Behold, my master wotteth not what is with me in the house, and he hath committed all that he hath to my hand; 9 There is none greater in this house than I; neither hath he kept back any thing from me but thee, because thou art his wife:how then can I do this great wickedness, and sin against God? 10 And it came to pass, as she spake to Joseph day by day, that he hearkened not unto her, to lie by her, or to be with her. 11 And it came to pass about this time, that Joseph went into the house to do his business; and there was none of the men of the house there within. 12 And she caught him by his garment, saying, Lie with me:and he left his garment in her hand, and fled, and got him out. 13 And it came to pass, when she saw that he had left his garment in her hand, and was fled forth, 14 That she called unto the men of her house, and spake unto them, saying, See, he hath brought in an Hebrew unto us to mock us; he came in unto me to lie with me, and I cried with a loud voice:15 And it came to pass, when he heard that I lifted up my voice and cried, that he left his garment with me, and fled, and got him out. 16 And she laid up his garment by her, until his lord came home. 17 And she spake unto him according to these words, saying, The Hebrew servant, which thou hast brought unto us, came in unto me to mock me:18 And it came to pass, as I lifted up my voice and cried, that he left his garment with me, and fled out. 19 And it came to pass, when his master heard the words of his wife, which she spake unto him, saying, After this manner did thy servant to me; that his wrath was kindled. 20 And Joseph's master took him, and put him into the prison, a place where the king's prisoners were bound:and he was there in the prison.
21 But the Lord was with Joseph, and shewed him mercy, and gave him favour in the sight of the keeper of the prison. 22 And the keeper of the prison committed to Joseph's hand all the prisoners that were in the prison; and whatsoever they did there, he was the doer of it. 23 The keeper of the prison looked not to any thing that was under his hand; because the Lord was with him, and that which he did, the Lord

made it to prosper.

Joshua 1

1 Now after the death of Moses the servant of the Lord it came to pass, that the Lord spake unto Joshua the son of Nun, Moses 'minister, saying, 2 Moses my servant is dead; now therefore arise, go over this Jordan, thou, and all this people, unto the land which I do give to them, even to the children of Israel. 3 Every place that the sole of your foot shall tread upon, that have I given unto you, as I said unto Moses. 4 From the wilderness and this Lebanon even unto the great river, the river Euphrates, all the land of the Hittites, and unto the great sea toward the going down of the sun, shall be your coast. 5 There shall not any man be able to stand before thee all the days of thy life:as I was with Moses, so I will be with thee:I will not fail thee, nor forsake thee. 6 Be strong and of a good courage:for unto this people shalt thou divide for an inheritance the land, which I sware unto their fathers to give them. 7 Only be thou strong and very courageous, that thou mayest observe to do according to all the law, which Moses my servant commanded thee:turn not from it to the right hand or to the left, that thou mayest prosper whithersoever thou goest. **8 This book of the law shall not depart out of thy mouth; but thou shalt meditate therein day and night, that thou mayest observe to do according to all that is written therein:for then thou shalt make thy way prosperous, and then thou shalt have good success.** 9 Have not I commanded thee? Be strong and of a good courage; be not afraid, neither be thou dismayed:for the Lord thy God is with thee whithersoever thou goest.
10 Then Joshua commanded the officers of the people, saying, 11 Pass through the host, and command the people, saying, Prepare you victuals; for within three days ye shall pass over this Jordan, to go in to possess the land, which the Lord your God giveth you to possess it. 12 And to the Reubenites, and to the Gadites, and to half the tribe of Manasseh, spake Joshua, saying, 13 Remember the word which

Moses the servant of the Lord commanded you, saying, The Lord your God hath given you rest, and hath given you this land. 14 Your wives, your little ones, and your cattle, shall remain in the land which Moses gave you on this side Jordan; but ye shall pass before your brethren armed, all the mighty men of valour, and help them; 15 Until the Lord have given your brethren rest, as he hath given you, and they also have possessed the land which the Lord your God giveth them:then ye shall return unto the land of your possession, and enjoy it, which Moses the Lord' s servant gave you on this side Jordan toward the sunrising.

16 And they answered Joshua, saying, All that thou commandest us we will do, and whithersoever thou sendest us, we will go. 17 According as we hearkened unto Moses in all things, so will we hearken unto thee:only the Lord thy God be with thee, as he was with Moses. 18 Whosoever he be that doth rebel against thy commandment, and will not hearken unto thy words in all that thou commandest him, he shall be put to death:only be strong and of a good courage.

Judges 18
1 In those days there was no king in Israel:and in those days the tribe of the Danites sought them an inheritance to dwell in; for unto that day all their inheritance had not fallen unto them among the tribes of Israel. 2 And the children of Dan sent of their family five men from their coasts, men of valour, from Zorah, and from Eshtaol, to spy out the land, and to search it; and they said unto them, Go, search the land:who when they came to mount Ephraim, to the house of Micah, they lodged there. 3 When they were by the house of Micah, they knew the voice of the young man the Levite:and they turned in thither, and said unto him, Who brought thee hither? and what makest thou in this place? and what hast thou here? 4 And he said unto them, Thus and thus dealeth Micah with me, and hath hired me, and I am his priest. **5 And they said unto him, Ask counsel, we pray thee, of**

God, that we may know whether our way which we go shall be prosperous. 6 And the priest said unto them, Go in peace:before the Lord is your way wherein ye go. 7 Then the five men departed, and came to Laish, and saw the people that were therein, how they dwelt careless, after the manner of the Zidonians, quiet and secure; and there was no magistrate in the land, that might put them to shame in any thing; and they were far from the Zidonians, and had no business with any man. 8 And they came unto their brethren to Zorah and Eshtaol:and their brethren said unto them, What say ye? 9 And they said, Arise, that we may go up against them:for we have seen the land, and, behold, it is very good:and are ye still? be not slothful to go, and to enter to possess the land. 10 When ye go, ye shall come unto a people secure, and to a large land:for God hath given it into your hands; a place where there is no want of any thing that is in the earth. 11 And there went from thence of the family of the Danites, out of Zorah and out of Eshtaol, six hundred men appointed with weapons of war. 12 And they went up, and pitched in Kirjathjearim, in Judah:wherefore they called that place Mahanehdan unto this day:behold, it is behind Kirjathjearim. 13 And they passed thence unto mount Ephraim, and came unto the house of Micah. 14 Then answered the five men that went to spy out the country of Laish, and said unto their brethren, Do ye know that there is in these houses an ephod, and teraphim, and a graven image, and a molten image? now therefore consider what ye have to do. 15 And they turned thitherward, and came to the house of the young man the Levite, even unto the house of Micah, and saluted him. 16 And the six hundred men appointed with their weapons of war, which were of the children of Dan, stood by the entering of the gate. 17 And the five men that went to spy out the land went up, and came in thither, and took the graven image, and the ephod, and the teraphim, and the molten image:and the priest stood in the entering of the gate with the six hundred men that were appointed with weapons of war. 18 And these went into Micah's house, and fetched the carved image, the ephod, and the teraphim, and the molten image. Then said the priest unto them, What do ye? 19 And they said unto him, Hold thy peace, lay thine hand upon thy mouth, and go with us, and be to us a father and a priest:is it better for thee to be a priest unto the house of one man, or that thou be a priest unto a tribe and a family in Israel? 20 And the priest's heart was glad, and he took the ephod, and the teraphim, and the graven image, and went in the midst of the people. 21 So they turned and departed, and put the little ones and the cattle and the carriage before them. 22 And when they were a good way from the house of Micah, the men that were in the houses near to Micah's house were gathered together, and overtook the children of Dan. 23 And they cried unto the children of Dan. And they turned their faces, and said unto Micah, What aileth thee, that thou comest with such a company? 24 And he said, Ye have taken away my gods which I made, and the priest, and ye are gone away:and what have I more? and what is this that ye say unto me, What aileth thee? 25 And the children of Dan said unto him, Let not thy voice be heard among us, lest angry fellows run upon thee, and thou lose thy life, with the lives of thy household. 26 And the children of Dan went their way:and when Micah saw that they were too strong for him, he turned and went back unto his house. 27 And they took the things which Micah had made, and the priest which he had, and came unto Laish, unto a people that were at quiet and secure:and they smote them with the edge of the sword, and burnt the city with fire. 28 And there was no deliverer, because it was far from Zidon, and they had no business with any man; and it was in the valley that lieth by Bethrehob. And they built a city, and dwelt therein. 29 And they called the name of the city Dan, after the name of Dan their father, who was born unto Israel:howbeit the name of the city was Laish at the first. 30 And the children of Dan set up the graven image:and Jonathan, the son of Gershom, the son of Manasseh, he and his sons were priests to the tribe of Dan until the day of the captivity of the land. 31 And they set them up Micah's graven image, which he made, all the time that the house of God was in Shiloh.

Job 8

1 Then answered Bildad the Shuhite, and said,
2 How long wilt thou speak these things?
and how long shall the words of thy mouth be like a strong wind?
3 Doth God pervert judgment?
or doth the Almighty pervert justice?
4 If thy children have sinned against him,
and he have cast them away for their transgression;
5 If thou wouldest seek unto God betimes,
and make thy supplication to the Almighty;
**6 If thou wert pure and upright;
surely now he would awake for thee,
and make the habitation of thy righteousness prosperous.
7 Though thy beginning was small,**
yet thy latter end should greatly increase.
8 For enquire, I pray thee, of the former age,
and prepare thyself to the search of their fathers:
9 (For we are but of yesterday, and know nothing,
because our days upon earth are a shadow:)
10 Shall not they teach thee,
and tell thee, and utter words out of their heart?
11 Can the rush grow up without mire?
can the flag grow without water?
12 Whilst it is yet in his greenness, and not cut down,
it withereth before any other herb.
13 So are the paths of all that forget God;
and the hypocrite's hope shall perish:
14 Whose hope shall be cut off,
and whose trust shall be a spider's web.
15 He shall lean upon his house, but it shall not stand:
he shall hold it fast, but it shall not endure.
16 He is green before the sun,
and his branch shooteth forth in his garden.
17 His roots are wrapped about the heap,
and seeth the place of stones.
18 If he destroy him from his place,
then it shall deny him, saying, I have not seen thee.
19 Behold, this is the joy of his way,
and out of the earth shall others grow.

20 Behold, God will not cast away a perfect man,
neither will he help the evil doers:
21 Till he fill thy mouth with laughing,
and thy lips with rejoicing.
22 They that hate thee shall be clothed with shame;
and the dwelling place of the wicked shall come to nought.

Isaiah 48

1 Hear ye this, O house of Jacob,
which are called by the name of Israel,
and are come forth out of the waters of Judah,
which swear by the name of the Lord,
and make mention of the God of Israel,
but not in truth, nor in righteousness.
2 For they call themselves of the holy city,
and stay themselves upon the God of Israel;
The Lord of hosts is his name.
3 I have declared the former things from the beginning;
and they went forth out of my mouth, and I shewed them;
I did them suddenly, and they came to pass.
4 Because I knew that thou art obstinate,
and thy neck is an iron sinew,
and thy brow brass;
5 I have even from the beginning declared it to thee;
before it came to pass I shewed it thee:
lest thou shouldest say, Mine idol hath done them,
and my graven image, and my molten image, hath commanded them.
6 Thou hast heard, see all this; and will not ye declare it? I have
shewed thee new things from this time, even hidden things, and thou
didst not know them.
7 They are created now, and not from the beginning;
even before the day when thou heardest them not;
lest thou shouldest say, Behold, I knew them.
8 Yea, thou heardest not; yea, thou knewest not;
yea, from that time that thine ear was not opened:
for I knew that thou wouldest deal very treacherously,
and wast called a transgressor from the womb.
9 For my name's sake will I defer mine anger,

and for my praise will I refrain for thee,
that I cut thee not off.
10 Behold, I have refined thee, but not with silver;
I have chosen thee in the furnace of affliction.
11 For mine own sake, even for mine own sake, will I do it:
for how should my name be polluted?
and I will not give my glory unto another.
12 Hearken unto me, O Jacob and Israel, my called;
I am he; I am the first, I also am the last.
13 Mine hand also hath laid the foundation of the earth,
and my right hand hath spanned the heavens:
when I call unto them, they stand up together.
14 All ye, assemble yourselves, and hear;
which among them hath declared these things?
The Lord hath loved him:
he will do his pleasure on Babylon,
and his arm shall be on the Chaldeans.
15 I, even I, have spoken; yea, I have called him:
I have brought him, and he shall make his way prosperous.
16 Come ye near unto me, hear ye this;
I have not spoken in secret from the beginning;
from the time that it was, there am I:
and now the Lord God, and his Spirit, hath sent me.
17 Thus saith the Lord, thy Redeemer, the Holy One of Israel;
I am the Lord thy God which teacheth thee to profit,
which leadeth thee by the way that thou shouldest go.
18 O that thou hadst hearkened to my commandments! then had thy
peace been as a river, and thy righteousness as the waves of the sea:
19 Thy seed also had been as the sand,
and the offspring of thy bowels like the gravel thereof;
his name should not have been cut off nor destroyed from before me.
20 Go ye forth of Babylon, flee ye from the Chaldeans,
with a voice of singing declare ye, tell this,
utter it even to the end of the earth;
say ye, The Lord hath redeemed his servant Jacob.
21 And they thirsted not when he led them through the deserts:
he caused the waters to flow out of the rock for them:
he clave the rock also, and the waters gushed out.
22 There is no peace, saith the Lord, unto the wicked.

Zechariah 8

1 Again the word of the Lord of hosts came to me, saying,
2 Thus saith the Lord of hosts;
I was jealous for Zion with great jealousy,
and I was jealous for her with great fury.
3 Thus saith the Lord; I am returned unto Zion,
and will dwell in the midst of Jerusalem:
and Jerusalem shall be called a city of truth;
and the mountain of the Lord of hosts the holy mountain.
4 Thus saith the Lord of hosts;
There shall yet old men and old women dwell in the streets of
Jerusalem,
and every man with his staff in his hand for very age.
5 And the streets of the city shall be full of boys and girls
playing in the streets thereof.
6 Thus saith the Lord of hosts;
If it be marvellous in the eyes of the remnant of this people in these
days,
should it also be marvellous in mine eyes? saith the Lord of hosts.
7 Thus saith the Lord of hosts;
Behold, I will save my people from the east country,
and from the west country;
8 And I will bring them, and they shall dwell in the midst of
Jerusalem:
and they shall be my people, and I will be their God,
in truth and in righteousness.
9 Thus saith the Lord of hosts; Let your hands be strong, ye that hear
in these days these words by the mouth of the prophets, which were in
the day that the foundation of the house of the Lord of hosts was laid,
that the temple might be built. 10 For before these days there was no
hire for man, nor any hire for beast; neither was there any peace to
him that went out or came in because of the affliction:for I set all men
every one against his neighbour. 11 But now I will not be unto the
residue of this people as in the former days, saith the Lord of hosts. **12
For the seed shall be prosperous; the vine shall give her fruit, and
the ground shall give her increase, and the heavens shall give
their dew; and I will cause the remnant of this people to possess
all these things.** 13 And it shall come to pass, that as ye were a curse
among the heathen, O house of Judah, and house of Israel; so will I

save you, and ye shall be a blessing:fear not, but let your hands be strong. 14 For thus saith the Lord of hosts; As I thought to punish you, when your fathers provoked me to wrath, saith the Lord of hosts, and I repented not:15 So again have I thought in these days to do well unto Jerusalem and to the house of Judah:fear ye not.

16 These are the things that ye shall do; Speak ye every man the truth to his neighbour; execute the judgment of truth and peace in your gates:17 And let none of you imagine evil in your hearts against his neighbour; and love no false oath:for all these are things that I hate, saith the Lord. 18 And the word of the Lord of hosts came unto me, saying, 19 Thus saith the Lord of hosts; The fast of the fourth month, and the fast of the fifth, and the fast of the seventh, and the fast of the tenth, shall be to the house of Judah joy and gladness, and cheerful feasts; therefore love the truth and peace. 20 Thus saith the Lord of hosts; It shall yet come to pass, that there shall come people, and the inhabitants of many cities: 21 And the inhabitants of one city shall go to another, saying, Let us go speedily to pray before the Lord, and to seek the Lord of hosts:I will go also. 22 Yea, many people and strong nations shall come to seek the Lord of hosts in Jerusalem, and to pray before the Lord. 23 Thus saith the Lord of hosts; In those days it shall come to pass, that ten men shall take hold out of all languages of the nations, even shall take hold of the skirt of him that is a Jew, saying, We will go with you:for we have heard that God is with you.

Romans 1

1 Paul, a servant of Jesus Christ, called to be an apostle, separated unto the gospel of God, 2 (Which he had promised afore by his prophets in the holy scriptures,) 3 Concerning his Son Jesus Christ our Lord, which was made of the seed of David according to the flesh; 4 And declared to be the Son of God with power, according to the spirit of holiness, by the resurrection from the dead:5 By whom we have received grace and apostleship, for obedience to the faith among all nations, for his name:6 Among whom are ye also the called of Jesus Christ: 7 To all that be in Rome, beloved of God, called to be saints:Grace to you and peace from God our Father, and the Lord Jesus Christ. 8 First, I thank my God through Jesus Christ for you all, that your faith is spoken of throughout the whole world. 9 For God is

my witness, whom I serve with my spirit in the gospel of his Son, that without ceasing I make mention of you always in my prayers; **10 Making request, if by any means now at length I might have a prosperous journey by the will of God to come unto you.** 11 For I long to see you, that I may impart unto you some spiritual gift, to the end ye may be established; 12 That is, that I may be comforted together with you by the mutual faith both of you and me.

13 Now I would not have you ignorant, brethren, that oftentimes I purposed to come unto you, (but was let hitherto,) that I might have some fruit among you also, even as among other Gentiles. 14 I am debtor both to the Greeks, and to the Barbarians; both to the wise, and to the unwise. 15 So, as much as in me is, I am ready to preach the gospel to you that are at Rome also.

16 For I am not ashamed of the gospel of Christ:for it is the power of God unto salvation to every one that believeth; to the Jew first, and also to the Greek. 17 For therein is the righteousness of God revealed from faith to faith:as it is written, The just shall live by faith.

18 For the wrath of God is revealed from heaven against all ungodliness and unrighteousness of men, who hold the truth in unrighteousness; 19 Because that which may be known of God is manifest in them; for God hath shewed it unto them. 20 For the invisible things of him from the creation of the world are clearly seen, being understood by the things that are made, even his eternal power and Godhead; so that they are without excuse:21 Because that, when they knew God, they glorified him not as God, neither were thankful; but became vain in their imaginations, and their foolish heart was darkened. 22 Professing themselves to be wise, they became fools, 23 And changed the glory of the uncorruptible God into an image made like to corruptible man, and to birds, and fourfooted beasts, and creeping things.

24 Wherefore God also gave them up to uncleanness through the lusts of their own hearts, to dishonour their own bodies between themselves:25 Who changed the truth of God into a lie, and worshipped and served the creature more than the Creator, who is blessed for ever. Amen.

26 For this cause God gave them up unto vile affections:for even their women did change the natural use into that which is against nature:27 And likewise also the men, leaving the natural use of the woman, burned in their lust one toward another; men with men working that

which is unseemly, and receiving in themselves that recompence of their error which was meet.

28 And even as they did not like to retain God in their knowledge, God gave them over to a reprobate mind, to do those things which are not convenient; 29 Being filled with all unrighteousness, fornication, wickedness, covetousness, maliciousness; full of envy, murder, debate, deceit, malignity; whisperers, 30 Backbiters, haters of God, despiteful, proud, boasters, inventors of evil things, disobedient to parents, 31 Without understanding, covenantbreakers, without natural affection, implacable, unmerciful:32 Who knowing the judgment of God, that they which commit such things are worthy of death, not only do the same, but have pleasure in them that do them.

Wisdom Keys – When much is given much is required

Chapter 7

Chapters on Prosperously

Prosperously

2 Chronicles 7

1 Now when Solomon had made an end of praying, the fire came down from heaven, and consumed the burnt offering and the sacrifices; and the glory of the Lord filled the house. 2 And the priests could not enter into the house of the Lord, because the glory of the Lord had filled the Lord 's house. 3 And when all the children of Israel saw how the fire came down, and the glory of the Lord upon the house, they bowed themselves with their faces to the ground upon the pavement, and worshipped, and praised the Lord, saying, For he is good; for his mercy endureth for ever.

4 Then the king and all the people offered sacrifices before the Lord. 5 And king Solomon offered a sacrifice of twenty and two thousand oxen, and an hundred and twenty thousand sheep:so the king and all the people dedicated the house of God. 6 And the priests waited on their offices:the Levites also with instruments of musick of the Lord, which David the king had made to praise the Lord, because his mercy endureth for ever, when David praised by their ministry; and the priests sounded trumpets before them, and all Israel stood. 7 Moreover Solomon hallowed the middle of the court that was before the house of the Lord:for there he offered burnt offerings, and the fat of the peace offerings, because the brasen altar which Solomon had made was not able to receive the burnt offerings, and the meat offerings, and the fat. 8 Also at the same time Solomon kept the feast seven days, and all Israel with him, a very great congregation, from

the entering in of Hamath unto the river of Egypt. 9 And in the eighth day they made a solemn assembly:for they kept the dedication of the altar seven days, and the feast seven days. 10 And on the three and twentieth day of the seventh month he sent the people away into their tents, glad and merry in heart for the goodness that the Lord had shewed unto David, and to Solomon, and to Israel his people. **11 Thus Solomon finished the house of the Lord, and the king's house:and all that came into Solomon's heart to make in the house of the Lord, and in his own house, he prosperously effected.** 12 And the Lord appeared to Solomon by night, and said unto him, I have heard thy prayer, and have chosen this place to myself for an house of sacrifice. 13 If I shut up heaven that there be no rain, or if I command the locusts to devour the land, or if I send pestilence among my people; 14 If my people, which are called by my name, shall humble themselves, and pray, and seek my face, and turn from their wicked ways; then will I hear from heaven, and will forgive their sin, and will heal their land. 15 Now mine eyes shall be open, and mine ears attent unto the prayer that is made in this place. 16 For now have I chosen and sanctified this house, that my name may be there for ever:and mine eyes and mine heart shall be there perpetually. 17 And as for thee, if thou wilt walk before me, as David thy father walked, and do according to all that I have commanded thee, and shalt observe my statutes and my judgments; 18 Then will I stablish the throne of thy kingdom, according as I have covenanted with David thy father, saying, There shall not fail thee a man to be ruler in Israel. 19 But if ye turn away, and forsake my statutes and my commandments, which I have set before you, and shall go and serve other gods, and worship them; 20 Then will I pluck them up by the roots out of my land which I have given them; and this house, which I have sanctified for my name, will I cast out of my sight, and will make it to be a proverb and a byword among all nations. 21 And this house, which is high, shall be an astonishment to every one that passeth by it; so that he shall say, Why hath the Lord done thus unto this land, and unto this house? 22 And it shall be answered, Because they forsook the Lord God of their fathers, which brought them forth out of the land of Egypt, and laid hold on other gods, and worshipped them, and served them:therefore hath he brought all this evil upon them.

Psalms 45

To the chief Musician upon Shoshannim, for the sons of Korah, Maschil, A Song of loves.

1 My heart is inditing a good matter:

I speak of the things which I have made touching the king:my tongue is the pen of a ready writer.

2 Thou art fairer than the children of men:

grace is poured into thy lips:

therefore God hath blessed thee for ever.

3 Gird thy sword upon thy thigh, O most mighty,

with thy glory and thy majesty.

4 And in thy majesty ride prosperously

because of truth and meekness and righteousness;

and thy right hand shall teach thee terrible things.

5 Thine arrows are sharp

in the heart of the king's enemies;

whereby the people fall under thee.

6 Thy throne, O God, is for ever and ever:

the sceptre of thy kingdom is a right sceptre.

7 Thou lovest righteousness, and hatest wickedness:

therefore God, thy God, hath anointed thee

with the oil of gladness above thy fellows.

8 All thy garments smell of myrrh, and aloes, and cassia,

out of the ivory palaces, whereby they have made thee glad.

9 Kings 'daughters were among thy honourable women:

upon thy right hand did stand the queen in gold of Ophir.

10 Hearken, O daughter, and consider, and incline thine ear;

forget also thine own people, and thy father's house;

11 So shall the king greatly desire thy beauty:

for he is thy Lord; and worship thou him.

12 And the daughter of Tyre shall be there with a gift;
even the rich among the people shall intreat thy favour.
13 The king's daughter is all glorious within:
her clothing is of wrought gold.
14 She shall be brought unto the king in raiment of needlework:
the virgins her companions that follow her shall be brought unto thee.
15 With gladness and rejoicing shall they be brought:
they shall enter into the king's palace.
16 Instead of thy fathers shall be thy children,
whom thou mayest make princes in all the earth.
17 I will make thy name to be remembered in all generations:
therefore shall the people praise thee for ever and ever.

Chapter 8

Scriptures on the Hebrew word towb (H2896)

Listed in this chapter will be all translated English, Hebrew and Aramaic words associated with the word prosperity. The numbers gives the reference to the Hebrew original word. The word before the number in the Scripture reference is the English word translated. See example below:

Gen 1:10
And God called the dry land Earth; and the gathering together of the waters called he Seas: and God saw that it was **good. H2896**

The word good is followed by H2986

The original Hebrew word for good is **towb** (H2986), This Hebrew word (towb) is also translated prosperity in other verses of the Bible. Therefore, all words listed in this chapter have the same meaning as prosperity. It is important in our bible study go back to the original Hebrew, Greek and Aramaic word for definition purpose. In one place the word prosperity might have a total different meaning depending on the original Hebrew, Greek and Aramaic word.

Example 2:

Deu 23:6
Thou shalt not seek their peace nor their **prosperity H2896** all thy days for ever.

In this example the translator used the word prosperity for the Hebrew word **towb (H2896)**. With these two examples, the words prosperity and good are used. They both come from the same Hebrew word towb (H2896). This will help us to understand how the bible was translated to our English language.

This bible study guide will help you to increase your faith in the word of God. The Holy Spirit will give you the understanding you need to comprehend his divine word. Faith comes by hearing and hearing with understanding from God Word. I encourage you to study to show yourself approved unto God.

These words include the following number of Scripture References:

- Good (61 times)
- Better (72 times)
- Well (20 times)
- Goodness (16 times)
- Goodly (9 times)
- Best (8 times)
- Merry (7 times)
- Fair (7 times)
- Prosperity (6 times)
- Fine (3 times)
- Precious (4 times)
- Wealth (3 times)
- Beautiful (2 times)
- Fairer (2 times)
- Favour (2 times)
- Glad (2 times)

- Misc. (35* times)

*Indicates more than one word used

Sum: good (361x), better (72x), well (20x), goodness (16x), goodly (9x), best (8x), merry (7x), fair (7x), prosperity (6x), precious (4x), fine (3x), wealth (3x), beautiful (2x), fairer (2x), favour (2x), glad (2x), misc (35x).

Find below English words translated from the Hebrew word towb

1. **H 2986 - towb**

2. **Strong Definition:**

From 2895; good (as an adjective) in the widest sense; used likewise as a noun, both in the masculine and the feminine, the singular and the plural (good, a good or good thing, a good man or woman; the good, goods or good things, good men or women), also as an adverb (well):--beautiful, best, better, bountiful, cheerful, at ease, X fair (word), (be in) favour, fine, glad, good (deed, -lier, liest, -ly, -ness, -s), graciously, joyful, kindly, kindness, liketh (best), loving, merry, X most, pleasant, + pleaseth, pleasure, precious, prosperity, ready, sweet, wealth, welfare, (be) well ([-favoured]).

English Definition of the word most used for 2896 (towb)

1. Having admirable, pleasing, superior, or positive qualities, not negative, bad or mediocre: a good idea; a good teacher.

2. a. morally excellent or admirable; virtuous; righteous: a good man.

b. (as collective noun; preceded by the): the good.

3. Suitable or efficient for a purpose: a good secretary; a good winter coat.

4. Beneficial or advantageous: vegetables are good for you.

5. Not ruined or decayed; sound or whole: the meat is still good.

6. Kindly, generous, or approving: you are good to him.

7. Right or acceptable: your qualifications are good for the job.

8. Rich and fertile: good land.

9. Valid or genuine: I would not do this without good reason.

10. Honorable or held in high esteem: a good family.

11. Commercially or financially secure, sound, or safe: good securities; a good investment.

12. (Banking & Finance) (of a draft) drawn for a stated sum

13. (Banking & Finance) (Of debts) expected to be fully paid

14. Clever, competent, or talented: he's good at science.

15. Obedient or well-behaved: a good dog.

16. Reliable, safe, or recommended: a good make of clothes.

17. Affording material pleasure or indulgence: the good things in life; the good life.

18. Having a well-proportioned, beautiful, or generally fine appearance: a good figure; a good complexion.

19. Complete; full: I took a good look round the house.

20. Propitious; opportune: a good time to ask the manager for a rise.

21. Satisfying or gratifying: a good rest.

22. Comfortable: did you have a good night?

23. Newest or of the best quality: to keep the good plates for important guests.

24. Fairly large, extensive, or long: a good distance away.

25. Sufficient; ample: we have a good supply of food.

26. (Cookery) US (of meat) of the third government grade, above standard and below choice

27. Serious or intellectual: good music.

28. used in a traditional description: the good ship ``America''.

29. Used in polite or patronizing phrases or to express anger (often intended ironically): how is your good lady?; look here, my good man!.

30. A good one

a. an unbelievable assertion

b. a very funny joke

31. As good as virtually; practically: it's as good as finished.

32. As good as gold excellent; very good indeed

33. Be as good as to be so good as to would you please

34. Come good to recover and perform well after a bad start or setback

35. Good and (intensifier): good and mad.

36. (Intensifier; used in mild oaths): good grief!; good heavens!.

37. An exclamation of approval, agreement, pleasure, etc.

38. Moral or material advantage or use; benefit or profit: for the good of our workers; what is the good of worrying?

39. Positive moral qualities; goodness; virtue; righteousness; piety

40. (Sometimes capital) moral qualities seen as a single abstract entity: we must pursue the Good.

41. A good thing

42. (Economics) economics a commodity or service that satisfies a human need

43. For good for good and all forever; permanently: I have left them for good.

44. Make good

a. to recompense or repair damage or injury

b. to be successful

c. to demonstrate or prove the truth of (a statement or accusation)

d. to secure and retain (a position)

e. to effect or fulfil (something intended or promised)

45. Good on you good for you well done, well said, etc.: a term of congratulation

46. Get any good of get some good of

a. to handle to good effect: I never got any good of this machine.

b. to understand properly: I could never get any good of him.

c. to receive cooperation from

[Old English gōd; related to Old Norse gōthr, Old High German guot good]

3. Translated to English words 559 times

Good (351x), better (72x), well (20x), goodness (16x), goodly (9x), best (8x), merry (7x), fair (7x), prosperity (6x), precious (4x), fine (3x), wealth (3x), beautiful (2x), fairer (2x), favour (2x), misc (35x)

4. **Strong's Number H2896** matches the Hebrew בוט (towb), which occurs 559 times in 517 verses in the Hebrew concordance of the KJV

5. Scriptures references with Hebrew reference number behind word: (Example – good H2896)

Gen 1:4

And God saw the light, that it was **good: H2896** and God divided the light from the darkness.

Gen 1:10

And God called the dry land Earth; and the gathering together of the waters called he Seas: and God saw that it was **good. H2896**

Gen 1:12

And the earth brought forth grass, and herb yielding seed after his kind, and the tree yielding fruit, whose seed was in itself, after his kind: and God saw that it was good. H2896

Gen 1:18

And to rule over the day and over the night, and to divide the light from the darkness: and God saw that it was good. H2896

Gen 1:21
And God created great whales, and every living creature that moveth, which the waters brought forth abundantly, after their kind, and every winged fowl after his kind: and God saw that it was good. H2896

Gen 1:25
And God made the beast of the earth after his kind, and cattle after their kind, and every thing that creepeth upon the earth after his kind: and God saw that it was good. H2896

Gen 1:31
And God saw every thing that he had made, and, behold, it was very good. H2896 And the evening and the morning were the sixth day.

Gen 2:9
And out of the ground made the LORD God to grow every tree that is pleasant to the sight, and good H2896 for food; the tree of life also in the midst of the garden, and the tree of knowledge of good H2896 and evil.

Gen 2:12
And the gold of that land is good: H2896 there is bdellium and the onyx stone.

Gen 2:17
But of the tree of the knowledge of good H2896 and evil, thou shalt not eat of it: for in the day that thou eatest thereof thou shalt surely die.

Gen 2:18
And the LORD God said, It is not good H2896 that the man should be alone; I will make him an help meet for him.

Gen 3:5
For God doth know that in the day ye eat thereof, then your eyes shall
be opened, and ye shall be as gods, knowing good H2896 and evil.

Gen 3:6
And when the woman saw that the tree was good H2896 for food, and
that it was pleasant to the eyes, and a tree to be desired to make one
wise, she took of the fruit thereof, and did eat, and gave also unto her
husband with her; and he did eat.

Gen 3:22
And the LORD God said, Behold, the man is become as one of us, to
know good H2896 and evil: and now, lest he put forth his hand, and
take also of the tree of life, and eat, and live for ever:

Gen 6:2
That the sons of God saw the daughters of men that they were fair;
H2896 and they took them wives of all which they chose.

Gen 15:15
And thou shalt go to thy fathers in peace; thou shalt be buried in a
good H2896 old age.

Gen 16:6
But Abram said unto Sarai, Behold, thy maid is in thy hand; do to her
as it pleaseth thee. H2896 And when Sarai dealt hardly with her, she
fled from her face.

Gen 18:7
And Abraham ran unto the herd, and fetcht a calf tender and good,
H2896 and gave it unto a young man; and he hasted to dress it.

Gen 19:8
Behold now, I have two daughters which have not known man; let

me, I pray you, bring them out unto you, and do ye to them as is good H2896 in your eyes: only unto these men do nothing; for therefore came they under the shadow of my roof.

Gen 20:15
And Abimelech said, Behold, my land is before thee: dwell where it pleaseth H2896 thee.

Gen 24:16
And the damsel was very fair H2896 to look upon, a virgin, neither had any man known her: and she went down to the well, and filled her pitcher, and came up.

Gen 24:50
Then Laban and Bethuel answered and said, The thing proceedeth from the LORD: we cannot speak unto thee bad or good. H2896

Gen 25:8
Then Abraham gave up the ghost, and died in a good H2896 old age, an old man, and full of years; and was gathered to his people.

Gen 26:7
And the men of the place asked him of his wife; and he said, She is my sister: for he feared to say, She is my wife; lest, said he, the men of the place should kill me for Rebekah; because she was fair H2896 to look upon.

Gen 26:29
That thou wilt do us no hurt, as we have not touched thee, and as we have done unto thee nothing but good, H2896 and have sent thee away in peace: thou art now the blessed of the LORD.

Gen 27:9
Go now to the flock, and fetch me from thence two good H2896 kids

of the goats; and I will make them savoury meat for thy father, such as he loveth:

Gen 29:19
And Laban said, It is better H2896 that I give her to thee, than that I should give her to another man: abide with me.

Gen 30:20
And Leah said, God hath endued me with a good H2896 dowry; now will my husband dwell with me, because I have born him six sons: and she called his name Zebulun.

Gen 31:24
And God came to Laban the Syrian in a dream by night, and said unto him, Take heed that thou speak not to Jacob either good H2896 or bad.

Gen 31:29
It is in the power of my hand to do you hurt: but the God of your father spake unto me yesternight, saying, Take thou heed that thou speak not to Jacob either good H2896 or bad.

Gen 40:16
When the chief baker saw that the interpretation was good, H2896 he said unto Joseph, I also was in my dream, and, behold, I had three white baskets on my head:

Gen 41:5
And he slept and dreamed the second time: and, behold, seven ears of corn came up upon one stalk, rank and good. H2896

Gen 41:22
And I saw in my dream, and, behold, seven ears came up in one stalk, full and good: H2896

Gen 41:24
And the thin ears devoured the seven good H2896 ears: and I told this
unto the magicians; but there was none that could declare it to me.

Gen 41:26
The seven good H2896 kine are seven years; and the seven good
H2896 ears are seven years: the dream is one.

Gen 41:35
And let them gather all the food of those good H2896 years that
come, and lay up corn under the hand of Pharaoh, and let them keep
food in the cities.

Gen 44:4
And when they were gone out of the city, and not yet far off, Joseph
said unto his steward, Up, follow after the men; and when thou dost
overtake them, say unto them, Wherefore have ye rewarded evil for
good? H2896

Gen 49:15
And he saw that rest was good, H2896 and the land that it was
pleasant; and bowed his shoulder to bear, and became a servant unto
tribute.

Gen 50:20
But as for you, ye thought evil against me; but God meant it unto
good, H2896 to bring to pass, as it is this day, to save much people
alive.

Exd 2:2
And the woman conceived, and bare a son: and when she saw him
that he was a goodly H2896 child, she hid him three months.

Exd 3:8
And I am come down to deliver them out of the hand of the
Egyptians, and to bring them up out of that land unto a good H2896
land and a large, unto a land flowing with milk and honey; unto the
place of the Canaanites, and the Hittites, and the Amorites, and the
Perizzites, and the Hivites, and the Jebusites.

Exd 14:12
Is not this the word that we did tell thee in Egypt, saying, Let us
alone, that we may serve the Egyptians? For it had been better H2896
for us to serve the Egyptians, than that we should die in the
wilderness.

Exd 18:9
And Jethro rejoiced for all the goodness H2896 which the LORD had
done to Israel, whom he had delivered out of the hand of the
Egyptians.

Exd 18:17
And Moses' father in law said unto him, The thing that thou doest is
not good. H2896

Lev 27:10
He shall not alter it, nor change it, a good H2896 for a bad, or a bad
for a good: H2896 and if he shall at all change beast for beast, then it
and the exchange thereof shall be holy.

Lev 27:12
And the priest shall value it, whether it be good H2896 or bad: as thou
valuest it, who art the priest, so shall it be.

Lev 27:14
And when a man shall sanctify his house to be holy unto the LORD,
then the priest shall estimate it, whether it be good H2896 or bad: as

the priest shall estimate it, so shall it stand.

Lev 27:33
He shall not search whether it be good H2896 or bad, neither shall he
change it: and if he change it at all, then both it and the change thereof
shall be holy; it shall not be redeemed.

Num 10:29
And Moses said unto Hobab, the son of Raguel the Midianite, Moses'
father in law, We are journeying unto the place of which the LORD
said, I will give it you: come thou with us, and we will do thee good:
for the LORD hath spoken good H2896 concerning Israel.

Num 10:32
And it shall be, if thou go with us, yea, it shall be, that what goodness
H2896 the LORD shall do unto us, the same will we do unto thee.

Strong's Number H2896 matches the Hebrew טוֹב (towb),
which occurs 559 times in 517 verses in the Hebrew concordance of
the KJV
Page 2 / 11 (Num 13:19–Rth 2:22)

Num 13:19
And what the land is that they dwell in, whether it be good H2896 or
bad; and what cities they be that they dwell in, whether in tents, or in
strong holds;

Num 14:3
And wherefore hath the LORD brought us unto this land, to fall by
the sword, that our wives and our children should be a prey? were it
not better H2896 for us to return into Egypt?

Num 14:7
And they spake unto all the company of the children of Israel, saying,
The land, which we passed through to search it, is an exceeding good
H2896 land.

Num 24:13
If Balak would give me his house full of silver and gold, I cannot go
beyond the commandment of the LORD, to do either good H2896 or
bad of mine own mind; but what the LORD saith, that will I speak?

Num 36:6
This is the thing which the LORD doth command concerning the
daughters of Zelophehad, saying, Let them marry to whom they think
best; H2896 only to the family of the tribe of their father shall they
marry.

Deu 1:14
And ye answered me, and said, The thing which thou hast spoken is
good H2896 for us to do.

Deu 1:25
And they took of the fruit of the land in their hands, and brought it
down unto us, and brought us word again, and said, It is a good
H2896 land which the LORD our God doth give us.

Deu 1:35
Surely there shall not one of these men of this evil generation see that
good H2896 land, which I sware to give unto your fathers,

Deu 1:39
Moreover your little ones, which ye said should be a prey, and your
children, which in that day had no knowledge between good H2896
and evil, they shall go in thither, and unto them will I give it, and they
shall possess it.

Deu 3:25
I pray thee, let me go over, and see the good H2896 land that is
beyond Jordan, that goodly H2896 mountain, and Lebanon.

Deu 4:21
Furthermore the LORD was angry with me for your sakes, and sware
that I should not go over Jordan, and that I should not go in unto that
good H2896 land, which the LORD thy God giveth thee for an
inheritance:

Deu 4:22
But I must die in this land, I must not go over Jordan: but ye shall go
over, and possess that good H2896 land.

Deu 6:10
And it shall be, when the LORD thy God shall have brought thee into
the land which he sware unto thy fathers, to Abraham, to Isaac, and to
Jacob, to give thee great and goodly H2896 cities, which thou
buildedst not,

Deu 6:18
And thou shalt do that which is right and good H2896 in the sight of
the LORD: that it may be well with thee, and that thou mayest go in
and possess the good H2896 land which the LORD sware unto thy
fathers,

Deu 6:24
And the LORD commanded us to do all these statutes, to fear the
LORD our God, for our good H2896 always, that he might preserve
us alive, as it is at this day.

Deu 8:7
For the LORD thy God bringeth thee into a good H2896 land, a land
of brooks of water, of fountains and depths that spring out of valleys

and hills;

Deu 8:10
When thou hast eaten and art full, then thou shalt bless the LORD thy God for the good H2896 land which he hath given thee.

Deu 8:12
Lest when thou hast eaten and art full, and hast built goodly H2896 houses, and dwelt therein;

Deu 9:6
Understand therefore, that the LORD thy God giveth thee not this good H2896 land to possess it for thy righteousness; for thou art a stiffnecked people.

Deu 10:13
To keep the commandments of the LORD, and his statutes, which I command thee this day for thy good? H2896

Deu 11:17
And then the LORD'S wrath be kindled against you, and he shut up the heaven, that there be no rain, and that the land yield not her fruit; and lest ye perish quickly from off the good H2896 land which the LORD giveth you.

Deu 12:28
Observe and hear all these words which I command thee, that it may go well with thee, and with thy children after thee for ever, when thou doest that which is good H2896 and right in the sight of the LORD thy God.

Deu 23:6
Thou shalt not seek their peace nor their prosperity H2896 all thy

days for ever.

Deu 23:16
He shall dwell with thee, even among you, in that place which he shall choose in one of thy gates, where it liketh him best: H2896 thou shalt not oppress him.

Deu 26:11
And thou shalt rejoice in every good H2896 thing which the LORD thy God hath given unto thee, and unto thine house, thou, and the Levite, and the stranger that is among you.

Deu 28:11
And the LORD shall make thee plenteous in goods, H2896 in the fruit of thy body, and in the fruit of thy cattle, and in the fruit of thy ground, in the land which the LORD sware unto thy fathers to give thee.

Deu 28:12
The LORD shall open unto thee his good H2896 treasure, the heaven to give the rain unto thy land in his season, and to bless all the work of thine hand: and thou shalt lend unto many nations, and thou shalt not borrow.

Deu 30:9
And the LORD thy God will make thee plenteous in every work of thine hand, in the fruit of thy body, and in the fruit of thy cattle, and in the fruit of thy land, for good: H2896 for the LORD will again rejoice over thee for good, H2896 as he rejoiced over thy fathers:

Deu 30:15
See, I have set before thee this day life and good, H2896 and death and evil;

Jos 7:21
When I saw among the spoils a goodly H2896 Babylonish garment,
and two hundred shekels of silver, and a wedge of gold of fifty
shekels weight, then I coveted them, and took them; and, behold, they
are hid in the earth in the midst of my tent, and the silver under it.

Jos 9:25
And now, behold, we are in thine hand: as it seemeth good H2896 and
right unto thee to do unto us, do.

Jos 21:45
There failed not ought of any good H2896 thing which the LORD had
spoken unto the house of Israel; all came to pass.

Jos 23:13
Know for a certainty that the LORD your God will no more drive out
any of these nations from before you; but they shall be snares and
traps unto you, and scourges in your sides, and thorns in your eyes,
until ye perish from off this good H2896 land which the LORD your
God hath given you.

Jos 23:14
And, behold, this day I am going the way of all the earth: and ye
know in all your hearts and in all your souls, that not one thing hath
failed of all the good H2896 things which the LORD your God spake
concerning you; all are come to pass unto you, and not one thing hath
failed thereof.

Jos 23:15
Therefore it shall come to pass, that as all good H2896 things are
come upon you, which the LORD your God promised you; so shall
the LORD bring upon you all evil things, until he have destroyed you
from off this good H2896 land which the LORD your God hath given
you.

Jos 23:16
When ye have transgressed the covenant of the LORD your God,
which he commanded you, and have gone and served other gods, and
bowed yourselves to them; then shall the anger of the LORD be
kindled against you, and ye shall perish quickly from off the good
H2896 land which he hath given unto you.

Jdg 8:2
And he said unto them, What have I done now in comparison of you?
Is not the gleaning of the grapes of Ephraim better H2896 than the
vintage of Abiezer?

Jdg 8:32
And Gideon the son of Joash died in a good H2896 old age, and was
buried in the sepulchre of Joash his father, in Ophrah of the
Abiezrites.

Jdg 8:35
Neither shewed they kindness to the house of Jerubbaal, namely,
Gideon, according to all the goodness H2896 which he had shewed
unto Israel.

Jdg 9:2
Speak, I pray you, in the ears of all the men of Shechem, Whether is
better H2896 for you, either that all the sons of Jerubbaal, which are
threescore and ten persons, reign over you, or that one reign over
you? remember also that I am your bone and your flesh.

Jdg 9:11
But the fig tree said unto them, Should I forsake my sweetness, and
my good H2896 fruit, and go to be promoted over the trees?

Jdg 9:16
Now therefore, if ye have done truly and sincerely, in that ye have

made Abimelech king, and if ye have dealt well H2896 with
Jerubbaal and his house, and have done unto him according to the
deserving of his hands;

Jdg 10:15
And the children of Israel said unto the LORD, We have sinned: do
thou unto us whatsoever seemeth good H2896 unto thee; deliver us
only, we pray thee, this day.

Jdg 11:25
And now art thou any thing better H2896 than Balak the son of
Zippor, king of Moab? did he ever strive against Israel, or did he ever
fight against them,

Jdg 15:2
And her father said, I verily thought that thou hadst utterly hated her;
therefore I gave her to thy companion: is not her younger sister fairer
H2896 than she? take her, I pray thee, instead of her.

Jdg 16:25
And it came to pass, when their hearts were merry, H2896 that they
said, Call for Samson, that he may make us sport. And they called for
Samson out of the prison house; and he made them sport: and they set
him between the pillars.

Jdg 18:9
And they said, Arise, that we may go up against them: for we have
seen the land, and, behold, it is very good: H2896 and are ye still? be
not slothful to go, and to enter to possess the land.

Jdg 18:19
And they said unto him, Hold thy peace, lay thine hand upon thy
mouth, and go with us, and be to us a father and a priest: is it better
H2896 for thee to be a priest unto the house of one man, or that thou

be a priest unto a tribe and a family in Israel?

Jdg 19:24
Behold, here is my daughter a maiden, and his concubine; them I will bring out now, and humble ye them, and do with them what seemeth good H2896 unto you: but unto this man do not so vile a thing.

Rth 2:22
And Naomi said unto Ruth her daughter in law, It is good, H2896 my daughter, that thou go out with his maidens, that they meet thee not in any other field.

Rth 3:13
Tarry this night, and it shall be in the morning, that if he will perform unto thee the part of a kinsman, well; H2896 let him do the kinsman's part: but if he will not do the part of a kinsman to thee, then will I do the part of a kinsman to thee, as the LORD liveth: lie down until the morning.

Rth 4:15
And he shall be unto thee a restorer of thy life, and a nourisher of thine old age: for thy daughter in law, which loveth thee, which is better H2896 to thee than seven sons, hath born him.

1Sa 1:8
Then said Elkanah her husband to her, Hannah, why weepest thou? and why eatest thou not? and why is thy heart grieved? am not I better H2896 to thee than ten sons?

1Sa 1:23
And Elkanah her husband said unto her, Do what seemeth thee good; H2896 tarry until thou have weaned him; only the LORD establish his word. So the woman abode, and gave her son suck until she weaned him.

1Sa 2:24
Nay, my sons; for it is no good H2896 report that I hear: ye make the LORD'S people to transgress.

1Sa 2:26
And the child Samuel grew on, and was in favour H2896 both with the LORD, and also with men.

1Sa 3:18
And Samuel told him every whit, and hid nothing from him. And he said, It is the LORD: let him do what seemeth him good. H2896

1Sa 8:14
And he will take your fields, and your vineyards, and your oliveyards, even the best H2896 of them, and give them to his servants.

1Sa 8:16
And he will take your menservants, and your maidservants, and your goodliest H2896 young men, and your asses, and put them to his work.

1Sa 9:2
And he had a son, whose name was Saul, a choice young man, and a goodly: H2896 and there was not among the children of Israel a goodlier H2896 person than he: from his shoulders and upward he was higher than any of the people.

1Sa 9:10
Then said Saul to his servant, Well H2896 said; come, let us go. So they went unto the city where the man of God was.

1Sa 11:10
Therefore the men of Jabesh said, To morrow we will come out unto

you, and ye shall do with us all that seemeth good H2896 unto you.

1Sa 12:23
Moreover as for me, God forbid that I should sin against the LORD in ceasing to pray for you: but I will teach you the good H2896 and the right way:

1Sa 14:36
And Saul said, Let us go down after the Philistines by night, and spoil them until the morning light, and let us not leave a man of them. And they said, Do whatsoever seemeth good H2896 unto thee. Then said the priest, Let us draw near hither unto God.

1Sa 14:40
Then said he unto all Israel, Be ye on one side, and I and Jonathan my son will be on the other side. And the people said unto Saul, Do what seemeth good H2896 unto thee.

1Sa 15:9
But Saul and the people spared Agag, and the best of the sheep, and of the oxen, and of the fatlings, and the lambs, and all that was good, H2896 and would not utterly destroy them: but every thing that was vile and refuse, that they destroyed utterly.

1Sa 15:22
And Samuel said, Hath the LORD as great delight in burnt offerings and sacrifices, as in obeying the voice of the LORD? Behold, to obey is better H2896 than sacrifice, and to hearken than the fat of rams.

1Sa 15:28
And Samuel said unto him, The LORD hath rent the kingdom of Israel from thee this day, and hath given it to a neighbour of thine, that is better H2896 than thou.

1Sa 16:12
And he sent, and brought him in. Now he was ruddy, and withal of a beautiful countenance, and goodly H2896 to look to. And the LORD said, Arise, anoint him: for this is he.

1Sa 19:4
And Jonathan spake good H2896 of David unto Saul his father, and said unto him, Let not the king sin against his servant, against David; because he hath not sinned against thee, and because his works have been to thee-ward very good: H2896

1Sa 20:7
If he say thus, It is well; H2896 thy servant shall have peace: but if he be very wroth, then be sure that evil is determined by him.

1Sa 24:17
And he said to David, Thou art more righteous than I: for thou hast rewarded me good, H2896 whereas I have rewarded thee evil.

1Sa 24:18
And thou hast shewed this day how that thou hast dealt well H2896 with me: forasmuch as when the LORD had delivered me into thine hand, thou killedst me not.

1Sa 24:19
For if a man find his enemy, will he let him go well H2896 away? wherefore the LORD reward thee good H2896 for that thou hast done unto me this day.

1Sa 25:3
Now the name of the man was Nabal; and the name of his wife Abigail: and she was a woman of good H2896 understanding, and of a beautiful countenance: but the man was churlish and evil in his doings; and he was of the house of Caleb.

1Sa 25:8
Ask thy young men, and they will shew thee. Wherefore let the young men find favour in thine eyes: for we come in a good H2896 day: give, I pray thee, whatsoever cometh to thine hand unto thy servants, and to thy son David.

1Sa 25:15
But the men were very good H2896 unto us, and we were not hurt, neither missed we any thing, as long as we were conversant with them, when we were in the fields:

1Sa 25:21
Now David had said, Surely in vain have I kept all that this fellow hath in the wilderness, so that nothing was missed of all that pertained unto him: and he hath requited me evil for good. H2896

1Sa 25:30
And it shall come to pass, when the LORD shall have done to my lord according to all the good H2896 that he hath spoken concerning thee, and shall have appointed thee ruler over Israel;

1Sa 25:36
And Abigail came to Nabal; and, behold, he held a feast in his house, like the feast of a king; and Nabal's heart was merry H2896 within him, for he was very drunken: wherefore she told him nothing, less or more, until the morning light.

1Sa 26:16
This thing is not good H2896 that thou hast done. As the LORD liveth, ye are worthy to die, because ye have not kept your master, the LORD'S anointed. And now see where the king's spear is, and the cruse of water that was at his bolster.

1Sa 27:1

And David said in his heart, I shall now perish one day by the hand of Saul: there is nothing better H2896 for me than that I should speedily escape into the land of the Philistines; and Saul shall despair of me, to seek me any more in any coast of Israel: so shall I escape out of his hand.

1Sa 29:6

Then Achish called David, and said unto him, Surely, as the LORD liveth, thou hast been upright, and thy going out and thy coming in with me in the host is good H2896 in my sight: for I have not found evil in thee since the day of thy coming unto me unto this day: nevertheless the lords favour H2896 thee not.

1Sa 29:9

And Achish answered and said to David, I know that thou art good H2896 in my sight, as an angel of God: notwithstanding the princes of the Philistines have said, He shall not go up with us to the battle.

2Sa 2:6

And now the LORD shew kindness and truth unto you: and I also will requite you this kindness, H2896 because ye have done this thing.

2Sa 3:13

And he said, Well; H2896 I will make a league with thee: but one thing I require of thee, that is, Thou shalt not see my face, except thou first bring Michal Saul's daughter, when thou comest to see my face.

2Sa 3:19

And Abner also spake in the ears of Benjamin: and Abner went also to speak in the ears of David in Hebron all that seemed good H2896 to Israel, and that seemed good to the whole house of Benjamin.

2Sa 3:36
And all the people took notice of it, and it pleased them: as whatsoever the king did **pleased** H2896 all the people.

2Sa 7:28
And now, O Lord GOD, thou art that God, and thy words be true, and thou hast promised this goodness H2896 unto thy servant:

2Sa 10:12
Be of good courage, and let us play the men for our people, and for the cities of our God: and the LORD do that which seemeth him good. H2896

2Sa 11:2
And it came to pass in an eveningtide, that David arose from off his bed, and walked upon the roof of the king's house: and from the roof he saw a woman washing herself; and the woman was very beautiful H2896 to look upon.

2Sa 13:22
And Absalom spake unto his brother Amnon neither good H2896 nor bad: for Absalom hated Amnon, because he had forced his sister Tamar.

2Sa 13:28
Now Absalom had commanded his servants, saying, Mark ye now when Amnon's heart is merry H2896 with wine, and when I say unto you, Smite Amnon; then kill him, fear not: have not I commanded you? be courageous, and be valiant.

2Sa 14:17
Then thine handmaid said, The word of my lord the king shall now be comfortable: for as an angel of God, so is my lord the king to discern good H2896 and bad: therefore the LORD thy God will be with thee.

2Sa 14:32

And Absalom answered Joab, Behold, I sent unto thee, saying, Come hither, that I may send thee to the king, to say, Wherefore am I come from Geshur? it had been good H2896 for me to have been there still: now therefore let me see the king's face; and if there be any iniquity in me, let him kill me.

2Sa 15:3

And Absalom said unto him, See, thy matters are good H2896 and right; but there is no man deputed of the king to hear thee.

2Sa 15:26

But if he thus say, I have no delight in thee; behold, here am I, let him do to me as seemeth good H2896 unto him.

2Sa 16:12

It may be that the LORD will look on mine affliction, and that the LORD will requite me good H2896 for his cursing this day.

2Sa 17:7

And Hushai said unto Absalom, The counsel that Ahithophel hath given is not good H2896 at this time.

2Sa 17:14

And Absalom and all the men of Israel said, The counsel of Hushai the Archite is better H2896 than the counsel of Ahithophel. For the LORD had appointed to defeat the good H2896 counsel of Ahithophel, to the intent that the LORD might bring evil upon Absalom.

2Sa 18:3

But the people answered, Thou shalt not go forth: for if we flee away, they will not care for us; neither if half of us die, will they care for us: but now thou art worth ten thousand of us: therefore now it is better

H2896 that thou succour us out of the city.

2Sa 18:27
And the watchman said, Me thinketh the running of the foremost is like the running of Ahimaaz the son of Zadok. And the king said, He is a good H2896 man, and cometh with good H2896 tidings.

2Sa 19:18
And there went over a ferry boat to carry over the king's household, and to do what he thought good. H2896 And Shimei the son of Gera fell down before the king, as he was come over Jordan;

2Sa 19:27
And he hath slandered thy servant unto my lord the king; but my lord the king is as an angel of God: do therefore what is good H2896 in thine eyes.

2Sa 19:35
I am this day fourscore years old: and can I discern between good H2896 and evil? can thy servant taste what I eat or what I drink? can I hear any more the voice of singing men and singing women? wherefore then should thy servant be yet a burden unto my lord the king?

2Sa 19:37
Let thy servant, I pray thee, turn back again, that I may die in mine own city, and be buried by the grave of my father and of my mother. But behold thy servant Chimham; let him go over with my lord the king; and do to him what shall seem good H2896 unto thee.

2Sa 19:38
And the king answered, Chimham shall go over with me, and I will do to him that which shall seem good H2896 unto thee: and whatsoever thou shalt require of me, that will I do for thee.

2Sa 24:22
And Araunah said unto David, Let my lord the king take and offer up
what seemeth good H2896 unto him: behold, here be oxen for burnt
sacrifice, and threshing instruments and other instruments of the oxen
for wood.

1Ki 1:6
And his father had not displeased him at any time in saying, Why hast
thou done so? and he also was a very goodly H2896 man; and his
mother bare him after Absalom.

1Ki 1:42
And while he yet spake, behold, Jonathan the son of Abiathar the
priest came: and Adonijah said unto him, Come in; for thou art a
valiant man, and bringest good H2896 tidings.

1Ki 2:18
And Bathsheba said, Well; H2896 I will speak for thee unto the king.

1Ki 2:32
And the LORD shall return his blood upon his own head, who fell
upon two men more righteous and better H2896 than he, and slew
them with the sword, my father David not knowing thereof, to wit,
Abner the son of Ner, captain of the host of Israel, and Amasa the son
of Jether, captain of the host of Judah.

1Ki 2:38
And Shimei said unto the king, The saying is good: H2896 as my lord
the king hath said, so will thy servant do. And Shimei dwelt in
Jerusalem many days.

1Ki 2:42
And the king sent and called for Shimei, and said unto him, Did I not
make thee to swear by the LORD, and protested unto thee, saying,

Know for a certain, on the day thou goest out, and walkest abroad any whither, that thou shalt surely die? and thou saidst unto me, The word that I have heard is good. H2896

1Ki 3:9
Give therefore thy servant an understanding heart to judge thy people, that I may discern between good H2896 and bad: for who is able to judge this thy so great a people?

1Ki 8:36
Then hear thou in heaven, and forgive the sin of thy servants, and of thy people Israel, that thou teach them the good H2896 way wherein they should walk, and give rain upon thy land, which thou hast given to thy people for an inheritance.

1Ki 8:56
Blessed be the LORD, that hath given rest unto his people Israel, according to all that he promised: there hath not failed one word of all his good H2896 promise, which he promised by the hand of Moses his servant.

1Ki 8:66
On the eighth day he sent the people away: and they blessed the king, and went unto their tents joyful and glad H2896 of heart for all the goodness H2896 that the LORD had done for David his servant, and for Israel his people.

1Ki 10:7
Howbeit I believed not the words, until I came, and mine eyes had seen it: and, behold, the half was not told me: thy wisdom and prosperity H2896 exceedeth the fame which I heard.

1Ki 12:7
And they spake unto him, saying, If thou wilt be a servant unto this

people this day, and wilt serve them, and answer them, and speak good H2896 words to them, then they will be thy servants for ever.

1Ki 14:13
And all Israel shall mourn for him, and bury him: for he only of Jeroboam shall come to the grave, because in him there is found some good H2896 thing toward the LORD God of Israel in the house of Jeroboam.

1Ki 14:15
For the LORD shall smite Israel, as a reed is shaken in the water, and he shall root up Israel out of this good H2896 land, which he gave to their fathers, and shall scatter them beyond the river, because they have made their groves, provoking the LORD to anger.

1Ki 18:24
And call ye on the name of your gods, and I will call on the name of the LORD: and the God that answereth by fire, let him be God. And all the people answered and said, It is well H2896 spoken.

1Ki 19:4
But he himself went a day's journey into the wilderness, and came and sat down under a juniper tree: and he requested for himself that he might die; and said, It is enough; now, O LORD, take away my life; for I am not better H2896 than my fathers.

1Ki 20:3
Thy silver and thy gold is mine; thy wives also and thy children, even the goodliest, H2896 are mine.

1Ki 21:2
And Ahab spake unto Naboth, saying, Give me thy vineyard, that I may have it for a garden of herbs, because it is near unto my house: and I will give thee for it a better H2896 vineyard than it; or, if it

seem good H2896 to thee, I will give thee the worth of it in money.

1Ki 22:8
And the king of Israel said unto Jehoshaphat, There is yet one man,
Micaiah the son of Imlah, by whom we may enquire of the LORD:
but I hate him; for he doth not prophesy good H2896 concerning me,
but evil. And Jehoshaphat said, Let not the king say so.

1Ki 22:13
And the messenger that was gone to call Micaiah spake unto him,
saying, Behold now, the words of the prophets declare good H2896
unto the king with one mouth: let thy word, I pray thee, be like the
word of one of them, and speak that which is good. H2896

1Ki 22:18
And the king of Israel said unto Jehoshaphat, Did I not tell thee that
he would prophesy no good H2896 concerning me, but evil?

2Ki 2:19
And the men of the city said unto Elisha, Behold, I pray thee, the
situation of this city is pleasant, H2896 as my lord seeth: but the water
is naught, and the ground barren.

2Ki 3:19
And ye shall smite every fenced city, and every choice city, and shall
fell every good H2896 tree, and stop all wells of water, and mar every
good H2896 piece of land with stones.

2Ki 3:25
And they beat down the cities, and on every good H2896 piece of
land cast every man his stone, and filled it; and they stopped all the
wells of water, and felled all the good H2896 trees: only in
Kirharaseth left they the stones thereof; howbeit the slingers went
about it, and smote it.

2Ki 5:12
Are not Abana and Pharpar, rivers of Damascus, better H2896 than all
the waters of Israel? may I not wash in them, and be clean? So he
turned and went away in a rage.

2Ki 10:3
Look even out the best H2896 and meetest of your master's sons, and
set him on his father's throne, and fight for your master's house.

2Ki 10:5
And he that was over the house, and he that was over the city, the
elders also, and the bringers up of the children, sent to Jehu, saying,
We are thy servants, and will do all that thou shalt bid us; we will not
make any king: do thou that which is good H2896 in thine eyes.

2Ki 20:3
I beseech thee, O LORD, remember now how I have walked before
thee in truth and with a perfect heart, and have done that which is
good H2896 in thy sight. And Hezekiah wept sore.

2Ki 20:13
And Hezekiah hearkened unto them, and shewed them all the house
of his precious things, the silver, and the gold, and the spices, and the
precious H2896 ointment, and all the house of his armour, and all that
was found in his treasures: there was nothing in his house, nor in all
his dominion, that Hezekiah shewed them not.

2Ki 20:19
Then said Hezekiah unto Isaiah, Good H2896 is the word of the
LORD which thou hast spoken. And he said, Is it not good, if peace
and truth be in my days?

2Ki 25:28
And he spake kindly H2896 to him, and set his throne above the

throne of the kings that were with him in Babylon;

1Ch 4:40
And they found fat pasture and good, H2896 and the land was wide, and quiet, and peaceable; for they of Ham had dwelt there of old.

1Ch 16:34
O give thanks unto the LORD; for he is good; H2896 for his mercy endureth for ever.

1Ch 17:26
And now, LORD, thou art God, and hast promised this goodness H2896 unto thy servant:

1Ch 19:13
Be of good courage, and let us behave ourselves valiantly for our people, and for the cities of our God: and let the LORD do that which is good H2896 in his sight.

1Ch 21:23
And Ornan said unto David, Take it to thee, and let my lord the king do that which is good H2896 in his eyes: lo, I give thee the oxen also for burnt offerings, and the threshing instruments for wood, and the wheat for the meat offering; I give it all.

1Ch 28:8
Now therefore in the sight of all Israel the congregation of the LORD, and in the audience of our God, keep and seek for all the commandments of the LORD your God: that ye may possess this good H2896 land, and leave it for an inheritance for your children after you for ever.

1Ch 29:28
And he died in a good H2896 old age, full of days, riches, and

honour: and Solomon his son reigned in his stead.

2Ch 3:5
And the greater house he cieled with fir tree, which he overlaid with
fine H2896 gold, and set thereon palm trees and chains.

2Ch 3:8
And he made the most holy house, the length whereof was according
to the breadth of the house, twenty cubits, and the breadth thereof
twenty cubits: and he overlaid it with fine H2896 gold, amounting to
six hundred talents.

2Ch 5:13
It came even to pass, as the trumpeters and singers were as one, to
make one sound to be heard in praising and thanking the LORD; and
when they lifted up their voice with the trumpets and cymbals and
instruments of musick, and praised the LORD, saying, For he is good;
H2896 for his mercy endureth for ever: that then the house was filled
with a cloud, even the house of the LORD;

2Ch 6:27
Then hear thou from heaven, and forgive the sin of thy servants, and
of thy people Israel, when thou hast taught them the good H2896 way,
wherein they should walk; and send rain upon thy land, which thou
hast given unto thy people for an inheritance.

2Ch 6:41
Now therefore arise, O LORD God, into thy resting place, thou, and
the ark of thy strength: let thy priests, O LORD God, be clothed with
salvation, and let thy saints rejoice in goodness. H2896

2Ch 7:3
And when all the children of Israel saw how the fire came down, and

the glory of the LORD upon the house, they bowed themselves with their faces to the ground upon the pavement, and worshipped, and praised the LORD, saying, For he is good; H2896 for his mercy endureth for ever.

2Ch 7:10
And on the three and twentieth day of the seventh month he sent the people away into their tents, glad and merry H2896 in heart for the goodness H2896 that the LORD had shewed unto David, and to Solomon, and to Israel his people.

2Ch 10:7
And they spake unto him, saying, If thou be kind H2896 to this people, and please them, and speak good H2896 words to them, they will be thy servants for ever.

2Ch 12:12
And when he humbled himself, the wrath of the LORD turned from him, that he would not destroy him altogether: and also in Judah things went well. H2896

2Ch 14:2
And Asa did that which was good H2896 and right in the eyes of the LORD his God:

2Ch 18:7
And the king of Israel said unto Jehoshaphat, There is yet one man, by whom we may enquire of the LORD: but I hate him; for he never prophesied good H2896 unto me, but always evil: the same is Micaiah the son of Imla. And Jehoshaphat said, Let not the king say so.

2Ch 18:12
And the messenger that went to call Micaiah spake to him, saying, Behold, the words of the prophets declare good H2896 to the king

with one assent; let thy word therefore, I pray thee, be like one of theirs, and speak thou good. H2896

2Ch 18:17
And the king of Israel said to Jehoshaphat, Did I not tell thee that he would not prophesy good H2896 unto me, but evil?

2Ch 19:3
Nevertheless there are good H2896 things found in thee, in that thou hast taken away the groves out of the land, and hast prepared thine heart to seek God.

2Ch 19:11
And, behold, Amariah the chief priest is over you in all matters of the LORD; and Zebadiah the son of Ishmael, the ruler of the house of Judah, for all the king's matters: also the Levites shall be officers before you. Deal courageously, and the LORD shall be with the good. H2896

2Ch 21:13
But hast walked in the way of the kings of Israel, and hast made Judah and the inhabitants of Jerusalem to go a whoring, like to the whoredoms of the house of Ahab, and also hast slain thy brethren of thy father's house, which were better H2896 than thyself:

2Ch 24:16
And they buried him in the city of David among the kings, because he had done good H2896 in Israel, both toward God, and toward his house.

2Ch 30:18
For a multitude of the people, even many of Ephraim, and Manasseh, Issachar, and Zebulun, had not cleansed themselves, yet did they eat the passover otherwise than it was written. But Hezekiah prayed for

them, saying, The good H2896 LORD pardon every one

2Ch 30:22
And Hezekiah spake comfortably unto all the Levites that taught the good H2896 knowledge of the LORD: and they did eat throughout the feast seven days, offering peace offerings, and making confession to the LORD God of their fathers.

2Ch 31:20
And thus did Hezekiah throughout all Judah, and wrought that which was good H2896 and right and truth before the LORD his God.

Ezr 3:11
And they sang together by course in praising and giving thanks unto the LORD; because he is good, H2896 for his mercy endureth for ever toward Israel. And all the people shouted with a great shout, when they praised the LORD, because the foundation of the house of the LORD was laid.

Ezr 7:9
For upon the first day of the first month began he to go up from Babylon, and on the first day of the fifth month came he to Jerusalem, according to the good H2896 hand of his God upon him.

Ezr 8:18
And by the good H2896 hand of our God upon us they brought us a man of understanding, of the sons of Mahli, the son of Levi, the son of Israel; and Sherebiah, with his sons and his brethren, eighteen;

Ezr 8:22
For I was ashamed to require of the king a band of soldiers and horsemen to help us against the enemy in the way: because we had spoken unto the king, saying, The hand of our God is upon all them for good H2896 that seek him; but his power and his wrath is against

all them that forsake him.

Ezr 8:27
Also twenty basons of gold, of a thousand drams; and two vessels of fine H2896 copper, precious as gold.

Ezr 9:12
Now therefore give not your daughters unto their sons, neither take their daughters unto your sons, nor seek their peace or their wealth H2896 for ever: that ye may be strong, and eat the good of the land, and leave it for an inheritance to your children for ever.

Neh 2:8
And a letter unto Asaph the keeper of the king's forest, that he may give me timber to make beams for the gates of the palace which appertained to the house, and for the wall of the city, and for the house that I shall enter into. And the king granted me, according to the good H2896 hand of my God upon me.

Neh 2:10
When Sanballat the Horonite, and Tobiah the servant, the Ammonite, heard of it, it grieved them exceedingly that there was come a man to seek the welfare H2896 of the children of Israel.

Neh 2:18
Then I told them of the hand of my God which was good H2896 upon me; as also the king's words that he had spoken unto me. And they said, Let us rise up and build. So they strengthened their hands for this good H2896 work.

Neh 5:9
Also I said, It is not good H2896 that ye do: ought ye not to walk in the fear of our God because of the reproach of the heathen our enemies?

Neh 5:19
Think upon me, my God, for good, H2896 according to all that I have
done for this people.

Neh 6:19
Also they reported his good deeds H2896 before me, and uttered my
words to him. And Tobiah sent letters to put me in fear.

Neh 9:13
Thou camest down also upon mount Sinai, and spakest with them
from heaven, and gavest them right judgments, and true laws, good
H2896 statutes and commandments:

Neh 9:20
Thou gavest also thy good H2896 spirit to instruct them, and
withheldest not thy manna from their mouth, and gavest them water
for their thirst.

Neh 13:31
And for the wood offering, at times appointed, and for the firstfruits.
Remember me, O my God, for good. H2896

Est 1:10
On the seventh day, when the heart of the king was merry H2896 with
wine, he commanded Mehuman, Biztha, Harbona, Bigtha, and
Abagtha, Zethar, and Carcas, the seven chamberlains that served in
the presence of Ahasuerus the king,

Est 1:11
To bring Vashti the queen before the king with the crown royal, to
shew the people and the princes her beauty: for she was fair H2896 to
look on.

Est 1:19

If it please the king, let there go a royal commandment from him, and
let it be written among the laws of the Persians and the Medes, that it
be not altered, That Vashti come no more before king Ahasuerus; and
let the king give her royal estate unto another that is better H2896
than she.

Est 2:2

Then said the king's servants that ministered unto him, Let there be
fair H2896 young virgins sought for the king:

Est 2:3

And let the king appoint officers in all the provinces of his kingdom,
that they may gather together all the fair H2896 young virgins unto
Shushan the palace, to the house of the women, unto the custody of
Hege the king's chamberlain, keeper of the women; and let their
things for purification be given them:

Est 2:7

And he brought up Hadassah, that is, Esther, his uncle's daughter: for
she had neither father nor mother, and the maid was fair and beautiful;
H2896 whom Mordecai, when her father and mother were dead, took
for his own daughter.

Est 2:9

And the maiden pleased him, and she obtained kindness of him; and
he speedily gave her her things for purification, with such things as
belonged to her, and seven maidens, which were meet to be given her,
out of the king's house: and he preferred her and her maids unto the
best H2896 place of the house of the women.

Est 3:11

And the king said unto Haman, The silver is given to thee, the people
also, to do with them as it seemeth good H2896 to thee.

Est 5:9

Then went Haman forth that day joyful and with a glad H2896 heart:
but when Haman saw Mordecai in the king's gate, that he stood not
up, nor moved for him, he was full of indignation against Mordecai.

Est 7:9

And Harbonah, one of the chamberlains, said before the king, Behold
also, the gallows fifty cubits high, which Haman had made for
Mordecai, who had spoken good H2896 for the king, standeth in the
house of Haman. Then the king said, Hang him thereon.

Est 8:5

And said, If it please H2896 the king, and if I have found favour in his
sight, and the thing seem right before the king, and I be pleasing
H2896 in his eyes, let it be written to reverse the letters devised by
Haman the son of Hammedatha the Agagite, which he wrote to
destroy the Jews which are in all the king's provinces:

Est 8:8

Write ye also for the Jews, as it liketh H2896 you, in the king's name,
and seal it with the king's ring: for the writing which is written in the
king's name, and sealed with the king's ring, may no man reverse.

Est 8:17

And in every province, and in every city, whithersoever the king's
commandment and his decree came, the Jews had joy and gladness, a
feast and a good H2896 day. And many of the people of the land
became Jews; for the fear of the Jews fell upon them.

Est 9:13

Then said Esther, If it please H2896 the king, let it be granted to the
Jews which are in Shushan to do to morrow also according unto this
day's decree, and let Haman's ten sons be hanged upon the gallows.

Est 9:19
Therefore the Jews of the villages, that dwelt in the unwalled towns, made the fourteenth day of the month Adar a day of gladness and feasting, and a good H2896 day, and of sending portions one to another.

Est 9:22
As the days wherein the Jews rested from their enemies, and the month which was turned unto them from sorrow to joy, and from mourning into a good H2896 day: that they should make them days of feasting and joy, and of sending portions one to another, and gifts to the poor.

Est 10:3
For Mordecai the Jew was next unto king Ahasuerus, and great among the Jews, and accepted of the multitude of his brethren, seeking the wealth H2896 of his people, and speaking peace to all his seed.

Job 2:10
But he said unto her, Thou speakest as one of the foolish women speaketh. What? shall we receive good H2896 at the hand of God, and shall we not receive evil? In all this did not Job sin with his lips.

Job 7:7
O remember that my life is wind: mine eye shall no more see good. H2896

Job 9:25
Now my days are swifter than a post: they flee away, they see no good. H2896

Job 21:13
They spend their days in wealth, H2896 and in a moment go down to

the grave.

Job 21:25
And another dieth in the bitterness of his soul, and never eateth with pleasure. H2896

Job 22:18
Yet he filled their houses with good H2896 things: but the counsel of the wicked is far from me.

Job 22:21
Acquaint now thyself with him, and be at peace: thereby good H2896 shall come unto thee.

Job 30:26
When I looked for good, H2896 then evil came unto me: and when I waited for light, there came darkness.

Job 34:4
Let us choose to us judgment: let us know among ourselves what is good. H2896

Job 36:11
If they obey and serve him, they shall spend their days in prosperity, H2896 and their years in pleasures.

Psa 4:6
There be many that say, Who will shew us any good? H2896 LORD, lift thou up the light of thy countenance upon us.

Psa 14:1
[[To the chief Musician, A Psalm of David.]] The fool hath said in his heart, There is no God. They are corrupt, they have done abominable works, there is none that doeth good. H2896

Psa 14:3
They are all gone aside, they are all together become filthy: there is
none that doeth good, H2896 no, not one.

Psa 16:2
O my soul, thou hast said unto the LORD, Thou art my Lord: my
goodness H2896 extendeth not to thee;

Psa 21:3
For thou preventest him with the blessings of goodness: H2896 thou
settest a crown of pure gold on his head.

Psa 23:6
Surely goodness H2896 and mercy shall follow me all the days of my
life: and I will dwell in the house of the LORD for ever.

Psa 25:8
Good H2896 and upright is the LORD: therefore will he teach sinners
in the way.

Psa 25:13
His soul shall dwell at ease; H2896 and his seed shall inherit the
earth.

Psa 34:8
O taste and see that the LORD is good: H2896 blessed is the man that
trusteth in him.

Psa 34:10
The young lions do lack, and suffer hunger: but they that seek the
LORD shall not want any good H2896 thing.

Psa 34:12
What man is he that desireth life, and loveth many days, that he may

see good? H2896

Psa 34:14
Depart from evil, and do good; H2896 seek peace, and pursue it.

Psa 35:12
They rewarded me evil for good H2896 to the spoiling of my soul.

Psa 36:4
He deviseth mischief upon his bed; he setteth himself in a way that is not good; H2896 he abhorreth not evil.

Psa 37:3
Trust in the LORD, and do good; H2896 so shalt thou dwell in the land, and verily thou shalt be fed.

Psa 37:16
A little that a righteous man hath is better H2896 than the riches of many wicked.

Psa 37:27
Depart from evil, and do good; H2896 and dwell for evermore.

Psa 38:20
They also that render evil for good H2896 are mine adversaries; because I follow the thing that good H2896 is.

Psa 39:2
I was dumb with silence, I held my peace, even from good; H2896 and my sorrow was stirred.

Psa 45:1
[[To the chief Musician upon Shoshannim, for the sons of Korah, Maschil, A Song of loves.]] My heart is inditing a good H2896

matter: I speak of the things which I have made touching the king: my tongue is the pen of a ready writer.

Psa 52:3
Thou lovest evil more than good; H2896 and lying rather than to speak righteousness. Selah.

Psa 52:9
I will praise thee for ever, because thou hast done it: and I will wait on thy name; for it is good H2896 before thy saints.

Psa 53:1
[[To the chief Musician upon Mahalath, Maschil, A Psalm of David.]] The fool hath said in his heart, There is no God. Corrupt are they, and have done abominable iniquity: there is none that doeth good. H2896

Psa 53:3
Every one of them is gone back: they are altogether become filthy; there is none that doeth good, H2896 no, not one.

Psa 54:6
I will freely sacrifice unto thee: I will praise thy name, O LORD; for it is good. H2896

Psa 63:3
Because thy lovingkindness is better H2896 than life, my lips shall praise thee.

Psa 65:11
Thou crownest the year with thy goodness; H2896 and thy paths drop fatness.

Psa 68:10
Thy congregation hath dwelt therein: thou, O God, hast prepared of

thy goodness H2896 for the poor.

Psa 69:16
Hear me, O LORD; for thy lovingkindness is good: H2896 turn unto me according to the multitude of thy tender mercies.

Psa 73:1
[[A Psalm of Asaph.]] Truly God is good H2896 to Israel, even to such as are of a clean heart.

Psa 73:28
But it is good H2896 for me to draw near to God: I have put my trust in the Lord GOD, that I may declare all thy works.

Psa 84:10
For a day in thy courts is better H2896 than a thousand. I had rather be a doorkeeper in the house of my God, than to dwell in the tents of wickedness.

Psa 84:11
For the LORD God is a sun and shield: the LORD will give grace and glory: no good H2896 thing will he withhold from them that walk uprightly.

Psa 85:12
Yea, the LORD shall give that which is good; H2896 and our land shall yield her increase.

Psa 86:5
For thou, Lord, art good, H2896 and ready to forgive; and plenteous in mercy unto all them that call upon thee.

Psa 86:17
Shew me a token for good; H2896 that they which hate me may see it,

and be ashamed: because thou, LORD, hast holpen me, and comforted me.

Psa 92:1
[[A Psalm or Song for the sabbath day.]] It is a good H2896 thing to give thanks unto the LORD, and to sing praises unto thy name, O most High:

Psa 100:5
For the LORD is good; H2896 his mercy is everlasting; and his truth endureth to all generations.

Psa 103:5
Who satisfieth thy mouth with good H2896 things; so that thy youth is renewed like the eagle's.

Psa 104:28
That thou givest them they gather: thou openest thine hand, they are filled with good. H2896

Psa 106:1
Praise ye the LORD. O give thanks unto the LORD; for he is good: H2896 for his mercy endureth for ever.

Psa 106:5
That I may see the good H2896 of thy chosen, that I may rejoice in the gladness of thy nation, that I may glory with thine inheritance.

Psa 107:1
O give thanks unto the LORD, for he is good: H2896 for his mercy endureth for ever.

Psa 107:9
For he satisfieth the longing soul, and filleth the hungry soul with

goodness. H2896

Psa 109:5
And they have rewarded me evil for good, H2896 and hatred for my love.

Psa 109:21
But do thou for me, O GOD the Lord, for thy name's sake: because thy mercy is good, H2896 deliver thou me.

Psa 111:10
The fear of the LORD is the beginning of wisdom: a good H2896 understanding have all they that do his commandments: his praise endureth for ever.

Psa 112:5
A good H2896 man sheweth favour, and lendeth: he will guide his affairs with discretion.

Psa 118:1
O give thanks unto the LORD; for he is good: H2896 because his mercy endureth for ever.

Psa 118:8
It is better H2896 to trust in the LORD than to put confidence in man.

Psa 118:9
It is better H2896 to trust in the LORD than to put confidence in princes.

Psa 118:29
O give thanks unto the LORD; for he is good: H2896 for his mercy endureth for ever.

Psa 119:39
Turn away my reproach which I fear: for thy judgments are good.
H2896

Psa 119:65
TETH. Thou hast dealt well H2896 with thy servant, O LORD,
according unto thy word.

Psa 119:68
Thou art good, H2896 and doest good; teach me thy statutes.

Psa 119:71
It is good H2896 for me that I have been afflicted; that I might learn
thy statutes.

Psa 119:72
The law of thy mouth is better H2896 unto me than thousands of gold
and silver.

Psa 119:122
Be surety for thy servant for good: H2896 let not the proud oppress
me.

Psa 122:9
Because of the house of the LORD our God I will seek thy good.
H2896

Psa 125:4
Do good, O LORD, unto those that be good, H2896 and to them that
are upright in their hearts.

Psa 128:2
For thou shalt eat the labour of thine hands: happy shalt thou be, and
it shall be well H2896 with thee.

Psa 133:1

[[A Song of degrees of David.]] Behold, how good H2896 and how pleasant it is for brethren to dwell together in unity!

Psa 133:2

It is like the precious H2896 ointment upon the head, that ran down upon the beard, even Aaron's beard: that went down to the skirts of his garments;

Psa 135:3

Praise the LORD; for the LORD is good: H2896 sing praises unto his name; for it is pleasant.

Psa 136:1

O give thanks unto the LORD; for he is good: H2896 for his mercy endureth for ever.

Psa 143:10

Teach me to do thy will; for thou art my God: thy spirit is good; H2896 lead me into the land of uprightness.

Psa 145:9

The LORD is good H2896 to all: and his tender mercies are over all his works.

Psa 147:1

Praise ye the LORD: for it is good H2896 to sing praises unto our God; for it is pleasant; and praise is comely.

Pro 2:9

Then shalt thou understand righteousness, and judgment, and equity; yea, every good H2896 path.

Pro 2:20

That thou mayest walk in the way of good H2896 men, and keep the paths of the righteous.

Pro 3:4
So shalt thou find favour and good H2896 understanding in the sight of God and man.

Pro 3:14
For the merchandise of it is better H2896 than the merchandise of silver, and the gain thereof than fine gold.

Pro 3:27
Withhold not good H2896 from them to whom it is due, when it is in the power of thine hand to do it.

Pro 4:2
For I give you good H2896 doctrine, forsake ye not my law.

Pro 8:11
For wisdom is better H2896 than rubies; and all the things that may be desired are not to be compared to it.

Pro 8:19
My fruit is better H2896 than gold, yea, than fine gold; and my revenue than choice silver.

Pro 11:23
The desire of the righteous is only good: H2896 but the expectation of the wicked is wrath.

Pro 11:27
He that diligently seeketh good H2896 procureth favour: but he that seeketh mischief, it shall come unto him.

Pro 12:2
A good H2896 man obtaineth favour of the LORD: but a man of wicked devices will he condemn.

Pro 12:9
He that is despised, and hath a servant, is better H2896 than he that honoureth himself, and lacketh bread.

Pro 12:14
A man shall be satisfied with good H2896 by the fruit of his mouth: and the recompence of a man's hands shall be rendered unto him.

Pro 12:25
Heaviness in the heart of man maketh it stoop: but a good H2896 word maketh it glad.

Pro 13:2
A man shall eat good H2896 by the fruit of his mouth: but the soul of the transgressors shall eat violence.

Pro 13:15
Good H2896 understanding giveth favour: but the way of transgressors is hard.

Pro 13:21
Evil pursueth sinners: but to the righteous good H2896 shall be repayed.

Pro 13:22
A good H2896 man leaveth an inheritance to his children's children: and the wealth of the sinner is laid up for the just.

Pro 14:14
The backslider in heart shall be filled with his own ways: and a good

H2896 man shall be satisfied from himself.

Pro 14:19
The evil bow before the good; H2896 and the wicked at the gates of
the righteous.

Pro 14:22
Do they not err that devise evil? but mercy and truth shall be to them
that devise good. H2896

Pro 15:3
The eyes of the LORD are in every place, beholding the evil and the
good. H2896

Pro 15:15
All the days of the afflicted are evil: but he that is of a merry H2896
heart hath a continual feast.

Pro 15:16
Better H2896 is little with the fear of the LORD than great treasure
and trouble therewith.

Pro 15:17
Better H2896 is a dinner of herbs where love is, than a stalled ox and
hatred therewith.

Pro 15:23
A man hath joy by the answer of his mouth: and a word spoken in due
season, how good H2896 is it!

Pro 15:30
The light of the eyes rejoiceth the heart: and a good H2896 report
maketh the bones fat.

Pro 16:8
Better H2896 is a little with righteousness than great revenues without right.

Pro 16:16
How much better H2896 is it to get wisdom than gold! and to get understanding rather to be chosen than silver!

Pro 16:19
Better H2896 it is to be of an humble spirit with the lowly, than to divide the spoil with the proud.

Pro 16:20
He that handleth a matter wisely shall find good: H2896 and whoso trusteth in the LORD, happy is he.

Pro 16:29
A violent man enticeth his neighbour, and leadeth him into the way that is not good. H2896

Pro 16:32
He that is slow to anger is better H2896 than the mighty; and he that ruleth his spirit than he that taketh a city.

Pro 17:1
Better H2896 is a dry morsel, and quietness therewith, than an house full of sacrifices with strife.

Pro 17:13
Whoso rewardeth evil for good, H2896 evil shall not depart from his house.

Pro 17:20
He that hath a froward heart findeth no good: H2896 and he that hath

a perverse tongue falleth into mischief.

Pro 17:26
Also to punish the just is not good, H2896 nor to strike princes for equity.

Pro 18:5
It is not good H2896 to accept the person of the wicked, to overthrow the righteous in judgment.

Pro 18:22
Whoso findeth a wife findeth a good H2896 thing, and obtaineth favour of the LORD.

Pro 19:1
Better H2896 is the poor that walketh in his integrity, than he that is perverse in his lips, and is a fool.

Pro 19:2
Also, that the soul be without knowledge, it is not good; H2896 and he that hasteth with his feet sinneth.

Pro 19:8
He that getteth wisdom loveth his own soul: he that keepeth understanding shall find good. H2896

Pro 19:22
The desire of a man is his kindness: and a poor man is better H2896 than a liar.

Pro 20:23
Divers weights are an abomination unto the LORD; and a false balance is not good. H2896

Pro 21:9
It is better H2896 to dwell in a corner of the housetop, than with a brawling woman in a wide house.

Pro 21:19
It is better H2896 to dwell in the wilderness, than with a contentious and an angry woman.

Pro 22:1
A good name is rather to be chosen than great riches, and loving H2896 favour rather than silver and gold.

Pro 22:9
He that hath a bountiful H2896 eye shall be blessed; for he giveth of his bread to the poor.

Pro 24:13
My son, eat thou honey, because it is good; H2896 and the honeycomb, which is sweet to thy taste:

Pro 24:23
These things also belong to the wise. It is not good H2896 to have respect of persons in judgment.

Pro 24:25
But to them that rebuke him shall be delight, and a good H2896 blessing shall come upon them.

Pro 25:7
For better H2896 it is that it be said unto thee, Come up hither; than that thou shouldest be put lower in the presence of the prince whom thine eyes have seen.

Pro 25:24
It is better H2896 to dwell in the corner of the housetop, than with a brawling woman and in a wide house.

Pro 25:25
As cold waters to a thirsty soul, so is good H2896 news from a far country.

Pro 25:27
It is not good H2896 to eat much honey: so for men to search their own glory is not glory.

Pro 27:5
Open rebuke is better H2896 than secret love.

Pro 27:10
Thine own friend, and thy father's friend, forsake not; neither go into thy brother's house in the day of thy calamity: for better H2896 is a neighbour that is near than a brother far off.

Pro 28:6
Better H2896 is the poor that walketh in his uprightness, than he that is perverse in his ways, though he be rich.

Pro 28:10
Whoso causeth the righteous to go astray in an evil way, he shall fall himself into his own pit: but the upright shall have good H2896 things in possession.

Pro 28:21
To have respect of persons is not good: H2896 for for a piece of bread that man will transgress.

Pro 31:12
She will do him good H2896 and not evil all the days of her life.
Pro 31:18
She perceiveth that her merchandise is good: H2896 her candle goeth
not out by night.

Ecc 2:1
I said in mine heart, Go to now, I will prove thee with mirth, therefore
enjoy pleasure: H2896 and, behold, this also is vanity.

Ecc 2:3
I sought in mine heart to give myself unto wine, yet acquainting mine
heart with wisdom; and to lay hold on folly, till I might see what was
that good H2896 for the sons of men, which they should do under the
heaven all the days of their life.

Ecc 2:24
There is nothing better H2896 for a man, than that he should eat and
drink, and that he should make his soul enjoy good H2896 in his
labour. This also I saw, that it was from the hand of God.

Ecc 2:26
For God giveth to a man that is good H2896 in his sight wisdom, and
knowledge, and joy: but to the sinner he giveth travail, to gather and
to heap up, that he may give to him that is good H2896 before God.
This also is vanity and vexation of spirit.

Ecc 3:12
I know that there is no good H2896 in them, but for a man to rejoice,
and to do good H2896 in his life.

Ecc 3:13
And also that every man should eat and drink, and enjoy the good
H2896 of all his labour, it is the gift of God.

Ecc 3:22
Wherefore I perceive that there is nothing better, H2896 than that a
man should rejoice in his own works; for that is his portion: for who
shall bring him to see what shall be after him?

Ecc 4:3
Yea, better H2896 is he than both they, which hath not yet been, who
hath not seen the evil work that is done under the sun.

Ecc 4:6
Better H2896 is an handful with quietness, than both the hands full
with travail and vexation of spirit.

Ecc 4:8
There is one alone, and there is not a second; yea, he hath neither
child nor brother: yet is there no end of all his labour; neither is his
eye satisfied with riches; neither saith he, For whom do I labour, and
bereave my soul of good? H2896 This is also vanity, yea, it is a sore
travail.

Ecc 4:9
Two are better H2896 than one; because they have a good H2896
reward for their labour.

Ecc 4:13
Better H2896 is a poor and a wise child than an old and foolish king,
who will no more be admonished.

Ecc 5:5
Better H2896 is it that thou shouldest not vow, than that thou
shouldest vow and not pay.

Ecc 5:11
When goods H2896 increase, they are increased that eat them: and

what good is there to the owners thereof, saving the beholding of them with their eyes?

Ecc 5:18
Behold that which I have seen: it is good H2896 and comely for one to eat and to drink, and to enjoy the good H2896 of all his labour that he taketh under the sun all the days of his life, which God giveth him: for it is his portion.

Ecc 6:3
If a man beget an hundred children, and live many years, so that the days of his years be many, and his soul be not filled with good, H2896 and also that he have no burial; I say, that an untimely birth is better H2896 than he.

Ecc 6:6
Yea, though he live a thousand years twice told, yet hath he seen no good: H2896 do not all go to one place?

Ecc 6:9
Better H2896 is the sight of the eyes than the wandering of the desire: this is also vanity and vexation of spirit.

Ecc 6:12
For who knoweth what is good H2896 for man in this life, all the days of his vain life which he spendeth as a shadow? for who can tell a man what shall be after him under the sun?

Ecc 7:1
A good name is better H2896 than precious H2896 ointment; and the day of death than the day of one's birth.

Ecc 7:2
It is better H2896 to go to the house of mourning, than to go to the

house of feasting: for that is the end of all men; and the living will lay it to his heart.

Ecc 7:3
Sorrow is better H2896 than laughter: for by the sadness of the countenance the heart is made better.

Ecc 7:5
It is better H2896 to hear the rebuke of the wise, than for a man to hear the song of fools.

Ecc 7:8
Better H2896 is the end of a thing than the beginning thereof: and the patient in spirit is better H2896 than the proud in spirit.

Ecc 7:10
Say not thou, What is the cause that the former days were better H2896 than these? for thou dost not enquire wisely concerning this.

Ecc 7:11
Wisdom is good H2896 with an inheritance: and by it there is profit to them that see the sun.

Ecc 7:14
In the day of prosperity H2896 be joyful, H2896 but in the day of adversity consider: God also hath set the one over against the other, to the end that man should find nothing after him.

Ecc 7:18
It is good H2896 that thou shouldest take hold of this; yea, also from this withdraw not thine hand: for he that feareth God shall come forth of them all.

Ecc 7:20
For there is not a just man upon earth, that doeth good, H2896 and sinneth not.

Ecc 7:26
And I find more bitter than death the woman, whose heart is snares and nets, and her hands as bands: whoso pleaseth H2896 God shall escape from her; but the sinner shall be taken by her.

Ecc 8:12
Though a sinner do evil an hundred times, and his days be prolonged, yet surely I know that it shall be well H2896 with them that fear God, which fear before him:

Ecc 8:13
But it shall not be well H2896 with the wicked, neither shall he prolong his days, which are as a shadow; because he feareth not before God.

Ecc 8:15
Then I commended mirth, because a man hath no better thing H2896 under the sun, than to eat, and to drink, and to be merry: for that shall abide with him of his labour the days of his life, which God giveth him under the sun.

Ecc 9:2
All things come alike to all: there is one event to the righteous, and to the wicked; to the good H2896 and to the clean, and to the unclean; to him that sacrificeth, and to him that sacrificeth not: as is the good, H2896 so is the sinner; and he that sweareth, as he that feareth an oath.

Ecc 9:4
For to him that is joined to all the living there is hope: for a living dog

is better H2896 than a dead lion.

Ecc 9:7
Go thy way, eat thy bread with joy, and drink thy wine with a merry
H2896 heart; for God now accepteth thy works.

Ecc 9:16
Then said I, Wisdom is better H2896 than strength: nevertheless the
poor man's wisdom is despised, and his words are not heard.

Ecc 9:18
Wisdom is better H2896 than weapons of war: but one sinner
destroyeth much good. H2896

Ecc 11:6
In the morning sow thy seed, and in the evening withhold not thine
hand: for thou knowest not whether shall prosper, either this or that,
or whether they both shall be alike good. H2896

Ecc 11:7
Truly the light is sweet, and a pleasant H2896 thing it is for the eyes
to behold the sun:

Ecc 12:14
For God shall bring every work into judgment, with every secret
thing, whether it be good, H2896 or whether it be evil.

Sgs 1:2
Let him kiss me with the kisses of his mouth: for thy love is better
H2896 than wine.

Sgs 1:3
Because of the savour of thy good H2896 ointments thy name is as
ointment poured forth, therefore do the virgins love thee.

Sgs 7:9
And the roof of thy mouth like the best H2896 wine for my beloved, that goeth down sweetly, causing the lips of those that are asleep to speak.

Isa 3:10
Say ye to the righteous, that it shall be well H2896 with him: for they shall eat the fruit of their doings.

Isa 5:9
In mine ears said the LORD of hosts, Of a truth many houses shall be desolate, even great and fair, H2896 without inhabitant.

Isa 5:20
Woe unto them that call evil good, H2896 and good H2896 evil; that put darkness for light, and light for darkness; that put bitter for sweet, and sweet for bitter!

Isa 7:15
Butter and honey shall he eat, that he may know to refuse the evil, and choose the good. H2896

Isa 7:16
For before the child shall know to refuse the evil, and choose the good, H2896 the land that thou abhorrest shall be forsaken of both her kings.

Isa 38:3
And said, Remember now, O LORD, I beseech thee, how I have walked before thee in truth and with a perfect heart, and have done that which is good H2896 in thy sight. And Hezekiah wept sore.

Isa 39:2
And Hezekiah was glad of them, and shewed them the house of his

precious things, the silver, and the gold, and the spices, and the precious H2896 ointment, and all the house of his armour, and all that was found in his treasures: there was nothing in his house, nor in all his dominion, that Hezekiah shewed them not.

Isa 39:8
Then said Hezekiah to Isaiah, Good H2896 is the word of the LORD which thou hast spoken. He said moreover, For there shall be peace and truth in my days.

Isa 41:7
So the carpenter encouraged the goldsmith, and he that smootheth with the hammer him that smote the anvil, saying, It is ready H2896 for the sodering: and he fastened it with nails, that it should not be moved.

Isa 52:7
How beautiful upon the mountains are the feet of him that bringeth good tidings, that publisheth peace; that bringeth good tidings of good, H2896 that publisheth salvation; that saith unto Zion, Thy God reigneth!

Isa 55:2
Wherefore do ye spend money for that which is not bread? and your labour for that which satisfieth not? hearken diligently unto me, and eat ye that which is good, H2896 and let your soul delight itself in fatness.

Isa 56:5
Even unto them will I give in mine house and within my walls a place and a name better H2896 than of sons and of daughters: I will give them an everlasting name, that shall not be cut off.

Isa 65:2
I have spread out my hands all the day unto a rebellious people, which walketh in a way that was not good, H2896 after their own thoughts;

Jer 5:25
Your iniquities have turned away these things, and your sins have withholden good H2896 things from you.

Jer 6:16
Thus saith the LORD, Stand ye in the ways, and see, and ask for the old paths, where is the good H2896 way, and walk therein, and ye shall find rest for your souls. But they said, We will not walk therein.

Jer 6:20
To what purpose cometh there to me incense from Sheba, and the sweet H2896 cane from a far country? your burnt offerings are not acceptable, nor your sacrifices sweet unto me.

Jer 8:15
We looked for peace, but no good H2896 came; and for a time of health, and behold trouble!

Jer 12:6
For even thy brethren, and the house of thy father, even they have dealt treacherously with thee; yea, they have called a multitude after thee: believe them not, though they speak fair words H2896 unto thee.

Jer 14:11
Then said the LORD unto me, Pray not for this people for their good. H2896

Jer 14:19
Hast thou utterly rejected Judah? hath thy soul lothed Zion? why hast thou smitten us, and there is no healing for us? we looked for peace,

and there is no good; H2896 and for the time of healing, and behold trouble!

Jer 15:11
The LORD said, Verily it shall be well H2896 with thy remnant; verily I will cause the enemy to entreat thee well in the time of evil and in the time of affliction.

Jer 17:6
For he shall be like the heath in the desert, and shall not see when good H2896 cometh; but shall inhabit the parched places in the wilderness, in a salt land and not inhabited.

Jer 18:10
If it do evil in my sight, that it obey not my voice, then I will repent of the good, H2896 wherewith I said I would benefit them.

Jer 18:20
Shall evil be recompensed for good? H2896 for they have digged a pit for my soul. Remember that I stood before thee to speak good H2896 for them, and to turn away thy wrath from them.

Jer 21:10
For I have set my face against this city for evil, and not for good, H2896 saith the LORD: it shall be given into the hand of the king of Babylon, and he shall burn it with fire.

Jer 22:15
Shalt thou reign, because thou closest thyself in cedar? did not thy father eat and drink, and do judgment and justice, and then it was well H2896 with him?

Jer 22:16
He judged the cause of the poor and needy; then it was well H2896 with him: was not this to know me? saith the LORD.

Jer 24:2
One basket had very good H2896 figs, even like the figs that are first
ripe: and the other basket had very naughty figs, which could not be
eaten, they were so bad.

Jer 24:3
Then said the LORD unto me, What seest thou, Jeremiah? And I said,
Figs; the good H2896 figs, very good; H2896 and the evil, very evil,
that cannot be eaten, they are so evil.

Jer 24:5
Thus saith the LORD, the God of Israel; Like these good H2896 figs,
so will I acknowledge them that are carried away captive of Judah,
whom I have sent out of this place into the land of the Chaldeans for
their good. H2896

Jer 24:6
For I will set mine eyes upon them for good, H2896 and I will bring
them again to this land: and I will build them, and not pull them
down; and I will plant them, and not pluck them up.

Jer 26:14
As for me, behold, I am in your hand: do with me as seemeth good
H2896 and meet unto you.

Jer 29:10
For thus saith the LORD, That after seventy years be accomplished at
Babylon I will visit you, and perform my good H2896 word toward
you, in causing you to return to this place.

Jer 29:32
Therefore thus saith the LORD; Behold, I will punish Shemaiah the
Nehelamite, and his seed: he shall not have a man to dwell among this
people; neither shall he behold the good H2896 that I will do for my

people, saith the LORD; because he hath taught rebellion against the LORD.

Jer 32:39
And I will give them one heart, and one way, that they may fear me for ever, for the good H2896 of them, and of their children after them:

Jer 32:42
For thus saith the LORD; Like as I have brought all this great evil upon this people, so will I bring upon them all the good H2896 that I have promised them.

Jer 33:9
And it shall be to me a name of joy, a praise and an honour before all the nations of the earth, which shall hear all the good H2896 that I do unto them: and they shall fear and tremble for all the goodness H2896 and for all the prosperity that I procure unto it.

Jer 33:11
The voice of joy, and the voice of gladness, the voice of the bridegroom, and the voice of the bride, the voice of them that shall say, Praise the LORD of hosts: for the LORD is good; H2896 for his mercy endureth for ever: and of them that shall bring the sacrifice of praise into the house of the LORD. For I will cause to return the captivity of the land, as at the first, saith the LORD.

Jer 33:14
Behold, the days come, saith the LORD, that I will perform that good H2896 thing which I have promised unto the house of Israel and to the house of Judah.

Jer 39:16
Go and speak to Ebedmelech the Ethiopian, saying, Thus saith the LORD of hosts, the God of Israel; Behold, I will bring my words

upon this city for evil, and not for good; H2896 and they shall be accomplished in that day before thee.

Jer 40:4
And now, behold, I loose thee this day from the chains which were upon thine hand. If it seem good H2896 unto thee to come with me into Babylon, come; and I will look well unto thee: but if it seem ill unto thee to come with me into Babylon, forbear: behold, all the land is before thee: whither it seemeth good H2896 and convenient for thee to go, thither go.

Jer 42:6
Whether it be good, H2896 or whether it be evil, we will obey the voice of the LORD our God, to whom we send thee; that it may be well with us, when we obey the voice of the LORD our God.

Jer 44:17
But we will certainly do whatsoever thing goeth forth out of our own mouth, to burn incense unto the queen of heaven, and to pour out drink offerings unto her, as we have done, we, and our fathers, our kings, and our princes, in the cities of Judah, and in the streets of Jerusalem: for then had we plenty of victuals, and were well, H2896 and saw no evil.

Jer 44:27
Behold, I will watch over them for evil, and not for good: H2896 and all the men of Judah that are in the land of Egypt shall be consumed by the sword and by the famine, until there be an end of them.

Jer 52:32
And spake kindly H2896 unto him, and set his throne above the throne of the kings that were with him in Babylon,

Lam 3:17
And thou hast removed my soul far off from peace: I forgat prosperity. H2896

Lam 3:25
The LORD is good H2896 unto them that wait for him, to the soul that seeketh him.

Lam 3:26
It is good H2896 that a man should both hope and quietly wait for the salvation of the LORD.

Lam 3:27
It is good H2896 for a man that he bear the yoke in his youth.

Lam 3:38
Out of the mouth of the most High proceedeth not evil and good? H2896

Lam 4:1
How is the gold become dim! how is the most H2896 fine gold changed! the stones of the sanctuary are poured out in the top of every street.

Lam 4:9
They that be slain with the sword are better H2896 than they that be slain with hunger: for these pine away, stricken through for want of the fruits of the field.

Eze 17:8
It was planted in a good H2896 soil by great waters, that it might bring forth branches, and that it might bear fruit, that it might be a goodly vine.

Eze 18:18
As for his father, because he cruelly oppressed, spoiled his brother by violence, and did that which is not good H2896 among his people, lo, even he shall die in his iniquity.

Eze 20:25
Wherefore I gave them also statutes that were not good, H2896 and judgments whereby they should not live;

Eze 24:4
Gather the pieces thereof into it, even every good H2896 piece, the thigh, and the shoulder; fill it with the choice bones.

Eze 31:16
I made the nations to shake at the sound of his fall, when I cast him down to hell with them that descend into the pit: and all the trees of Eden, the choice and best H2896 of Lebanon, all that drink water, shall be comforted in the nether parts of the earth.

Eze 34:14
I will feed them in a good H2896 pasture, and upon the high mountains of Israel shall their fold be: there shall they lie in a good H2896 fold, and in a fat pasture shall they feed upon the mountains of Israel.

Eze 34:18
Seemeth it a small thing unto you to have eaten up the good H2896 pasture, but ye must tread down with your feet the residue of your pastures? and to have drunk of the deep waters, but ye must foul the residue with your feet?

Eze 36:31
Then shall ye remember your own evil ways, and your doings that were not good, H2896 and shall lothe yourselves in your own sight

for your iniquities and for your abominations.

Dan 1:4
Children in whom was no blemish, but well H2896 favoured, and
skilful in all wisdom, and cunning in knowledge, and understanding
science, and such as had ability in them to stand in the king's palace,
and whom they might teach the learning and the tongue of the
Chaldeans.

Dan 1:15
And at the end of ten days their countenances appeared fairer H2896
and fatter in flesh than all the children which did eat the portion of the
king's meat.

Hsa 2:7
And she shall follow after her lovers, but she shall not overtake them;
and she shall seek them, but shall not find them: then shall she say, I
will go and return to my first husband; for then was it better H2896
with me than now.

Hsa 4:13
They sacrifice upon the tops of the mountains, and burn incense upon
the hills, under oaks and poplars and elms, because the shadow
thereof is good: H2896 therefore your daughters shall commit
whoredom, and your spouses shall commit adultery.

Hsa 8:3
Israel hath cast off the thing that is good: H2896 the enemy shall
pursue him.

Hsa 10:1
Israel is an empty vine, he bringeth forth fruit unto himself: according
to the multitude of his fruit he hath increased the altars; according to
the goodness H2896 of his land they have made goodly images.

Hsa 14:2
Take with you words, and turn to the LORD: say unto him, Take away all iniquity, and receive us graciously: H2896 so will we render the calves of our lips.

Joe 3:5
Because ye have taken my silver and my gold, and have carried into your temples my goodly H2896 pleasant things:

Strong's Number H2896 matches the Hebrew טוֹב (towb),
which occurs 559 times in 517 verses in the Hebrew concordance of the KJV
Page 11 / 11 (Amo 5:14–Mal 2:17)

Amo 5:14
Seek good, H2896 and not evil, that ye may live: and so the LORD, the God of hosts, shall be with you, as ye have spoken.

Amo 5:15
Hate the evil, and love the good, H2896 and establish judgment in the gate: it may be that the LORD God of hosts will be gracious unto the remnant of Joseph.

Amo 6:2
Pass ye unto Calneh, and see; and from thence go ye to Hamath the great: then go down to Gath of the Philistines: be they better H2896 than these kingdoms? or their border greater than your border?

Amo 9:4
And though they go into captivity before their enemies, thence will I command the sword, and it shall slay them: and I will set mine eyes upon them for evil, and not for good. H2896

Jon 4:3
Therefore now, O LORD, take, I beseech thee, my life from me; for it is better H2896 for me to die than to live.

Jon 4:8
And it came to pass, when the sun did arise, that God prepared a vehement east wind; and the sun beat upon the head of Jonah, that he fainted, and wished in himself to die, and said, It is better H2896 for me to die than to live.

Mic 1:12
For the inhabitant of Maroth waited carefully for good: H2896 but evil came down from the LORD unto the gate of Jerusalem.

Mic 3:2
Who hate the good, H2896 and love the evil; who pluck off their skin from off them, and their flesh from off their bones;

Mic 6:8
He hath shewed thee, O man, what is good; H2896 and what doth the LORD require of thee, but to do justly, and to love mercy, and to walk humbly with thy God?

Mic 7:4
The best H2896 of them is as a brier: the most upright is sharper than a thorn hedge: the day of thy watchmen and thy visitation cometh; now shall be their perplexity.

Nah 1:7
The LORD is good, H2896 a strong hold in the day of trouble; and he knoweth them that trust in him.

Nah 3:4
Because of the multitude of the whoredoms of the wellfavoured

H2896 harlot, the mistress of witchcrafts, that selleth nations through her whoredoms, and families through her witchcrafts.

Zec 1:13
And the LORD answered the angel that talked with me with good H2896 words and comfortable words.

Zec 1:17
Cry yet, saying, Thus saith the LORD of hosts; My cities through prosperity H2896 shall yet be spread abroad; and the LORD shall yet comfort Zion, and shall yet choose Jerusalem.

Zec 8:19
Thus saith the LORD of hosts; The fast of the fourth month, and the fast of the fifth, and the fast of the seventh, and the fast of the tenth, shall be to the house of Judah joy and gladness, and cheerful H2896 feasts; therefore love the truth and peace.

Zec 11:12
And I said unto them, If ye think good, H2896 give me my price; and if not, forbear. So they weighed for my price thirty pieces of silver.

Mal 2:17
Ye have wearied the LORD with your words. Yet ye say, Wherein have we wearied him? When ye say, Every one that doeth evil is good H2896 in the sight of the LORD, and he delighteth in them; or, Where is the God of judgment?

Wisdom Keys – You can do all things through Christ

Chapter 9

Scriptures on the Hebrew word shalown (7965)

In this chapter we will continue to define the word prosperity in its use with the Hebrew word **Shalown (7965)**.

1. *Shalowm – 7965*

2. Strong Definition

From 7999; *safe*, that is, (figuratively) *well*, *happy*, *friendly*; also (abstractly) *welfare*, that is, health, prosperity, peace:-- X do, familiar, X fare, favour, + friend, X greet, (good) health, (X perfect, such as be at) peace (-able, -ably), prosper (-ity, -ous), rest, safe (-ly), salute, welfare, (X all is, be) well, X wholly.

3. English Definition for the word Peace (translated 175 times)

—*noun*

1. the normal, nonwarring condition of a nation, group of nations, or the world.

2. (*often initial capital letter*) an agreement or treaty between warring or antagonistic nations, groups, etc., to end hostilities and abstain from further fighting or antagonism: *the Peace of Ryswick.*

3. a state of mutual harmony between people or groups, especially in personal relations: *Try to live in peace with your neighbors.*

4. the normal freedom from civil commotion and violence of a community; public order and security: *He was arrested for being drunk and disturbing the peace.*

5. cessation of or freedom from any strife or dissension.

6. freedom of the mind from annoyance, distraction, anxiety, an obsession, etc.; tranquillity; serenity.

7. a state of tranquillity or serenity: *May he rest in peace.*

8. a state or condition conducive to, proceeding from, or characterized by tranquillity: *the peace of a mountain resort.*

9. silence; stillness: *The cawing of a crow broke the afternoon's peace.*

10. (*initial capital letter, italics*) a comedy (421 b.c.) by Aristophanes.

—*interjection*

11. (used to express greeting or farewell or to request quietness or silence).

—*verb (used without object)*

12. *Obsolete.* to be or become silent.

—*Idioms*

13. at peace,

    a. in a state or relationship of nonbelligerence or concord; not at war.

      b. untroubled; tranquil; content.

      c. deceased.

14. hold / keep one's peace, to refrain from or cease speaking; keep silent: *He told her to hold her peace until he had finished.*

15. keep the peace, to maintain order; cause to refrain from creating a disturbance: *Several officers of the law were on hand to keep the peace.*

16. make one's peace with, to become reconciled with: *He repaired the fence he had broken and made his peace with the neighbor on whose property it stood.*

17. make peace, to ask for or arrange a cessation of hostilities or antagonism.

4. KJV Translations Count – Total 236 times

Peace (175x), Well (14 times), Peaceably (9x), Welfare (5x), Salute (4x), Prosperity (4x), Did (3x), Safe (3x), Health (2x), Peaceable (2x), Misc. (15x)

5. Scripture References

Gen 15:15
And thou shalt go to thy fathers in **peace**; H7965 thou shalt be buried in a good old age.

Gen 26:29
That thou wilt do us no hurt, as we have not touched thee, and as we
have done unto thee nothing but good, and have sent thee away in
peace: H7965 thou art now the blessed of the LORD.

Gen 26:31
And they rose up betimes in the morning, and sware one to another:
and Isaac sent them away, and they departed from him in peace.
H7965

Gen 28:21
So that I come again to my father's house in peace; H7965 then shall
the LORD be my God:

Gen 29:6
And he said unto them, Is he well? H7965 And they said, He is well:
H7965 and, behold, Rachel his daughter cometh with the sheep.

Gen 37:4
And when his brethren saw that their father loved him more than all
his brethren, they hated him, and could not speak peaceably H7965
unto him.

Gen 37:14
And he said to him, Go, I pray thee, see whether it be well H7965
with thy brethren, and well H7965 with the flocks; and bring me word
again. So he sent him out of the vale of Hebron, and he came to
Shechem.

Gen 41:16
And Joseph answered Pharaoh, saying, It is not in me: God shall give
Pharaoh an answer of peace. H7965

Gen 43:23

And he said, Peace H7965 be to you, fear not: your God, and the God of your father, hath given you treasure in your sacks: I had your money. And he brought Simeon out unto them.

Gen 43:27
And he asked them of their welfare, H7965 and said, Is your father well, H7965 the old man of whom ye spake? Is he yet alive?

Gen 43:28
And they answered, Thy servant our father is in good health, H7965 he is yet alive. And they bowed down their heads, and made obeisance.

Gen 44:17
And he said, God forbid that I should do so: but the man in whose hand the cup is found, he shall be my servant; and as for you, get you up in peace H7965 unto your father.

Exd 4:18
And Moses went and returned to Jethro his father in law, and said unto him, Let me go, I pray thee, and return unto my brethren which are in Egypt, and see whether they be yet alive. And Jethro said to Moses, Go in peace. H7965

Exd 18:7
And Moses went out to meet his father in law, and did obeisance, and kissed him; and they asked each other of their welfare; H7965 and they came into the tent.

Exd 18:23
If thou shalt do this thing, and God command thee so, then thou shalt be able to endure, and all this people shall also go to their place in peace. H7965

Lev 26:6
And I will give peace H7965 in the land, and ye shall lie down, and none shall make you afraid: and I will rid evil beasts out of the land, neither shall the sword go through your land.

Num 6:26
The LORD lift up his countenance upon thee, and give thee peace. H7965

Num 25:12
Wherefore say, Behold, I give unto him my covenant of peace: H7965

Deu 2:26
And I sent messengers out of the wilderness of Kedemoth unto Sihon king of Heshbon with words of peace, H7965 saying,

Deu 20:10
When thou comest nigh unto a city to fight against it, then proclaim peace H7965 unto it.

Deu 20:11
And it shall be, if it make thee answer of peace, H7965 and open unto thee, then it shall be, that all the people that is found therein shall be tributaries unto thee, and they shall serve thee.

Deu 23:6
Thou shalt not seek their peace H7965 nor their prosperity all thy days for ever.

Deu 29:19
And it come to pass, when he heareth the words of this curse, that he bless himself in his heart, saying, I shall have peace, H7965 though I walk in the imagination of mine heart, to add drunkenness to thirst:

Jos 9:15
And Joshua made peace H7965 with them, and made a league with them, to let them live: and the princes of the congregation sware unto them.

Jos 10:21
And all the people returned to the camp to Joshua at Makkedah in peace: H7965 none moved his tongue against any of the children of Israel.

Jdg 4:17
Howbeit Sisera fled away on his feet to the tent of Jael the wife of Heber the Kenite: for there was peace H7965 between Jabin the king of Hazor and the house of Heber the Kenite.

Jdg 6:23
And the LORD said unto him, Peace H7965 be unto thee; fear not: thou shalt not die.

Jdg 8:9
And he spake also unto the men of Penuel, saying, When I come again in peace, H7965 I will break down this tower.

Jdg 11:13
And the king of the children of Ammon answered unto the messengers of Jephthah, Because Israel took away my land, when they came up out of Egypt, from Arnon even unto Jabbok, and unto Jordan: now therefore restore those lands again peaceably. H7965

Jdg 11:31
Then it shall be, that whatsoever cometh forth of the doors of my house to meet me, when I return in peace H7965 from the children of Ammon, shall surely be the LORD'S, and I will offer it up for a burnt offering.

Jdg 18:6
And the priest said unto them, Go in peace: H7965 before the LORD
is your way wherein ye go.

Jdg 18:15
And they turned thitherward, and came to the house of the young man
the Levite, even unto the house of Micah, and saluted H7965 him.

Jdg 19:20
And the old man said, Peace H7965 be with thee; howsoever let all
thy wants lie upon me; only lodge not in the street.

Jdg 21:13
And the whole congregation sent some to speak to the children of
Benjamin that were in the rock Rimmon, and to call peaceably H7965
unto them.

1Sa 1:17
Then Eli answered and said, Go in peace: H7965 and the God of
Israel grant thee thy petition that thou hast asked of him.

1Sa 7:14
And the cities which the Philistines had taken from Israel were
restored to Israel, from Ekron even unto Gath; and the coasts thereof
did Israel deliver out of the hands of the Philistines. And there was
peace H7965 between Israel and the Amorites.

1Sa 10:4
And they will salute H7965 thee, and give thee two loaves of bread;
which thou shalt receive of their hands.

1Sa 16:4
And Samuel did that which the LORD spake, and came to Bethlehem.
And the elders of the town trembled at his coming, and said, Comest

thou peaceably? H7965

1Sa 16:5
And he said, Peaceably: H7965 I am come to sacrifice unto the
LORD: sanctify yourselves, and come with me to the sacrifice. And
he sanctified Jesse and his sons, and called them to the sacrifice.

1Sa 17:18
And carry these ten cheeses unto the captain of their thousand, and
look how thy brethren fare, H7965 and take their pledge.

1Sa 17:22
And David left his carriage in the hand of the keeper of the carriage,
and ran into the army, and came and saluted H7965 his brethren.

1Sa 20:7
If he say thus, It is well; thy servant shall have peace: H7965 but if he
be very wroth, then be sure that evil is determined by him.

1Sa 20:13
The LORD do so and much more to Jonathan: but if it please my
father to do thee evil, then I will shew it thee, and send thee away,
that thou mayest go in peace: H7965 and the LORD be with thee, as
he hath been with my father.

1Sa 20:21
And, behold, I will send a lad, saying, Go, find out the arrows. If I
expressly say unto the lad, Behold, the arrows are on this side of thee,
take them; then come thou: for there is peace H7965 to thee, and no
hurt; as the LORD liveth.

1Sa 20:42
And Jonathan said to David, Go in peace, H7965 forasmuch as we
have sworn both of us in the name of the LORD, saying, The LORD

be between me and thee, and between my seed and thy seed for ever. And he arose and departed: and Jonathan went into the city.

1Sa 25:5
And David sent out ten young men, and David said unto the young men, Get you up to Carmel, and go to Nabal, and greet H7965 him in my name:

1Sa 25:6
And thus shall ye say to him that liveth in prosperity, Peace H7965 be both to thee, and peace H7965 be to thine house, and peace H7965 be unto all that thou hast.

1Sa 25:35
So David received of her hand that which she had brought him, and said unto her, Go up in peace H7965 to thine house; see, I have hearkened to thy voice, and have accepted thy person.

1Sa 29:7
Wherefore now return, and go in peace, H7965 that thou displease not the lords of the Philistines.

1Sa 30:21
And David came to the two hundred men, which were so faint that they could not follow David, whom they had made also to abide at the brook Besor: and they went forth to meet David, and to meet the people that were with him: and when David came near to the people, he saluted H7965 them.

2Sa 3:21
And Abner said unto David, I will arise and go, and will gather all Israel unto my lord the king, that they may make a league with thee, and that thou mayest reign over all that thine heart desireth. And

David sent Abner away; and he went in peace. H7965

2Sa 3:22
And, behold, the servants of David and Joab came from pursuing a troop, and brought in a great spoil with them: but Abner was not with David in Hebron; for he had sent him away, and he was gone in peace. H7965

2Sa 3:23
When Joab and all the host that was with him were come, they told Joab, saying, Abner the son of Ner came to the king, and he hath sent him away, and he is gone in peace. H7965

2Sa 8:10
Then Toi sent Joram his son unto king David, to salute H7965 him, and to bless him, because he had fought against Hadadezer, and smitten him: for Hadadezer had wars with Toi. And Joram brought with him vessels of silver, and vessels of gold, and vessels of brass:

2Sa 11:7
And when Uriah was come unto him, David demanded of him how Joab did, H7965 and how the people did, H7965 and how the war prospered. H7965

2Sa 15:9
And the king said unto him, Go in peace. H7965 So he arose, and went to Hebron.

2Sa 15:27
The king said also unto Zadok the priest, Art not thou a seer? return into the city in peace, H7965 and your two sons with you, Ahimaaz thy son, and Jonathan the son of Abiathar.

2Sa 17:3
And I will bring back all the people unto thee: the man whom thou seekest is as if all returned: so all the people shall be in peace. H7965

2Sa 18:28
And Ahimaaz called, and said unto the king, All is well. H7965 And he fell down to the earth upon his face before the king, and said, Blessed be the LORD thy God, which hath delivered up the men that lifted up their hand against my lord the king.

2Sa 18:29
And the king said, Is the young man Absalom safe? H7965 And Ahimaaz answered, When Joab sent the king's servant, and me thy servant, I saw a great tumult, but I knew not what it was.

2Sa 18:32
And the king said unto Cushi, Is the young man Absalom safe? H7965 And Cushi answered, The enemies of my lord the king, and all that rise against thee to do thee hurt, be as that young man is.

2Sa 19:24
And Mephibosheth the son of Saul came down to meet the king, and had neither dressed his feet, nor trimmed his beard, nor washed his clothes, from the day the king departed until the day he came again in peace. H7965

2Sa 19:30
And Mephibosheth said unto the king, Yea, let him take all, forasmuch as my lord the king is come again in peace H7965 unto his own house.

2Sa 20:9
And Joab said to Amasa, Art thou in health, H7965 my brother? And Joab took Amasa by the beard with the right hand to kiss him.

1Ki 2:5
Moreover thou knowest also what Joab the son of Zeruiah did to me,
and what he did to the two captains of the hosts of Israel, unto Abner
the son of Ner, and unto Amasa the son of Jether, whom he slew, and
shed the blood of war in peace, H7965 and put the blood of war upon
his girdle that was about his loins, and in his shoes that were on his
feet.

1Ki 2:6
Do therefore according to thy wisdom, and let not his hoar head go
down to the grave in peace. H7965

1Ki 2:13
And Adonijah the son of Haggith came to Bathsheba the mother of
Solomon. And she said, Comest thou peaceably? H7965 And he said,
Peaceably. H7965

1Ki 2:33
Their blood shall therefore return upon the head of Joab, and upon the
head of his seed for ever: but upon David, and upon his seed, and
upon his house, and upon his throne, shall there be peace H7965 for
ever from the LORD.

1Ki 4:24
For he had dominion over all the region on this side the river, from
Tiphsah even to Azzah, over all the kings on this side the river: and he
had peace H7965 on all sides round about him.

1Ki 5:12
And the LORD gave Solomon wisdom, as he promised him: and there
was peace H7965 between Hiram and Solomon; and they two made a
league together.

1Ki 20:18
And he said, Whether they be come out for peace, H7965 take them alive; or whether they be come out for war, take them alive.

1Ki 22:17
And he said, I saw all Israel scattered upon the hills, as sheep that have not a shepherd: and the LORD said, These have no master: let them return every man to his house in peace. H7965

1Ki 22:27
And say, Thus saith the king, Put this fellow in the prison, and feed him with bread of affliction and with water of affliction, until I come in peace. H7965

1Ki 22:28
And Micaiah said, If thou return at all in peace, H7965 the LORD hath not spoken by me. And he said, Hearken, O people, every one of you.

2Ki 4:23
And he said, Wherefore wilt thou go to him to day? it is neither new moon, nor sabbath. And she said, It shall be well. H7965

2Ki 4:26
Run now, I pray thee, to meet her, and say unto her, Is it well H7965 with thee? is it well H7965 with thy husband? is it well H7965 with the child? And she answered, It is well. H7965

2Ki 5:19
And he said unto him, Go in peace. H7965 So he departed from him a little way.

2Ki 5:21
So Gehazi followed after Naaman. And when Naaman saw him

running after him, he lighted down from the chariot to meet him, and said, Is all well? H7965

2Ki 5:22
And he said, All is well. H7965 My master hath sent me, saying, Behold, even now there be come to me from mount Ephraim two young men of the sons of the prophets: give them, I pray thee, a talent of silver, and two changes of garments.

2Ki 9:11
Then Jehu came forth to the servants of his lord: and one said unto him, Is all well? H7965 wherefore came this mad fellow to thee? And he said unto them, Ye know the man, and his communication.

2Ki 9:17
And there stood a watchman on the tower in Jezreel, and he spied the company of Jehu as he came, and said, I see a company. And Joram said, Take an horseman, and send to meet them, and let him say, Is it peace? H7965

2Ki 9:18
So there went one on horseback to meet him, and said, Thus saith the king, Is it peace? H7965 And Jehu said, What hast thou to do with peace? H7965 turn thee behind me. And the watchman told, saying, The messenger came to them, but he cometh not again.

2Ki 9:19
Then he sent out a second on horseback, which came to them, and said, Thus saith the king, Is it peace? H7965 And Jehu answered, What hast thou to do with peace? H7965 turn thee behind me.

2Ki 9:22
And it came to pass, when Joram saw Jehu, that he said, Is it peace, H7965 Jehu? And he answered, What peace, H7965 so long as the

whoredoms of thy mother Jezebel and her witchcrafts are so many?
2Ki 9:31
And as Jehu entered in at the gate, she said, Had Zimri peace, H7965
who slew his master?

2Ki 10:13
Jehu met with the brethren of Ahaziah king of Judah, and said, Who
are ye? And they answered, We are the brethren of Ahaziah; and we
go down to salute H7965 the children of the king and the children of
the queen.

2Ki 20:19
Then said Hezekiah unto Isaiah, Good is the word of the LORD
which thou hast spoken. And he said, Is it not good, if peace H7965
and truth be in my days?

2Ki 22:20
Behold therefore, I will gather thee unto thy fathers, and thou shalt be
gathered into thy grave in peace; H7965 and thine eyes shall not see
all the evil which I will bring upon this place. And they brought the
king word again.

1Ch 12:17
And David went out to meet them, and answered and said unto them,
If ye be come peaceably H7965 unto me to help me, mine heart shall
be knit unto you: but if ye be come to betray me to mine enemies,
seeing there is no wrong in mine hands, the God of our fathers look
thereon, and rebuke it.

1Ch 12:18
Then the spirit came upon Amasai, who was chief of the captains, and
he said, Thine are we, David, and on thy side, thou son of Jesse:
peace, H7965 peace H7965 be unto thee, and peace H7965 be to thine
helpers; for thy God helpeth thee. Then David received them, and

made them captains of the band.

1Ch 18:10

He sent Hadoram his son to king David, to enquire of his welfare, H7965 and to congratulate him, because he had fought against Hadarezer, and smitten him; (for Hadarezer had war with Tou;) and with him all manner of vessels of gold and silver and brass.

1Ch 22:9

Behold, a son shall be born to thee, who shall be a man of rest; and I will give him rest from all his enemies round about: for his name shall be Solomon, and I will give peace H7965 and quietness unto Israel in his days.

2Ch 15:5

And in those times there was no peace H7965 to him that went out, nor to him that came in, but great vexations were upon all the inhabitants of the countries.

2Ch 18:16

Then he said, I did see all Israel scattered upon the mountains, as sheep that have no shepherd: and the LORD said, These have no master; let them return therefore every man to his house in peace. H7965

2Ch 18:26

And say, Thus saith the king, Put this fellow in the prison, and feed him with bread of affliction and with water of affliction, until I return in peace. H7965

2Ch 18:27

And Micaiah said, If thou certainly return in peace, H7965 then hath not the LORD spoken by me. And he said, Hearken, all ye people.

2Ch 19:1
And Jehoshaphat the king of Judah returned to his house in peace
H7965 to Jerusalem.

2Ch 34:28
Behold, I will gather thee to thy fathers, and thou shalt be gathered to
thy grave in peace, H7965 neither shall thine eyes see all the evil that
I will bring upon this place, and upon the inhabitants of the same. So
they brought the king word again.

Ezr 9:12
Now therefore give not your daughters unto their sons, neither take
their daughters unto your sons, nor seek their peace H7965 or their
wealth for ever: that ye may be strong, and eat the good of the land,
and leave it for an inheritance to your children for ever.

Est 2:11
And Mordecai walked every day before the court of the women's
house, to know how Esther did, H7965 and what should become of
her.

And he sent the letters unto all the Jews, to the hundred twenty and
seven provinces of the kingdom of Ahasuerus, with words of peace
H7965 and truth,

Est 10:3
For Mordecai the Jew was next unto king Ahasuerus, and great
among the Jews, and accepted of the multitude of his brethren,
seeking the wealth of his people, and speaking peace H7965 to all his
seed.

Job 5:24
And thou shalt know that thy tabernacle shall be in peace; H7965 and
thou shalt visit thy habitation, and shalt not sin.

Job 15:21
A dreadful sound is in his ears: in prosperity H7965 the destroyer shall come upon him.

Job 21:9
Their houses are safe H7965 from fear, neither is the rod of God upon them.

Job 25:2
Dominion and fear are with him, he maketh peace H7965 in his high places.

Psa 4:8
I will both lay me down in peace, H7965 and sleep: for thou, LORD, only makest me dwell in safety.

Psa 28:3
Draw me not away with the wicked, and with the workers of iniquity, which speak peace H7965 to their neighbours, but mischief is in their hearts.

Psa 29:11
The LORD will give strength unto his people; the LORD will bless his people with peace. H7965

Psa 34:14
Depart from evil, and do good; seek peace, H7965 and pursue it.

Psa 35:20
For they speak not peace: H7965 but they devise deceitful matters against them that are quiet in the land.

Psa 35:27
Let them shout for joy, and be glad, that favour my righteous cause: yea, let them say continually, Let the LORD be magnified, which hath pleasure in the prosperity H7965 of his servant.

Psa 37:11
But the meek shall inherit the earth; and shall delight themselves in the abundance of peace. H7965

Psa 37:37
Mark the perfect man, and behold the upright: for the end of that man is peace. H7965

Psa 38:3
There is no soundness in my flesh because of thine anger; neither is there any rest H7965 in my bones because of my sin.

Psa 41:9
Yea, mine own familiar H7965 friend, in whom I trusted, which did eat of my bread, hath lifted up his heel against me.

Psa 55:18
He hath delivered my soul in peace H7965 from the battle that was against me: for there were many with me.

Psa 55:20
He hath put forth his hands against such as be at peace H7965 with him: he hath broken his covenant.

Psa 69:22
Let their table become a snare before them: and that which should have been for their welfare, H7965 let it become a trap.

Psa 72:3

The mountains shall bring peace H7965 to the people, and the little hills, by righteousness.

Psa 72:7
In his days shall the righteous flourish; and abundance of peace H7965 so long as the moon endureth.

Psa 73:3
For I was envious at the foolish, when I saw the prosperity H7965 of the wicked.

Psa 85:8
I will hear what God the LORD will speak: for he will speak peace H7965 unto his people, and to his saints: but let them not turn again to folly.

Psa 85:10
Mercy and truth are met together; righteousness and peace H7965 have kissed each other.

Psa 119:165
Great peace H7965 have they which love thy law: and nothing shall offend them.

Psa 120:6
My soul hath long dwelt with him that hateth peace. H7965

Psa 120:7
I am for peace: H7965 but when I speak, they are for war.

Psa 122:6
Pray for the peace H7965 of Jerusalem: they shall prosper that love thee.

Psa 122:7
Peace H7965 be within thy walls, and prosperity within thy palaces.

Psa 122:8
For my brethren and companions' sakes, I will now say, Peace H7965
be within thee.

Psa 125:5
As for such as turn aside unto their crooked ways, the LORD shall
lead them forth with the workers of iniquity: but peace H7965 shall be
upon Israel.

Psa 128:6
Yea, thou shalt see thy children's children, and peace H7965 upon
Israel.

Psa 147:14
He maketh peace H7965 in thy borders, and filleth thee with the finest
of the wheat.

Pro 3:2
For length of days, and long life, and peace, H7965 shall they add to
thee.

Pro 3:17
Her ways are ways of pleasantness, and all her paths are peace.
H7965

Pro 12:20
Deceit is in the heart of them that imagine evil: but to the counsellors
of peace H7965 is joy.

Ecc 3:8
A time to love, and a time to hate; a time of war, and a time of peace.

H7965

Sgs 8:10
I am a wall, and my breasts like towers: then was I in his eyes as one that found favour. H7965

Isa 9:6
For unto us a child is born, unto us a son is given: and the government shall be upon his shoulder: and his name shall be called Wonderful, Counsellor, The mighty God, The everlasting Father, The Prince of Peace. H7965

Isa 9:7
Of the increase of his government and peace H7965 there shall be no end, upon the throne of David, and upon his kingdom, to order it, and to establish it with judgment and with justice from henceforth even for ever. The zeal of the LORD of hosts will perform this.

Isa 26:3
Thou wilt keep him in perfect H7965 peace, H7965 whose mind is stayed on thee: because he trusteth in thee.

Isa 26:12
LORD, thou wilt ordain peace H7965 for us: for thou also hast wrought all our works in us.

Isa 27:5
Or let him take hold of my strength, that he may make peace H7965 with me; and he shall make peace H7965 with me.

Isa 32:17
And the work of righteousness shall be peace; H7965 and the effect of righteousness quietness and assurance for ever.

Isa 32:18
And my people shall dwell in a peaceable H7965 habitation, and in
sure dwellings, and in quiet resting places;
Isa 33:7
Behold, their valiant ones shall cry without: the ambassadors of peace
H7965 shall weep bitterly.

Isa 38:17
Behold, for peace H7965 I had great bitterness: but thou hast in love
to my soul delivered it from the pit of corruption: for thou hast cast all
my sins behind thy back.

Isa 39:8
Then said Hezekiah to Isaiah, Good is the word of the LORD which
thou hast spoken. He said moreover, For there shall be peace H7965
and truth in my days.

Isa 41:3
He pursued them, and passed safely; H7965 even by the way that he
had not gone with his feet.

Isa 45:7
I form the light, and create darkness: I make peace, H7965 and create
evil: I the LORD do all these things.

Strong's Number H7965 matches the Hebrew שָׁלוֹם (shalowm),
which occurs 236 times in 208 verses in the Hebrew concordance of
the KJV
Page 4 / 5 (Isa 48:18–Hag 2:9)

Isa 48:18
O that thou hadst hearkened to my commandments! then had thy
peace H7965 been as a river, and thy righteousness as the waves of

the sea:

Isa 48:22
There is no peace, H7965 saith the LORD, unto the wicked.

Isa 52:7
How beautiful upon the mountains are the feet of him that bringeth good tidings, that publisheth peace; H7965 that bringeth good tidings of good, that publisheth salvation; that saith unto Zion, Thy God reigneth!

Isa 53:5
But he was wounded for our transgressions, he was bruised for our iniquities: the chastisement of our peace H7965 was upon him; and with his stripes we are healed.

Isa 54:10
For the mountains shall depart, and the hills be removed; but my kindness shall not depart from thee, neither shall the covenant of my peace H7965 be removed, saith the LORD that hath mercy on thee.

Isa 54:13
And all thy children shall be taught of the LORD; and great shall be the peace H7965 of thy children.

Isa 55:12
For ye shall go out with joy, and be led forth with peace: H7965 the mountains and the hills shall break forth before you into singing, and all the trees of the field shall clap their hands.

Isa 57:2
He shall enter into peace: H7965 they shall rest in their beds, each one walking in his uprightness.

Isa 57:19
I create the fruit of the lips; Peace, H7965 peace H7965 to him that is far off, and to him that is near, saith the LORD; and I will heal him.
Isa 57:21
There is no peace, H7965 saith my God, to the wicked.

Isa 59:8
The way of peace H7965 they know not; and there is no judgment in their goings: they have made them crooked paths: whosoever goeth therein shall not know peace. H7965

Isa 60:17
For brass I will bring gold, and for iron I will bring silver, and for wood brass, and for stones iron: I will also make thy officers peace, H7965 and thine exactors righteousness.

Isa 66:12
For thus saith the LORD, Behold, I will extend peace H7965 to her like a river, and the glory of the Gentiles like a flowing stream: then shall ye suck, ye shall be borne upon her sides, and be dandled upon her knees.

Jer 4:10
Then said I, Ah, Lord GOD! surely thou hast greatly deceived this people and Jerusalem, saying, Ye shall have peace; H7965 whereas the sword reacheth unto the soul.

Jer 6:14
They have healed also the hurt of the daughter of my people slightly, saying, Peace, H7965 peace; H7965 when there is no peace. H7965

Jer 8:11
For they have healed the hurt of the daughter of my people slightly, saying, Peace, H7965 peace; H7965 when there is no peace. H7965

Jer 8:15
We looked for peace, H7965 but no good came; and for a time of
health, and behold trouble!

Jer 9:8
Their tongue is as an arrow shot out; it speaketh deceit: one speaketh
peaceably H7965 to his neighbour with his mouth, but in heart he
layeth his wait.

Jer 12:5
If thou hast run with the footmen, and they have wearied thee, then
how canst thou contend with horses? and if in the land of peace,
H7965 wherein thou trustedst, they wearied thee, then how wilt thou
do in the swelling of Jordan?

Jer 12:12
The spoilers are come upon all high places through the wilderness: for
the sword of the LORD shall devour from the one end of the land
even to the other end of the land: no flesh shall have peace. H7965

Jer 13:19
The cities of the south shall be shut up, and none shall open them:
Judah shall be carried away captive all of it, it shall be wholly H7965
carried away captive.

Jer 14:13
Then said I, Ah, Lord GOD! behold, the prophets say unto them, Ye
shall not see the sword, neither shall ye have famine; but I will give
you assured peace H7965 in this place.

Jer 14:19
Hast thou utterly rejected Judah? hath thy soul lothed Zion? why hast
thou smitten us, and there is no healing for us? we looked for peace,
H7965 and there is no good; and for the time of healing, and behold

trouble!

Jer 15:5
For who shall have pity upon thee, O Jerusalem? or who shall bemoan thee? or who shall go aside to ask how thou doest? H7965

Jer 16:5
For thus saith the LORD, Enter not into the house of mourning, neither go to lament nor bemoan them: for I have taken away my peace H7965 from this people, saith the LORD, even lovingkindness and mercies.

Jer 20:10
For I heard the defaming of many, fear on every side. Report, say they, and we will report it. All my familiars H7965 watched for my halting, saying, Peradventure he will be enticed, and we shall prevail against him, and we shall take our revenge on him.

Jer 23:17
They say still unto them that despise me, The LORD hath said, Ye shall have peace; H7965 and they say unto every one that walketh after the imagination of his own heart, No evil shall come upon you.

Jer 25:37
And the peaceable H7965 habitations are cut down because of the fierce anger of the LORD.

Jer 28:9
The prophet which prophesieth of peace, H7965 when the word of the prophet shall come to pass, then shall the prophet be known, that the LORD hath truly sent him.

Jer 29:7
And seek the peace H7965 of the city whither I have caused you to be carried away captives, and pray unto the LORD for it: for in the peace H7965 thereof shall ye have peace. H7965

Jer 29:11
For I know the thoughts that I think toward you, saith the LORD, thoughts of peace, H7965 and not of evil, to give you an expected end.

Jer 30:5
For thus saith the LORD; We have heard a voice of trembling, of fear, and not of peace. H7965

Jer 33:6
Behold, I will bring it health and cure, and I will cure them, and will reveal unto them the abundance of peace H7965 and truth.

Jer 33:9
And it shall be to me a name of joy, a praise and an honour before all the nations of the earth, which shall hear all the good that I do unto them: and they shall fear and tremble for all the goodness and for all the prosperity H7965 that I procure unto it.

Jer 34:5
But thou shalt die in peace: H7965 and with the burnings of thy fathers, the former kings which were before thee, so shall they burn odours for thee; and they will lament thee, saying, Ah lord! for I have pronounced the word, saith the LORD.

Jer 38:4
Therefore the princes said unto the king, We beseech thee, let this man be put to death: for thus he weakeneth the hands of the men of war that remain in this city, and the hands of all the people, in

speaking such words unto them: for this man seeketh not the welfare H7965 of this people, but the hurt.

Jer 38:22
And, behold, all the women that are left in the king of Judah's house shall be brought forth to the king of Babylon's princes, and those women shall say, Thy friends H7965 have set thee on, and have prevailed against thee: thy feet are sunk in the mire, and they are turned away back.

Jer 43:12
And I will kindle a fire in the houses of the gods of Egypt; and he shall burn them, and carry them away captives: and he shall array himself with the land of Egypt, as a shepherd putteth on his garment; and he shall go forth from thence in peace. H7965

Lam 3:17
And thou hast removed my soul far off from peace: H7965 I forgat prosperity.

Eze 7:25
Destruction cometh; and they shall seek peace, H7965 and there shall be none.

Eze 13:10
Because, even because they have seduced my people, saying, Peace; H7965 and there was no peace; H7965 and one built up a wall, and, lo, others daubed it with untempered morter:

Eze 13:16
To wit, the prophets of Israel which prophesy concerning Jerusalem, and which see visions of peace H7965 for her, and there is no peace, H7965 saith the Lord GOD.

Eze 34:25

And I will make with them a covenant of peace, H7965 and will cause the evil beasts to cease out of the land: and they shall dwell safely in the wilderness, and sleep in the woods.

Eze 37:26

Moreover I will make a covenant of peace H7965 with them; it shall be an everlasting covenant with them: and I will place them, and multiply them, and will set my sanctuary in the midst of them for evermore.

Dan 10:19

And said, O man greatly beloved, fear not: peace H7965 be unto thee, be strong, yea, be strong. And when he had spoken unto me, I was strengthened, and said, Let my lord speak; for thou hast strengthened me.

Oba 1:7

All the men of thy confederacy have brought thee even to the border: the men that were at peace H7965 with thee have deceived thee, and prevailed against thee; they that eat thy bread have laid a wound under thee: there is none understanding in him.

Mic 3:5

Thus saith the LORD concerning the prophets that make my people err, that bite with their teeth, and cry, Peace; H7965 and he that putteth not into their mouths, they even prepare war against him.

Mic 5:5

And this man shall be the peace, H7965 when the Assyrian shall come into our land: and when he shall tread in our palaces, then shall we raise against him seven shepherds, and eight principal men.

Nah 1:15
Behold upon the mountains the feet of him that bringeth good tidings, that publisheth peace! H7965 O Judah, keep thy solemn feasts, perform thy vows: for the wicked shall no more pass through thee; he is utterly cut off.

Hag 2:9
The glory of this latter house shall be greater than of the former, saith the LORD of hosts: and in this place will I give peace, H7965 saith the LORD of hosts.

Even he shall build the temple of the LORD; and he shall bear the glory, and shall sit and rule upon his throne; and he shall be a priest upon his throne: and the counsel of peace H7965 shall be between them both.

Zec 8:10
For before these days there was no hire for man, nor any hire for beast; neither was there any peace H7965 to him that went out or came in because of the affliction: for I set all men every one against his neighbour.

Zec 8:12
For the seed shall be prosperous; H7965 the vine shall give her fruit, and the ground shall give her increase, and the heavens shall give their dew; and I will cause the remnant of this people to possess all these things.

Zec 8:16
These are the things that ye shall do; Speak ye every man the truth to his neighbour; execute the judgment of truth and peace H7965 in your gates:

Zec 8:19
Thus saith the LORD of hosts; The fast of the fourth month, and the fast of the fifth, and the fast of the seventh, and the fast of the tenth, shall be to the house of Judah joy and gladness, and cheerful feasts; therefore love the truth and peace. H7965

Zec 9:10
And I will cut off the chariot from Ephraim, and the horse from Jerusalem, and the battle bow shall be cut off: and he shall speak peace H7965 unto the heathen: and his dominion shall be from sea even to sea, and from the river even to the ends of the earth.

Mal 2:5
My covenant was with him of life and peace; H7965 and I gave them to him for the fear wherewith he feared me, and was afraid before my name.

Mal 2:6
The law of truth was in his mouth, and iniquity was not found in his lips: he walked with me in peace H7965 and equity, and did turn many away from iniquity.

Wisdom Keys – The Joy of the Lord is your strength

Chapter 10

Scriptures on Hebrew shelve (H7959) and tsalach (6743)

1.   H 7959 (shelev)

2. **Strong Definition**

From 7951: security. Prosperity

3. **Prosperity** (English) / Hebrew shelve

4. **Strong's Number** H7959 found only one time

5. **Translation** – shelve to prosperity

6. **Scripture reference** (one reference only)

Psa 30:6
And in my **prosperity** H7959 I said, I shall never be moved.

Find Listed below Hebrew (tsalach) H6743 translated to English words:

Prosper, come, prosperous, come mightily, effected, good, meet, break out, went over

1. H6743 (tsalach)

2.Strong's Definition – A primitive root; to push forward, break out, come (mightily), go over, be good, be meet, be profitable, prosper

3. Translated to English words 65 times

KJV Translation Count — Total: 65x
The KJV translates Strongs H6743 in the following manner: **prosper** (44x), **come** (6x), **prosperous** (5x), **come mightily** (2x), **effected** (1x), **good** (1x), **meet** (1x), **break out** (1x), **went over** (1x), **misc** (3x).

4.Scripture References

Gen 24:21
And the man wondering at her held his peace, to wit whether the LORD had made H6743 his journey **prosperous** H6743 or not.

Gen 24:40
And he said unto me, The LORD, before whom I walk, will send his angel with thee, and **prosper** H6743 thy way; and thou shalt take a wife for my son of my kindred, and of my father's house:

Gen 24:42
And I came this day unto the well, and said, O LORD God of my master Abraham, if now thou do prosper H6743 my way which I go:

Gen 24:56
And he said unto them, Hinder me not, seeing the LORD hath prospered H6743 my way; send me away that I may go to my master.

Gen 39:2
And the LORD was with Joseph, and he was a prosperous H6743 man; and he was in the house of his master the Egyptian.

Gen 39:3
And his master saw that the LORD was with him, and that the LORD made all that he did to prosper H6743 in his hand.

Gen 39:23
The keeper of the prison looked not to any thing that was under his hand; because the LORD was with him, and that which he did, the LORD made it to prosper. H6743

Num 14:41
And Moses said, Wherefore now do ye transgress the commandment of the LORD? but it shall not prosper. H6743

Deu 28:29
And thou shalt grope at noonday, as the blind gropeth in darkness, and thou shalt not prosper H6743 in thy ways: and thou shalt be only oppressed and spoiled evermore, and no man shall save thee.

Jos 1:8
This book of the law shall not depart out of thy mouth; but thou shalt meditate therein day and night, that thou mayest observe to do according to all that is written therein: for then thou shalt make H6743 thy way prosperous, H6743 and then thou shalt have good success.

Jdg 14:6
And the Spirit of the LORD came mightily H6743 upon him, and he
rent him as he would have rent a kid, and he had nothing in his hand:
but he told not his father or his mother what he had done.

Jdg 14:19
And the Spirit of the LORD came H6743 upon him, and he went
down to Ashkelon, and slew thirty men of them, and took their spoil,
and gave change of garments unto them which expounded the riddle.
And his anger was kindled, and he went up to his father's house.

Jdg 15:14
And when he came unto Lehi, the Philistines shouted against him: and
the Spirit of the LORD came mightily H6743 upon him, and the cords
that were upon his arms became as flax that was burnt with fire, and
his bands loosed from off his hands.

Jdg 18:5
And they said unto him, Ask counsel, we pray thee, of God, that we
may know whether our way which we go shall be prosperous. H6743

1Sa 10:6
And the Spirit of the LORD will come H6743 upon thee, and thou
shalt prophesy with them, and shalt be turned into another man.

1Sa 10:10
And when they came thither to the hill, behold, a company of
prophets met him; and the Spirit of God came H6743 upon him, and
he prophesied among them.

1Sa 11:6
And the Spirit of God came H6743 upon Saul when he heard those
tidings, and his anger was kindled greatly.

1Sa 16:13
Then Samuel took the horn of oil, and anointed him in the midst of his brethren: and the Spirit of the LORD came H6743 upon David from that day forward. So Samuel rose up, and went to Ramah.

1Sa 18:10
And it came to pass on the morrow, that the evil spirit from God came H6743 upon Saul, and he prophesied in the midst of the house: and David played with his hand, as at other times: and there was a javelin in Saul's hand.

2Sa 19:17
And there were a thousand men of Benjamin with him, and Ziba the servant of the house of Saul, and his fifteen sons and his twenty servants with him; and they went over H6743 Jordan before the king.

1Ki 22:12
And all the prophets prophesied so, saying, Go up to Ramothgilead, and prosper: H6743 for the LORD shall deliver it into the king's hand.

1Ki 22:15
So he came to the king. And the king said unto him, Micaiah, shall we go against Ramothgilead to battle, or shall we forbear? And he answered him, Go, and prosper: H6743 for the LORD shall deliver it into the hand of the king.

1Ch 22:11
Now, my son, the LORD be with thee; and prosper H6743 thou, and build the house of the LORD thy God, as he hath said of thee.

1Ch 22:13
Then shalt thou prosper, H6743 if thou takest heed to fulfil the statutes and judgments which the LORD charged Moses with concerning Israel: be strong, and of good courage; dread not, nor be

dismayed.

1Ch 29:23
Then Solomon sat on the throne of the LORD as king instead of
David his father, and prospered; H6743 and all Israel obeyed him.

2Ch 7:11
Thus Solomon finished the house of the LORD, and the king's house:
and all that came into Solomon's heart to make in the house of the
LORD, and in his own house, he prosperously effectcd. H6743

2Ch 13:12
And, behold, God himself is with us for our captain, and his priests
with sounding trumpets to cry alarm against you. O children of Israel,
fight ye not against the LORD God of your fathers; for ye shall not
prosper. H6743

2Ch 14:7
Therefore he said unto Judah, Let us build these cities, and make
about them walls, and towers, gates, and bars, while the land is yet
before us; because we have sought the LORD our God, we have
sought him, and he hath given us rest on every side. So they built and
prospered. H6743

2Ch 18:11
And all the prophets prophesied so, saying, Go up to Ramothgilead,
and prosper: H6743 for the LORD shall deliver it into the hand of the
king.

2Ch 18:14
And when he was come to the king, the king said unto him, Micaiah,
shall we go to Ramothgilead to battle, or shall I forbear? And he said,
Go ye up, and prosper, H6743 and they shall be delivered into your

hand.

2Ch 20:20
And they rose early in the morning, and went forth into the wilderness of Tekoa: and as they went forth, Jehoshaphat stood and said, Hear me, O Judah, and ye inhabitants of Jerusalem; Believe in the LORD your God, so shall ye be established; believe his prophets, so shall ye prosper. H6743

2Ch 24:20
And the Spirit of God came upon Zechariah the son of Jehoiada the priest, which stood above the people, and said unto them, Thus saith God, Why transgress ye the commandments of the LORD, that ye cannot prosper? H6743 because ye have forsaken the LORD, he hath also forsaken you.

2Ch 26:5
And he sought God in the days of Zechariah, who had understanding in the visions of God: and as long as he sought the LORD, God made him to prosper. H6743

2Ch 31:21
And in every work that he began in the service of the house of God, and in the law, and in the commandments, to seek his God, he did it with all his heart, and prospered. H6743

2Ch 32:30
This same Hezekiah also stopped the upper watercourse of Gihon, and brought it straight down to the west side of the city of David. And Hezekiah prospered H6743 in all his works.

Neh 1:11
O Lord, I beseech thee, let now thine ear be attentive to the prayer of thy servant, and to the prayer of thy servants, who desire to fear thy

name: and prosper, H6743 I pray thee, thy servant this day, and grant him mercy in the sight of this man. For I was the king's cupbearer.

Neh 2:20
Then answered I them, and said unto them, The God of heaven, he will prosper H6743 us; therefore we his servants will arise and build: but ye have no portion, nor right, nor memorial, in Jerusalem.

Psa 1:3
And he shall be like a tree planted by the rivers of water, that bringeth forth his fruit in his season; his leaf also shall not wither; and whatsoever he doeth shall prosper. H6743

Psa 37:7
Rest in the LORD, and wait patiently for him: fret not thyself because of him who prospereth H6743 in his way, because of the man who bringeth wicked devices to pass.

Psa 45:4
And in thy majesty ride prosperously H6743 because of truth and meekness and righteousness; and thy right hand shall teach thee terrible things.

Psa 118:25
Save now, I beseech thee, O LORD: O LORD, I beseech thee, send now prosperity. H6743

Pro 28:13
He that covereth his sins shall not prosper: H6743 but whoso confesseth and forsaketh them shall have mercy.

Isa 48:15
I, even I, have spoken; yea, I have called him: I have brought him, and he shall make his way prosperous. H6743

Isa 53:10
Yet it pleased the LORD to bruise him; he hath put him to grief: when thou shalt make his soul an offering for sin, he shall see his seed, he shall prolong his days, and the pleasure of the LORD shall prosper H6743 in his hand.

Isa 54:17
No weapon that is formed against thee shall prosper; H6743 and every tongue that shall rise against thee in judgment thou shalt condemn. This is the heritage of the servants of the LORD, and their righteousness is of me, saith the LORD.

Isa 55:11
So shall my word be that goeth forth out of my mouth: it shall not return unto me void, but it shall accomplish that which I please, and it shall prosper H6743 in the thing whereto I sent it.

Jer 2:37
Yea, thou shalt go forth from him, and thine hands upon thine head: for the LORD hath rejected thy confidences, and thou shalt not prosper H6743 in them.

Jer 5:28
They are waxen fat, they shine: yea, they overpass the deeds of the wicked: they judge not the cause, the cause of the fatherless, yet they prosper; H6743 and the right of the needy do they not judge.

Jer 12:1
Righteous art thou, O LORD, when I plead with thee: yet let me talk with thee of thy judgments: Wherefore doth the way of the wicked prosper? H6743 wherefore are all they happy that deal very treacherously?

Jer 13:7
Then I went to Euphrates, and digged, and took the girdle from the place where I had hid it: and, behold, the girdle was marred, it was profitable H6743 for nothing.

This evil people, which refuse to hear my words, which walk in the imagination of their heart, and walk after other gods, to serve them, and to worship them, shall even be as this girdle, which is good H6743 for nothing.

Jer 22:30
Thus saith the LORD, Write ye this man childless, a man that shall not prosper H6743 in his days: for no man of his seed shall prosper, H6743 sitting upon the throne of David, and ruling any more in Judah.

Jer 32:5
And he shall lead Zedekiah to Babylon, and there shall he be until I visit him, saith the LORD: though ye fight with the Chaldeans, ye shall not prosper. H6743

Eze 15:4
Behold, it is cast into the fire for fuel; the fire devoureth both the ends of it, and the midst of it is burned. Is it meet H6743 for any work?

Eze 16:13
Thus wast thou decked with gold and silver; and thy raiment was of fine linen, and silk, and broidered work; thou didst eat fine flour, and honey, and oil: and thou wast exceeding beautiful, and thou didst prosper H6743 into a kingdom.

Eze 17:9
Say thou, Thus saith the Lord GOD; Shall it prosper? H6743 shall he not pull up the roots thereof, and cut off the fruit thereof, that it

wither? it shall wither in all the leaves of her spring, even without great power or many people to pluck it up by the roots thereof.

Eze 17:10
Yea, behold, being planted, shall it prosper? H6743 shall it not utterly wither, when the east wind toucheth it? it shall wither in the furrows where it grew.

Eze 17:15
But he rebelled against him in sending his ambassadors into Egypt, that they might give him horses and much people. Shall he prosper? H6743 shall he escape that doeth such things? or shall he break the covenant, and be delivered?

Dan 8:12
And an host was given him against the daily sacrifice by reason of transgression, and it cast down the truth to the ground; and it practised, and prospered. H6743

Dan 8:24
And his power shall be mighty, but not by his own power: and he shall destroy wonderfully, and shall prosper, H6743 and practise, and shall destroy the mighty and the holy people.

Dan 8:25
And through his policy also he shall cause craft to prosper H6743 in his hand; and he shall magnify himself in his heart, and by peace shall destroy many: he shall also stand up against the Prince of princes; but he shall be broken without hand.

Dan 11:27
And both these kings' hearts shall be to do mischief, and they shall speak lies at one table; but it shall not prosper: H6743 for yet the end shall be at the time appointed.

Dan 11:36
And the king shall do according to his will; and he shall exalt himself, and magnify himself above every god, and shall speak marvellous things against the God of gods, and shall prosper H6743 till the indignation be accomplished: for that that is determined shall be done.

Amo 5:6
Seek the LORD, and ye shall live; lest he break out H6743 like fire in the house of Joseph, and devour it, and there be none to quench it in Bethel.

Chapter 11

Scripture on Hebrew word shalvah (H7962) and shalev (7961)

Find Listed below H7962 (Shalvah) translated to English words:

Prosperity, peaceably, quietness, abundance, and peace

1. **H7962**
2. **Strong Definition** – security, abundance, peace, prosperity, quietness
3. **Translated to English 8 times**

The KJV translates Strongs H7962 in the following manner: prosperity (3x), peaceably (2x), quietness (1x), abundance (1x), peace (1x).

4. Scripture References

Psa 122:7
Peace be within thy walls, and **prosperity** H7962 within thy palaces.

Pro 1:32
For the turning away of the simple shall slay them, and the prosperity H7962 of fools shall destroy them.

Pro 17:1
Better is a dry morsel, and **quietness** H7962 therewith, than an house full of sacrifices with strife.

Jer 22:21
I spake unto thee in thy prosperity; H7962 but thou saidst, I will not hear. This hath been thy manner from thy youth, that thou obeyedst not my voice.

Eze 16:49
Behold, this was the iniquity of thy sister Sodom, pride, fulness of bread, and **abundance** H7962 of idleness was in her and in her daughters, neither did she strengthen the hand of the poor and needy.

Dan 8:25
And through his policy also he shall cause craft to prosper in his hand; and he shall magnify himself in his heart, and by peace H7962 shall destroy many: he shall also stand up against the Prince of princes; but he shall be broken without hand.

Dan 11:21
And in his estate shall stand up a vile person, to whom they shall not give the honour of the kingdom: but he shall come in peaceably, H7962 and obtain the kingdom by flatteries.

Dan 11:24
He shall enter peaceably H7962 even upon the fattest places of the province; and he shall do that which his fathers have not done, nor his fathers' fathers; he shall scatter among them the prey, and spoil, and riches: yea, and he shall forecast his devices against the strong holds, even for a time.

Scriptures on Hebrew word shalev (H7961)

Find listed below Hebrew (shalev) H7961 translated to English words:

At ease, peaceable, quietness, prosperity, quiet, prosper, wealthy

1.H7961 (shalev)

2. Strong Definition – To be tranquil, that is, secure or successful: - be happy, prosper, be in safety

3. Translated to English 8 times

KJV Translation Count — Total: 8x
The KJV translates Strongs H7961 in the following manner: **at ease** (2x), **peaceable** (1x), **quietness** (1x), **prosperity** (1x), **quiet** (1x), **prosper** (1x), **wealthy** (1x).

4. **Scripture References**

1Ch 4:40
And they found fat pasture and good, and the land was wide, and quiet, and peaceable; H7961 for they of Ham had dwelt there of old.

Job 16:12
I was at ease, H7961 but he hath broken me asunder: he hath also taken me by my neck, and shaken me to pieces, and set me up for his mark.

Job 20:20

Surely he shall not feel quietness H7961 in his belly, he shall not save of that which he desired.

Job 21:23
One dieth in his full strength, being wholly at ease and quiet. H7961

Psa 73:12
Behold, these are the ungodly, who prosper H7961 in the world; they increase in riches.

Jer 49:31
Arise, get you up unto the wealthy H7961 nation, that dwelleth without care, saith the LORD, which have neither gates nor bars, which dwell alone.

Eze 23:42
And a voice of a multitude being at ease H7961 was with her: and with the men of the common sort were brought Sabeans from the wilderness, which put bracelets upon their hands, and beautiful crowns upon their heads.

Zec 7:7
Should ye not hear the words which the LORD hath cried by the former prophets, when Jerusalem was inhabited and in prosperity, H7961 and the cities thereof round about her, when men inhabited the south and the plain?

About the Author

Dr. Michael Grant is the dynamic founder of King Jesus Worship Center (KJWC), a global ministry organization located in Winnsboro, Louisiana. King Jesus Worship Center is one church in multiple locations. The headquarters in Winnsboro is a 2000 seat facility in a town of less than six thousand in population. Pastor Grant is the pastor of both the Winnsboro and Monroe locations in Louisiana. He is the Bishop or overseer of all other King Jesus locations. Dr. Grant life goal is preach the good news of the kingdom and reveal to the body of Christ who they are on their God side of the family. Through the King Jesus television and Internet broadcasts, this gospel is being preached throughout the world.

Pastor Grant founded King Jesus Bible College to prepare ministers, evangelist, ministry leaders, pastors, and other for the work of the kingdom. Dr. Grant is the president of the bible college. The bible college offer 2-year associate and 4 year bachelor degrees in Basic Bible Studies (BBS). Dr. Grant received his Doctor of Divinity from Christian Bible College in Baton Rouge Louisiana. He also holds a BS Degree in Plant and Soil Science from Southern University Baton Rouge, Louisiana.

Dr. Grant is the founder of Ministers United for Christ Fellowship. Members have access to a long list of benefits, support services, and ministry resources designed to optimize their effectiveness in ministry. One of the ministry tools provided to fellowship members is the IWORD NETWORK (iwordnetwork.net). This network gives ministries a portal to have their own internet channel for live streaming, online TV, on demand, scheduled streaming, and online Radio. Dr. Grant speaks at revivals, conferences, public speakings, and any various other engagements throughout the Country. "When I see all the people of the world are hurting and in darkness," he says. "I will not stop until this gospel of the kingdom is exposed to every person on the planet."

For more information:

King Jesus Worship Center
P. O. Box 64
Winnsboro, La. 71295
318.435.9010
ministersunited@yahoo.com
kingjesusworship.org

Other Books by Dr. Michael Grant

1. Christ Body Revealed
2. Words are Seed Containing Your Future
3. Prayers That Breakthrough
4. The Saving Blood of King Jesus

Prayer for Salvation

Dear Lord Jesus, I thank you for paying the price for my sins. I believe you died and after three days you were raised from the dead. Please forgive me of all I have done wrong. Come into my heart and save me. I submit to you as my Lord and my God. I believe I am born again. Thank you for not remembering my sins forever. I thank you for giving me everlasting life.

Prayer for the Holy Ghost

Father I come to you in the name of Jesus. I thank you for giving me a new spirit and heart. Holy Spirit come into my heart and fill me up with your Spirit. I need more power in my life. I believe by faith I am filled with the Holy Ghost. By faith I will speak with unknown tongues. As I speak, fill me up with your wisdom, knowledge, understanding, and power. Thank you Holy Spirit.

CPSIA information can be obtained
at www.ICGtesting.com
Printed in the USA
FSHW02n2007310518
48924FS